INSURANCE AND B\

This book looks at the behavior of \
decision makers, and policy makers   ..vels
involved in the selling, buying, and \   ..c. It compares
their actions to those predicted by be\   ..iodels of choice derived
from classical economic theory. When actual choices stray from predictions, the behavior is considered anomalous. Howard C. Kunreuther, Mark
V. Pauly, and Stacey McMorrow attempt to understand why these anomalies
sometimes occur and sometimes do not, in many cases using insights from
behavioral economics. The authors then consider if and how such behavioral anomalies could be modified.

This book is in no way a defense of the insurance industry nor an attack
on it. Neither is it a consumer guide to purchasing insurance, although the
authors believe that consumers will benefit from the insights it contains.
Rather, this book describes situations in which both public policy and the
insurance industry's collective posture need to change. This may require
incentives, rules, and institutions to help reduce inefficient and anomalous
behavior, thereby encouraging behavior that will improve individual and
social welfare.

Howard C. Kunreuther is the James G. Dinan Professor of Decision Sciences
and Business and Public Policy at the Wharton School, University of
Pennsylvania, and co-director of the Wharton Risk Management and Decision
Processes Center. Dr. Kunreuther is a member of the World Economic Forum's
Global Agenda Council on Insurance and Asset Management for 2011–12, a
Fellow of the American Association for the Advancement of Science, and a
distinguished Fellow of the Society for Risk Analysis, which honored him
with a Distinguished Achievement Award in 2001.

Mark V. Pauly is the Bendheim Professor in the Department of Health Care
Management at the Wharton School of the University of Pennsylvania. One
of the leading health economists in the United States, he is a former commissioner on the Physician Payment Review Commission and is a co-editor-
in-chief of the *International Journal of Health Care Finance and Economics*
and an associate editor of the *Journal of Risk and Uncertainty*. Professor
Pauly has served on Institute of Medicine panels on public accountability
for health insurers under Medicare.

Stacey McMorrow is a research associate in the Health Policy Center at the
Urban Institute, Washington, DC. She has studied a variety of factors that
affect health insurance coverage and access to care and has analyzed the
potential impacts of national health reforms on employers and individuals.

Insurance and Behavioral Economics

Improving Decisions in the Most Misunderstood Industry

HOWARD C. KUNREUTHER

University of Pennsylvania

MARK V. PAULY

University of Pennsylvania

STACEY McMORROW

The Urban Institute

CAMBRIDGE
UNIVERSITY PRESS

CAMBRIDGE UNIVERSITY PRESS
Cambridge, New York, Melbourne, Madrid, Cape Town,
Singapore, São Paulo, Delhi, Mexico City

Cambridge University Press
32 Avenue of the Americas, New York, NY 10013-2473, USA

www.cambridge.org
Information on this title: www.cambridge.org/9780521608268

First published 2013

Printed in the United States of America

A catalog record for this publication is available from the British Library.

Library of Congress Cataloging in Publication data
Kunreuther, Howard.
Insurance and behavioral economics : improving decisions in the most misunderstood
industry / Howard C. Kunreuther, Mark V. Pauly, Stacey McMorrow.
pages   cm
Includes bibliographical references and index.
ISBN 978-0-521-84572-4 – ISBN 978-0-521-60826-8 (pbk.)
1. Risk (Insurance)   2. Insurance – Decision making.   3. Consumer behavior.
I. Howard C. Kunreuther, 1938–   II. Mark V. Pauly, 1941–   III. Stacey McMorrow, 1978–
HG8054.5.K858   2012
368–dc23   2012006486

ISBN 978-0-521-84572-4 Hardback
ISBN 978-0-521-60826-8 Paperback

Contents

Preface

This book looks at the behavior of individuals at risk, insurance industry decision makers, and policy makers at the local, state, and federal levels involved in the selling, buying, and regulating of insurance. It compares their actions to those predicted by benchmark models of choice derived from classical economic theory. Where actual choices stray from predictions, the behavior is considered to be *anomalous*. We attempt to understand why these anomalies sometimes occur and sometimes do not, in many cases using insights from behavioral economics. We then consider if and how such behavioral anomalies could be modified.

This book is in no way a defense of the insurance industry nor an attack on it. Neither is it a consumer guide to purchasing insurance, although we believe that consumers will benefit from the insights it contains. Rather, we describe in this book situations in which public policy and the insurance industry's collective posture need to change. This may require incentives, rules, and institutions that will help reduce inefficient and anomalous behaviors and encourage behavior that will improve individual and social welfare.

A key element for achieving comfort is transparency, so that insurance plays its proper roles: providing a signal for safety; rewarding individuals for taking responsibility for their safety, financial well-being, and health; and providing proper compensation in a timely manner when misfortune strikes. While the principles and strategies we propose are sometimes intended to help decision makers conform more closely to the benchmark models of choice, we recognize that economic and political circumstances may make other choices preferable. We will be pleased if this book simply helps eliminate much of the confusion and mistrust that characterizes this most misunderstood industry.

A ROADMAP OF THE BOOK

Part I, *Contrasting Ideal and Real Worlds of Insurance*, provides a set of examples of insurance in practice. First, Chapter 1 discusses the purposes of the book and the roots of misunderstanding of insurance. Chapter 2 lays out the precepts of classical economics by formulating benchmark models of demand and supply of insurance. Using these models as reference points, Chapter 3 provides examples of insurance decision making in real-world settings and defines what we mean by "anomalous behavior." In Chapter 4, we identify situations in which the benchmark models work reasonably well on both the demand side (consumer behavior) and the supply side (firm and investor behavior).

Part II, *Understanding Consumer and Insurer Behavior*, focuses on the many real-world complications that conflict with some of the assumptions that guide the benchmark models of choice. These include imperfect information or misinformation on the risk, information asymmetry between buyers and sellers, and correlated losses. Chapter 5 characterizes what insurance markets should look like when these real-world conditions are present.

When the benchmark models fail to correctly predict consumer and industry responses, we develop alternative models using concepts from behavioral economics. In Chapter 6, we develop a model of choice that characterizes demand for insurance by focusing on the importance of goals and plans in making decisions under uncertainty. Chapter 7 then provides examples of demand-side anomalies indicating why they are likely to occur.

In Chapter 8, we turn to the supply side by developing descriptive models of insurers' behavior with respect to pricing their product and determining what coverage to offer, and the role that capital markets and rating agencies play in the process, indicating anomalies we observe along the way. By understanding why insurers deviate from benchmark models of choice, it is easier to understand the types of supply-side anomalies that currently exist. In Chapter 9, terrorism and natural hazards are used to illustrate why insurers have behaved in ways that appear to be anomalous.

Part III, *The Future of Insurance*, relies on our understanding of consumer and firm behavior to provide answers to questions both narrow and broad. What information could be provided to help consumers decide what types of coverage they should consider buying? What steps can insurance firms take to continue to offer coverage at reasonable premiums even after large losses occur? How should capital markets be structured so that insurance firms can offer coverage for the widest range of situations at premiums that both investors and consumers find attractive? What role should the public sector play in encouraging or possibly requiring consumers and/or firms to undertake steps so their behavior conforms more closely to the relevant benchmark model?

In Chapter 10, we address the question as to who should bear the losses from untoward events and then look at ways to reduce the likelihood and costs of these risks. This can be accomplished by allocating resources efficiently and distributing them equitably and fairly. We then develop a set of information and design principles for evaluating the role that insurance can play with other policy tools for reducing risks and providing funds should a loss occur. Chapter 11 proposes a set of policies for correcting anomalies on the demand and supply sides by focusing on why consumers and insurers behave as they do and then suggesting ways in which they can be persuaded to improve their own welfare as well as that of society.

The next three chapters focus on insurance strategies for reducing risk. Chapter 12 proposes multiyear homeowners' insurance policies tied to property as a way of encouraging adoption of cost-effective, risk-reducing measures. Chapter 13 examines possible anomalous behavior in health insurance markets and how such behavior might be modified to keep medical costs and premiums at appropriate levels. Finally, Chapter 14 suggests how political and market frameworks might be structured so that insurance markets can improve individual and social welfare.

Acknowledgments

During the five years that we have formulated concepts and ideas for this book, we have learned a great deal from interactions with our colleagues and friends at the University of Pennsylvania and researchers interested in the role that insurance can play as part of the policy process. At the same time, we gained considerable insight from discussions with those who deal with insurance issues on a daily basis in real-world settings. They provided us with the nature of the institutional arrangements and decision-making processes that inform actual choices.

Special thanks go to Tom Baker, Debra Ballen, Jeffrey R. Brown, Cary Coglianese, Keith Crocker, Neil Doherty, Ken Froot, Jim Gallagher, Victor Goldberg, Gary Grant, Scott Harrington, Robert Hartwig, Eric Johnson, Robert W. Klein, Paul Kleindorfer, David Krantz, Michael Liersch, Jim MacDonald, Robert Meyer, Erwann Michel-Kerjan, Olivia Mitchell, Eric Nelson, Ed Pasterick, Jim Poterba, Richard Roth, Jr., Joshua Teitelbaum, Richard Thomas, and Joel Wooten for their insights and critical comments. Many of the concepts and ideas discussed in this book were critically evaluated by members of the Extreme Events project of the Wharton Risk Center, who helped us craft guiding principles and their implications. Many other concepts originated from discussions with colleagues at conferences and meetings, notably the National Bureau of Economic Research (NBER) Insurance Workshop. We are also grateful for financial support from the Wharton Risk Management and Decision Processes Center that enabled us to write this book.

A special note of thanks goes to Hugh Hoikwang Kim for his research assistance, and to Douglas R. Sease for his careful editing of the manuscript and expert guidance on ways to present this material. We are very grateful for the encouragement and support that Scott Parris, our editor at Cambridge University Press, has given us throughout the process, which was longer than he or we envisioned. Special appreciation goes to Carol Heller, who edited and commented on the manuscript during the many stages of the process with able assistance from Allison Hedges and Ann Miller.

Finally, Howard and Mark thank our wives, Gail and Kitty, for their support and encouragement throughout the process of writing this book. We kept telling them that the manuscript was almost finished, but they came to understand the long-term nature of the process. The strategies and principles for improving behavior that form the last part of the book were stimulated by our own misperceptions as to how long it would take us to complete this book.

Howard C. Kunreuther
Mark V. Pauly
Stacey McMorrow
September 2012

PART I

CONTRASTING IDEAL AND REAL
WORLDS OF INSURANCE

1

Purposes of This Book

Our goal in this book is to identify and analyze examples of behavior on the parts of consumers, insurance companies, investors, and regulators that could be characterized as "anomalous" if judged by standards of *rational behavior*. In this book, the term *rationality* is defined as economists have traditionally used it when analyzing decisions that involve risk and uncertainty. We characterize behavior as anomalous when it violates these standards.

Even though the economist's notion of rationality is well established, it is not the only or even the best way to portray what people may mean by appropriate behavior. In fact, we ourselves often behave in ways that do not conform to these formal principles of rationality and can provide good reasons or excuses for these deviations. We and others (Cutler and Zeckhauser 2004; Kunreuther and Pauly 2006; Liebman and Zeckhauser 2008) have noted examples of behavior by consumers and suppliers of insurance that violate the economic models of rational choice.

The main message from the behavioral economics revolution is that real-world agents often do not make choices in the way that economic models of rationality suggest they should. In evaluating the results of such behavior and suggesting what strategies one should pursue, researchers still normally turn to the conventional economic models as normative benchmarks. For this reason, formal economic models of demand and supply developed over decades are often used as benchmarks for evaluating the behavior of those who are considering purchasing insurance and those who decide whether or not to offer coverage for specific risks.

Given the intellectual history, logical consistency, and strategic implications of these rational economic models, we use them as a standard in this book. However, there may be times when it is appropriate to deviate from these *benchmark models*. In fact we sometimes argue that, even as normative standards, the benchmark models may not be logically or politically appropriate. We will therefore examine the nature of consumer and insurer behavior, explain their actions or inaction to the extent we can, and offer prescriptions for improving choices.

We have three broad goals for this book. We want buyers of insurance to have a firmer grasp as to how they can improve their decisions on whether to purchase specific types of insurance and if so, how much coverage to buy. We want insurance companies to understand more about their customers' motivations and biases and thus how to better construct and market their products. We also want legislators and regulators to make better decisions about how and when to intervene in private insurance markets.

THE ROOTS OF MISUNDERSTANDING OF INSURANCE

The fact that insurance expenditures in the United States are in the trillions of dollars does not imply that consumers obtaining coverage and companies selling policies are making the voluntary decisions implied by classical economics textbooks. The most obvious reason, already noted, is that decision makers may not use these models in determining how much coverage (if any) to demand or what price to charge when supplying insurance. A less obvious reason is that many insurance purchases are not made voluntarily by the individuals at risk, but are often required by institutional arrangements or made financially attractive by firms to their employees, sometimes in response to tax incentives. For example, banks and financial institutions normally require insurance against property damage as a condition for a mortgage. Almost every state mandates proof of third-party automobile insurance when registering a car and requires firms to purchase workers' compensation insurance to cover their employees against the costs of on-the-job accidents. Many employers offer their workers some tax-free life insurance and subsidize the cost of employees' health insurance, so that there is no reason for any person to calculate the resulting costs and expected benefits of this coverage. In these cases, individuals are merely responding to legal requirements or financial incentives.

For those insurance policies purchased by individuals voluntarily, decisions as to whether to buy coverage still might not fit the standard economic models. Some types of individually chosen insurance are said to be *overpurchased*, such as warranty protection and low-deductible coverage on one's home, health, and automobile. On the other hand, many consumers and firms *underpurchase* protection against catastrophic losses to property or against very expensive medical procedures. And while mortgage lenders require standard homeowners' coverage, they do not require earthquake protection; few residents in seismic areas of California purchase this coverage today. Many financial institutions also do not enforce the requirement that residents in flood-prone areas with federally insured mortgages purchase flood insurance.

The supply side of the market is also subject to behavior that diverges from what one would expect based on economic models. Insurers are often reluctant to continue offering coverage against risks from which they have recently suffered severe losses, as illustrated by the refusal of many insurers to continue to offer terrorism coverage following the attacks of 9/11 or the reluctance of insurers to continue to offer coverage in Florida against wind damage from hurricanes after Hurricane Andrew in 1992. There are a number of possible explanations for such behaviors, which we will examine in later chapters of this book.

One major cause of misunderstanding about insurance among consumers is an unrealistic expectation about how they will feel about losses they may (or may not) experience. People often choose coverage that does not fully protect them in order to keep their premiums low, but when they suffer a loss they are unhappy that not all the damage is covered. However, they are also unhappy when they have paid a premium and a loss does *not* occur because they perceive that the insurance was an unwise investment.

It is inevitable that most buyers of insurance will not get anything back on their policies in any given year or nearly as much as they paid in premiums over time. That is the nature of the insurance business. When purchasing insurance, a person's mantra should be *the best return is no return at all,* knowing that one is protected financially against a potential loss.

But consumers often lose sight of the fundamental goal of buying coverage. It is the separation in time between paying for insurance and getting back benefits that confuses and frustrates consumers. When they have voluntarily purchased policies for several years without experiencing any losses, they often do not renew their policies. In the case of flood insurance, homeowners at risk are likely to cancel this coverage after several no-loss years, even doing so illegally when required by lenders to purchase and maintain a policy.

When insured individuals do suffer a loss, they are naturally inclined to seek the most generous benefits they can, even when their policy explicitly limits the type of losses for which they are allowed to file claims. Consider homeowners inundated by the Florida storms in 2004 and Hurricanes Katrina, Rita, and Wilma in 2005 who did not have flood insurance. Many of these victims tried to collect on water damage caused by the storms' surges even though their policies specifically restricted coverage to wind damage, not water damage. These homeowners had insurance, but not the right coverage.

Of course, if people had known in advance that a hurricane would hit, they might have paid attention to the fine print and bought flood insurance to cover storm surge and other water damage from the storm. If they knew they would never have a fire in their home during their lifetime, they would not voluntarily buy fire insurance. The realization that you cannot know the future with certainty spills over as irritation with insurance. People fail to recognize that this product is designed to help them cope with this uncertainty by giving up a modest amount of money in most circumstances in order to be able to return many multiples of the premium in the event of rare bad luck. It is thus not surprising that consumers are much less likely to report being satisfied with insurance than with products that give them tangible benefits they enjoy immediately after purchase.

Another source of confusion and misunderstanding that leads to disappointment is the often complex and ambiguous language in insurance contracts. Much of the billions of dollars of damage wrought by Hurricane Katrina on the Gulf Coast of Mississippi occurred when

Katrina's huge storm surge damaged or destroyed thousands of homes and businesses. Homeowners, infuriated when they realized that their policies covered wind – not water – damage, teamed with their state governments to sue insurance carriers. They argued that, even if they had understood that their insurance did not cover water damage, it still should pay because Katrina's screaming winds drove a wall of water that damaged their property. The homeowners lost the suit, but the insurance industry lost much credibility and people became more concerned that their coverage was much less than it appeared to be on paper.

With respect to the supply side, insurance executives often appear to misunderstand their own product in part because of uncertainty: they cannot predict catastrophic weather events, health care cost inflation, or the amount of interest they will earn on their reserves. Paradoxically, managers in the business of bearing other peoples' risks often appear to think (or hope) that they can avoid most of these risks. They also exhibit a poor understanding of their customers' motivations and biases.

The industry has made some astoundingly simple mistakes in the past from which it has learned the hard way. How difficult is it to recognize that Florida will be hit by hurricanes and that damage along its heavily developed coast will be extensive and expensive? Prior to Hurricane Andrew in 1992, many insurers were willing to offer coverage to those who requested it without determining the likelihood that they would suffer catastrophic losses from the next severe hurricane to make landfall in Florida. It was only after Hurricane Andrew, when nine property insurers became insolvent, that there was a recognition that companies would have to charge much higher premiums to protect coastal property against hurricanes.

This general misunderstanding of the fundamental purpose of insurance, along with some legitimate confusion regarding insurance policy details by consumers, contributes to the sometimes anomalous decisions on the demand side. Insurers, for their part, misunderstand how to predict rare events and therefore sometimes make decisions that appear to ignore risks altogether. Alternatively, they sometimes fixate on the magnitude of recent losses and claims without weighting these figures by an estimate of the likelihood of another catastrophe occurring. This behavior suggests that insurance is hard even for those in the business to understand. Clearing up these misunderstandings and suggesting ways to cope with these issues is what this book is about.

COMPARING ACTUAL BEHAVIOR WITH BENCHMARK MODELS

We will shed light on how buyers and sellers of insurance, and regulators who oversee the insurance industry, do and should make decisions. We start by comparing actual behavior with what benchmark models of rational behavior indicate decision makers *should* do in the face of uncertainty.

On the demand side, classical economic theory assumes that consumers with accurate information about risks decide on insurance purchases by making explicit tradeoffs between the expected benefits and the costs of different policies. Economists use the well-developed *expected utility theory of choice* to indicate how individuals should make decisions under uncertainty; this is the basis for our benchmark model of *demand*.

On the supply side, classical theory assumes perfect competition among insurers, the freedom to set prices, and knowledgeable investors who diversify their risk across many projects and supply capital for investments that provide the highest expected return. Economists assume that firms will behave in such a way as to maximize their expected long-run profits and, thus, the value of the firm; this is the basis for our benchmark model of *supply*. Regulators are expected to step in only in the case of widespread inefficiency and to deal with situations where the actions of a firm affect the actions of others (i.e., *externalities*), imperfect flows of information, and transaction costs that may cause the competitive market to fail.

Consumers, the insurance industry, and those who oversee it are unlikely to make the kinds of rational decisions that classical economics would predict, even in markets with voluntary and free choice on the supply and demand sides. Therefore, we turn to the emerging field of behavioral economics, which focuses on systematic biases and heuristics (rules of thumb) that lead consumers, managers, investors, and regulators to make choices that deviate from the benchmark models derived from classical economics.

Behavioral economics takes into account emotions and biases such as fear and anxiety, the demonstrated tendency to value losses more than gains, and the propensity of decision makers to maintain the status quo even when circumstances indicate they should change. In other words, behavioral economics does *not* assume a person always or usually makes decisions based on classical models of choice, or even based on carefully organized calculations. It allows for feelings, emotions, fuzzy thinking, limited information processing abilities, and imperfect foresight.

The tension between classical economic theory and behavioral economics with respect to choices made by consumers and insurers is highlighted in Daniel Kahneman's compelling book *Thinking, Fast and Slow* where he characterizes two modes of thinking which he labels *System 1* and *System 2*:

- System 1 operates automatically and quickly with little or no effort and no sense of voluntary control. It uses simple associations, including emotional reactions that have been acquired by personal experience with events and their consequences.
- System 2 allocates attention to effortful and intentional mental activities including simple or complex computations or formal logic.

Many of the biases and simplified decision rules that characterize judgment and choice under uncertainty that we describe in this book are due to operation of the more automatic and less analytic System 1. Expected utility theory and expected profit maximization require the decision maker to utilize System 2 to make deliberative choices. But even when a consumer or an insurer devotes considerable time and effort in making choices, emotions can be so strong as to overwhelm a systematic decision process.

These attributes are especially likely with insurance, because the decision maker deals with risks where there is considerable uncertainty regarding the likelihood and consequences of loss-producing events. Prospective policyholders tend not to understand insurance well and often do not trust the sellers. Those at risk have a low tolerance for ambiguity and often purchase insurance to gain peace of mind. They then regret having bought coverage if they do not collect on their policy.

We believe the contrast between these two approaches – the elegance of classical economic theory versus the real-world applications of behavioral economics – provides a useful introduction to a more general debate that promises to stimulate discussion among social scientists and will impact the field of economics for years to come. There is an ongoing intellectual tug of war between economists who use the classical model and those who have joined the behavioral camp, although in most cases it is a matter of proportion and benefit of the doubt, rather than methodological purity. More practically, we believe that examining the insurance industry through the lenses of both approaches enables us to offer ideas as to what policies and programs can correct, or at least modify, behavior that appears to be irrational.

SUMMARY

Insurance is an extraordinarily useful tool to manage risk, but it is broadly misunderstood by consumers, regulators, and insurance executives, who all engage in behavior that does not conform to classical economic predictions of rationality. Yet to a great extent, the benefits of insurance to individuals and society rest on both buyers and sellers behaving rationally and predictably. With considerable sums of money at stake in consumer premiums and insurance company payouts, it is important to understand the reasons for anomalous behavior. Insurance contracts should be structured to prevent or minimize choices that can be costly to those who make these decisions and to the general public as it impacts social welfare.

We examine these behaviors through the lens of classical economics, which predicts how decision makers should make choices, and also through the lens of behavioral economics, which takes into account emotions, biases, and simplified decision rules. We then make recommendations for policies and programs to correct or at least modify what appears to be irrational behavior.

2

An Introduction to Insurance in Practice and Theory

When Judy's sister discovered she had cancer, Judy was frightened. Their mother had died of cancer and Judy became preoccupied with the possibility that a genetic link might endanger her, too. Not long after her sister's diagnosis, Judy bought an expensive insurance policy that promised to pay her money on top of any medical benefits if she got cancer (but not if she contracted another disease).

Doug's new car, an expensive Lexus sports car, was his dream come true. He maintained it meticulously and, thinking ahead, took out an insurance policy on the car with a very low $500 deductible, even though that increased his premium considerably. That way, he figured, repairs to his car would be nearly covered even if someone in a parking lot simply dented his fender. Three months later, Doug's attention momentarily lapsed when his cell phone rang and he plowed into the car ahead of him at a stoplight. The body shop estimated damages to the Lexus at $1,500, well over Doug's $500 deductible. Yet Doug chose to pay the entire cost out of pocket, fearful that making a claim would drive his insurance premiums even higher.

After a series of hurricanes battered Florida's long, low-lying coastline in 2004 and 2005, a number of property insurers decided the risk of insuring homes and hotels on the coast just wasn't worth it and began to cut back their coverage in hurricane-prone areas within the state. Florida responded in 2007 by setting up its own government-backed insurance company, the Citizens Property Insurance Corporation, to supply coverage to coastal residents who couldn't obtain a policy from commercial insurers. Better yet for the residents, the coverage was highly subsidized and much cheaper than policies offered by the private sector. By the end of 2010, Citizens stood as the largest provider of wind coverage in Florida.

No one will forget the attacks on the Twin Towers of the World Trade Center (WTC) and the Pentagon on September 11, 2001. But this wasn't the first time terrorists struck in the United States. On February 26, 1993, terrorists drove a truck laden with explosives into the basement of the North Tower of the WTC and detonated it. They failed to topple the Towers as they intended, but they killed six people and injured more than a thousand. Repairs to the office towers cost millions, dislocated many business and government offices for months, and cost insurers $725 million in claims. Two years after the 1993 World Trade Center attack, Timothy McVeigh detonated a huge bomb in front of the Alfred P. Murrah Federal Building in downtown Oklahoma City, killing 168 people, including babies in a nursery in the building.

Yet when Al-Qaeda terrorists struck the Twin Towers in 2001, terrorism was not named as a separate risk in the "all perils" insurance policies held by the WTC's firms, and thus insurers did not charge specific premiums for it. But immediately after 9/11, even if frightened property owners wanted to buy separate insurance against a terrorist attack, few companies would sell it to them – and then only at extremely high premiums.

Each of these cases illustrates a fundamental misunderstanding by those considering purchasing insurance about what coverage to acquire, and by those selling policies about what premiums they should charge. On the demand side, Judy could have bought a policy that would cover costs from cancer as well as any other illness for which she might be hospitalized. By not submitting a claim, Doug behaved as if he had purchased a much less expensive high-deductible policy than his current low-deductible policy. His premiums would have been much lower had he chosen a high-deductible policy in the first place. Deciding not to make any claim at all on this expensive insurance after an accident appears even less logical.

On the supply side, the legislators who approved the state-run Citizens Property Insurance Corporation with its subsidized rates in hurricane-prone areas of Florida made coastal homeowners very happy. But the rest of Florida's taxpayers won't be pleased the next time a hurricane hits and they find themselves paying for repairs to all those seaside mansions because the state-run company did not take in enough premiums to cover its losses. And one wonders why, despite the attack on the World Trade Center in 1993 and the Oklahoma City bombing in 1995, insurers continued to include terrorism as an unnamed peril in their policies, so they did not collect any premiums for covering terrorism losses from the 2001 attack. Moreover, why was something previously offered for no additional charge now suddenly either not available or enormously expensive?

Insurance is one of mankind's greatest inventions, an extraordinarily useful tool to reduce risk. When it works as intended, it provides financial protection for individuals and a profitable business model for insurance firms and their investors. But at every level, confusion about insurance produces behavior that cannot be easily understood based on models of choice that assume individuals and firms are behaving sensibly by making relevant tradeoffs.

Uncertainty creates both the demand for and supply of insurance. If you knew for sure that you would *never* damage your car through your own fault, you would be better off not paying for collision coverage. If an insurer knew that it would have to pay a claim of a specified amount with certainty, it would not offer coverage at a premium less than the claim it would have to pay. But in reality, there is some risk that you will have an accident. If your car never suffers damage, you'll be slightly worse off if you paid a premium for the policy. But if you total your car, you are much better off, because the insurance company will pay for a new one. The insurance company shoulders the risk of you damaging your car in exchange for premium payments that are normally considerably less than the value of a new car. If the company calculates the price of its insurance policies correctly, it takes in enough premium dollars and earns enough on the investments it makes to cover your claim, as well as all its other claims, and still makes a profit.

To a large extent, the benefits of insurance to individuals and society rest on people behaving rationally and predictably. It often comes down to the kinds of maxims we've all heard and hated as children: "You should have thought of that beforehand" (and bought adequate coverage), or "What if everybody behaved that way?" (and tried to collect more on a claim than the actual loss).

Suppose I am a bit of a hypochondriac and can persuade my doctor to prescribe an expensive test for a disease that I know I probably don't have. If my insurance covers the costs of the test, I can achieve peace of mind. If I am the only one who wants such a test, then my premiums will not change. But if everyone in my insurance group follows suit, all of our insurance premiums will rise sharply; we will then end up shelling out a lot of money for tests that are hard to justify on medical grounds.

Homeowners without flood insurance who suffer water damage want the government to bail them out – figuratively and literally. Government officials recognized this and so provided an economic incentive in the form of a subsidy to induce those residing in flood-prone areas to purchase coverage. But even though flood insurance costs considerably less than what it would if premiums reflected risk, many residents in flood-prone areas do not buy coverage voluntarily.

Thus, despite the apparent simplicity of insurance, misconceptions abound, sometimes for good reasons, often for no reason. Consumers appear to get it wrong, lawmakers and regulators often misperceive the role of insurance, and even insurance executives themselves sometimes behave in ways that conflict with the basic principles of the product they are supplying. With considerable sums of money at stake in consumer premiums and insurance company payouts, we should strive to make wise choices about the types of insurance to purchase, how much coverage to buy, and what kinds of policies are sold at what price. As our examples illustrate, however, what people do when they buy or sell insurance often does not appear to be based on systematic thinking, much less on clear and simple decision-making rules.

If insurance is bought and sold properly, it can do an enormous amount of good for consumer well-being and for the health of the economy. Hence, if one can improve the decision-making processes of consumers who are at risk and insurers who supply protection, then both individual and social welfare will be improved. To better judge behavior we will develop benchmark models of supply and demand that indicate what choices should be made on the basis of classical economic theory.

INSURANCE AND THE U.S. ECONOMY

Insurance is a very large industry and involves trillions of dollars in expenditures. How important is the insurance industry in the U.S. economy? Usually, we answer this question using an industry's revenues or sales relative to total gross domestic product (GDP) or some other financial measure of economic activity. Those revenues also serve as a rough measure of the share of national resources (labor and capital) employed by a given industry.

Insurance needs to be viewed differently. As we have already noted, people pay premiums to be able to receive insurance benefit payments. This means that the bulk of revenues that come in the front door of an insurance company as premiums, subsequently (and appropriately) go out the other door to pay claims, with only a fraction of those revenues covering the costs of the labor and capital that facilitated this web of transactions. This means that the economy's share of real resources used by insurance is much smaller than its share of revenues.

The importance of these special characteristics of the private insurance sector in the U.S. economy is indicated in Table 2.1. On one hand, it shows that the flow of revenues into insurance companies is large in both absolute terms (nearly \$2 trillion) and relative to the total \$14 trillion U.S. economy. On the other hand, the number of workers in this industry, while 2.3 million strong, is a more modest share of the total U.S. workforce. Similarly, the government's calculation of value added in this industry (value added is the difference between revenues and costs) is less than half of total revenues, at \$392 billion, because the main cost to insurers is the cost of paying claims. Finally, insurers accumulate substantial amounts of capital both as reserves against unusually high future claims and (in annuity and life insurance) as investments whose returns are used to pay benefits to people who buy and retain insurance over time. Those assets amounted to more than \$6 trillion in 2007, large in absolute terms, but only about four percent of total U.S. financial assets.

Table 2.1. *Premium revenues, employment, and financial assets of private insurance companies, 2007 (total and relative to the economy)*

Premium revenues, by type	
Private health insurance and managed care	$760 billion
Life and health companies[a]	$667 billion
Property/casualty companies[b]	$448 billion
TOTAL	$1.875 trillion
TOTAL percentage of U.S. GDP	13.3%
Insurance industry employment	2.3 million
Total percentage of U.S. workforce (full- and part-time)	1.6%
Financial assets and value added	
Insurance industry assets (excl. pension)	$6.3 trillion
Insurance assets as percent of total financial assets	4.2%
Value added by insurance carriers	$392 billion
As percent of GDP	2.8%

Sources: data on private health insurance and managed care from the Center for Medicare and Medicaid Services, National Health Expenditures Projections; data on life and health companies from the Insurance Information Institute, *Online Insurance Fact Book* 2010; data on property/casualty companies from the U.S. Statistical Abstract 2010, Table 1185 (original data from ISO and Highline Data LLC); data on insurance industry employment from the Bureau of Economic Analysis, Industry Economic Accounts (full-time and part-time employment by industry); data on insurance industry assets from the U.S. Statistical Abstract 2010, Table 1129 (original data from the Board of Governors of the Federal Reserve); data on the value added by insurance carriers from the Bureau of Economic Analysis, Industry Economic Accounts (value added by industry).
[a] Premiums are direct premiums written.
[b] Premiums are net premiums written.

It is important to note, however, that these measures of funds flowing through the insurance sector are, at best, an imperfect proxy for the importance of insurance to the economy. The reason is that insurance is often a necessary ingredient in a large transaction, and it provides a commensurate benefit. It is often worth much more than it costs.[1] To illustrate, insurance is crucial for protecting home buyers' investments as well as their lenders' financial commitments against damage to the structure from natural and man-made causes. Without that protection, the bank would not have issued a mortgage.

Table 2.2 elaborates on the information in Table 2.1 to show that some parts of the industry are large relative to others. Health insurance is the

Table 2.2. *Insurance premiums written, by line, 2007*

Private health insurance	$760 billion
Property/casualty[a]	$448 billion
Automobile	$186 billion
Homeowners	$57 billion
Commercial, multiple peril	$31 billion
Marine	$13 billion
Workers' compensation	$41 billion
Medical Malpractice	$10 billion
Other liability	$41 billion
Reinsurance	$12 billion
Other lines	$57 billion
Life/health (2008)[b]	$667 billion
Life insurance	$184 billion
Annuities	$328 billion[c]
Accident and health	$155 billion

Sources: data on private health insurance from the CMS National Health Expenditures Projections; data on property/casualty insurance from the U.S. Statistical Abstract 2010, Table 1185 (original data from ISO and Highline Data LLC); data on life and health insurance from the Insurance Information Institute Online Insurance Fact Book 2010.

[a] Premiums are net premiums written.

[b] Premiums are direct premiums written.

[c] Represents both immediate annuities (insurance) and deferred annuity retirement funds (investments).

single largest subsector, with premiums of $760 billion (nearly sixty-five percent of total private health spending) in 2007. Slightly more than half of the $448 billion in property-casualty premiums goes for automobile and homeowners' insurance to protect people against damage to their property and against legal liability for negligent behavior. The rest is accounted for by a variety of coverage types as illustrated in Table 2.2. Life insurance and annuities represent $512 billion of the $667 billion in direct premiums written in 2007 for life and health insurance. The remainder represents premiums for accident and health policies.

In addition to private insurance, there are some important social insurance programs in which premiums exceed those provided by the private sector. In the health area, Medicare and Medicaid premiums at $813 billion per year are greater than private health insurance premiums[2] and Social Security, at $805 billion, is much larger than private pension programs (Federal OASDI Board of Trustees 2009; Truffer et al. 2010).

THE BENCHMARK MODEL OF SUPPLY

The benchmark model of supply assumes that insurance companies are maximizing long-run expected profits for their owners in a competitive insurance market. In this environment, there are many insurance firms, each of which can charge any premium for a prespecified amount of coverage. The assumption of competition implies that the premiums they charge will be just enough to allow the insurers to cover their costs and make a normal or marketwide competitive profit.

Potential customers at risk and the insurers providing protection are assumed to have accurate information on the likelihood of a loss and its consequences. In this idealized world, virtually every uncertain event of concern would be insured to some extent if the administrative (paperwork) cost of furnishing coverage was not high and consumers were sufficiently risk averse and maximized their expected utility (Arrow 1963). This would include the whole gamut of risky events: financial losses, poor health, uncertain career prospects, bad weather, and even bad luck in love. The only events that cannot be insured are those certain to occur, like the sun rising in the morning, or disasters that destroy all wealth such as Earth being hit by an asteroid.

In reality, consumers face most risks with incomplete financial protection – and some with no protection at all – in part because insurers do not offer coverage for all risky events. That raises an important question: Why is insurance supplied or offered for some risks and not for others? Why, for example, have property owners been covered against losses caused by hurricanes but not against a future terrorist attack following 9/11? For both risks, a large number of people and much property are exposed to a possible disaster. In this case, the explanation is fairly clear. Hurricanes occur periodically and provide insurers and catastrophe modeling firms with significant data that can be used to develop premiums that reflect risk. Furthermore, property owners are required by banks and financial institutions to purchase insurance against wind damage as a condition for a mortgage. Under the National Flood Insurance

Program (NFIP), the federal government also requires those residing in flood-prone areas to purchase coverage against water damage if they have a federally insured mortgage.

With respect to terrorism, however, most insurers determined after 9/11 that terroristic attacks were uninsurable by the private sector alone because of the difficulty they had in estimating the likelihood and consequences of future attacks.

As we will see in subsequent chapters, there are many other instances in which insurance is not offered when classical economics would predict that it should be. There are also a few cases in which insurance is offered by the private sector and purchased by many individuals when an analysis of the expected benefits of coverage relative to its cost suggest that this is an unwise purchase on financial grounds.

Fundamental Principles of Insurance Supply

A fundamental principle that determines the supply of insurance is that insurers pool risks where individuals are interested in protecting themselves. In insurance's simplest form, those facing a specific risk agree to pay a premium to an entity designated as an insurer. (This could be an individual or group of individuals rather than an insurance company.) Those premiums are then used to cover the losses of the unlikely victims. To illustrate, assume for a moment that there are no insurers and that there is a one in ten chance of each person losing $100 next year from a well-defined risk. On average, 10 out of 100 persons will lose money. Suppose next year everyone agrees to contribute ten dollars to a fund to help the unlucky losers. Under such an arrangement, if next year is an average year, 10 of 100 people will suffer a loss and each will collect ninety dollars from the pool. The ninety lucky winners will each be ten dollars poorer than would otherwise be the case. The net effect is that each person will lose ten dollars – but only ten dollars – no matter what happens. Under this mutual insurance arrangement the risk has disappeared, at a cost of ten dollars to each of the participants. In some years there will be less than ten losses and in other years there may be more than ten losses, but on average there will be ten losses.

To avoid the difficulty of collecting money after the fact from each of the winners to pay the losers, insurance firms will emerge and charge an annual premium of ten dollars to all those at risk before a disaster occurs to anyone. The insurer will then pay the full $100 loss to each loser. The expected loss is still ten dollars for everyone since there is a one in ten chance of losing $100 next year. The ten dollar premium collected from all 100 people, including those who later suffered losses, is just enough to cover the loss of $100 to the ten unlucky people. If there are more than ten losses in a given year, the amount collected from premiums will not be sufficient to pay every loss in full. The insuring organization may then assess additional premiums on all buyers who are members of the pool, or it will get investors to provide financial reserves to cover such events.

Sometimes a loss just means a reduction in the wealth a person owns. Sometimes the loss requires an outlay, as when I must pay for damages I caused to someone else. Even in this case, the insurer often pays the costs of repairing or paying the bill for a loss before it comes due, so the consumer does not have a cash flow problem. This system is financially feasible and stable: everyone at risk pays the same amount. The beautiful part is that a potentially large loss to each consumer has been converted into a much smaller sure thing – a fixed premium for all.

The Law of Large Numbers, Insurance Supply, and Competitive Equilibrium

Suppose everyone knew beforehand that the chance of a loss was one in ten and many people agreed to participate in this kind of arrangement. If the losses of each individual were statistically independent of the others, the so-called *law of large numbers* dictates that the average loss is virtually certain to be close to the *expected loss*. In this situation, an insurance firm would almost always be able to cover the losses without having to utilize other funds in its coffers (i.e., its reserves) or collect additional premiums from the population it covers.

Because this hypothetical premium does not take into account the administrative costs of collecting the premiums and paying the losses, and assumes zero expected profits, it is called an *actuarially fair premium*.[3] Of course, those who invest in for-profit insurance companies want to make money. In addition, there are administrative costs of collecting the premiums and verifying and paying claims, so that the actual price charged to individuals will be higher than the actuarially fair premium. If consumers are risk averse when it comes to losing large sums of money, they should be willing to pay something more than the expected loss or actuarially fair premium to avoid such an event.

More specifically, the actuarially fair premium is determined by the expected frequency of losses, that is, the loss probability (symbolized by p), and the dollar amount of the loss (designated as L). Thus, the actuarially fair premium and its equivalent, the expected loss, will equal pL dollars. How much more than pL each consumer would be willing to pay depends on how risk averse he or she is.

It is important to understand that insurance works by *pooling* risks, not by *exchanging* risks. That is, sellers of insurance do not have to be less risk averse than buyers of insurance for an exchange to occur at a given price. To the contrary, insurance can function well even if everyone has exactly the same wealth and the same attitude toward risk; all that is required is that the loss-producing events not be perfectly correlated.

The ideal situation is one in which losses are independent, so the law of large numbers characterizes the outcomes. More specifically, the occurrence of a loss for each person is uncorrelated with loss-producing events for the others. To illustrate how insurance works in this situation, suppose that the loss probability is fifty percent, and two people, Martin and Lewis, face the same kind of risky prospect. The first two rows in Table 2.3 show the risks Martin and Lewis face alone, without any kind of insurance arrangement: each faces a fifty percent chance of losing $100 and a fifty percent chance of losing nothing. Now suppose that Martin and Lewis pool their risks in the sense that they agree they will both pay half of any losses that occur, regardless of which person loses. The next four rows show the probabilities and the net losses for both parties for all possible combinations of events with risk pooling.

Note that, compared to no pooling, the chances of both Martin and Lewis losing $100 have been cut in half, from fifty percent to twenty-five percent. The most likely outcome now is a loss for each person of fifty dollars, which has a fifty percent chance of occurring; the best outcome, no loss, also becomes less likely. The point is that pooling risk has reduced

Table 2.3. *Numerical example of pooling*

	Probability	Loss/Person
Martin or Lewis	No Insurance	
No Loss	50%	$0
Loss	50%	$100
Martin, Lewis	Two-person Pool	
No Loss, No Loss	25%	$0
Loss, No Loss	25%	$50
No Loss, Loss	25%	$50
Loss, Loss	25%	$100

the chances of both the worst and the best outcomes, while increasing the likelihood that the loss per person will be close to the expected loss. If we added more people to the risk-sharing pool, it is obvious that the chances of each person bearing the maximum loss will decrease, and the chances that the losses are close to fifty dollars will rise. With thousands of people in the pool, the chance that the loss per person will deviate from fifty dollars will be very small.

This example shows how risk pooling can make risk-averse people better off. In real life, insurance plans such as the one just described have operated for years in the form of mutual insurers – firms owned by their policyholders. Some mutual health insurers in agricultural states were started by farmer-owned cooperatives that already existed to supply seed and fertilizer. Rather than trying to enforce agreements to share losses after the fact, they collect the premium up front and then later adjust charges if total losses differ from what was expected. Even with some administrative costs for arranging the mutual insurance pool, all risk-averse participants can be better off than if they were operating on their own. The key point is that the main role for the insurance entity is to arrange and implement a mechanism in which bad fortunes are ameliorated.

In contrast to mutual insurance firms, stockholders who finance publicly traded insurers face a small risk that they may lose all or part of their investment if the insurer becomes insolvent because its losses exceed the premiums collected and the company's reserves. However, if the insurer's portfolio consists of a large number of independent events, the risk that these stockholders bear is so minimal that there really is little difference between this institutional arrangement and a mutual insurance firm.

Although risk pooling and the law of large numbers make it unlikely that actual losses from independent risks will deviate significantly from expected losses, it still is possible that, on occasion, total claims in a given time period will exceed premiums collected. Sometimes you toss the dice several times and snake eyes emerge more than once, even though each toss is independent; some years an unexpectedly large number of households might have kitchen fires and the insurer providing coverage against this risk has more claims than anticipated. In the Martin and Lewis example, if both people committed by putting fifty dollars into the pool at the outset, there would not be enough to fully cover the one in four chance of both experiencing a loss.

The occurrence of many more than the expected number of independent losses is so unlikely when there are a large number of insured individuals that when it happens we search for some additional explanation as to why these losses appear to be simultaneous or correlated. In the case of kitchen fires, perhaps there was a Chinese cooking craze that led many people to use woks carelessly and set the oil ablaze. To say that, on rare occasions, lightning does strike twice in the same place never seems adequate even if we know it is a possibility.

If the insurer is to fulfill its contract to pay claims in full in these rare cases, it needs to have additional resources to cover this kind of contingency. It can line up reserves before the event, try to borrow money, or sell stock after such a catastrophe. Having liquid funds on hand for such emergencies is far simpler than other options and generally cheaper. In the case of a large number of independent risks, charging a premium that reflects the expected loss will provide enough funds to pay virtually the total loss.[4] Only small amounts of additional capital will be needed in the form of reserves to pay claims, just in case the actual frequency of losses or the magnitude of the losses is higher than expected. In a setting where losses are not independent, the likelihood of unusually large claims is higher, and so more capital is needed to provide the same level of protection to policyholders and to the insurance company.

Solving Two Interrelated Problems

The insurance firm thus has to solve two interrelated problems: how large its reserve of capital should be, and how it can obtain that capital at the lowest possible cost. Any additional real expense associated with obtaining capital (for example, commissions to brokers who arrange the transaction) will push the break-even premium above the actuarially fair level to reflect the costs of having reserves available. Of course, suppliers of capital will require a potential return or profit on their investment. To trace out the insurance firm or market long-run supply curve, we also need to know how the additional cost per dollar of coverage changes with the total volume of coverage supplied.

Let us begin by considering a baseline case. Suppose the firm can obtain capital by promising to pay those who supply these funds a return equal to what the suppliers of capital would have received if they had invested their resources somewhere else in the private market, plus an additional amount equal to the expected value of the claims on that capital. For example, suppose the market return on investment is ten percent and the probability that a dollar of their capital will be needed to pay claims next year is one tenth of one percent (or one in a thousand), so they will lose that investment and any return on it. Investors who supply capital to insurance companies will then need a nominal return of a little more than 10.1 percent.[5]

Suppose each policy sold has a maximum loss that the insurer agrees to pay. Then the maximum claims that the insurance company will have to pay would be the maximum loss on each policy, multiplied by the number of policies in force. Suppose that all policyholders suffer a maximum loss simultaneously and the insurer needs sufficient capital to cover all those claims. If the company can obtain that much additional capital by promising to pay 10.1 percent and setting its premium at a level that allows it to do so, it will be positioned to avoid insolvency and default on its contracts to policyholders.

When the insurer adds the dollar of capital to its reserves, it increases the amount of benefits it will pay in this one in one thousand case and so can increase its actuarially fair premium. That increase will just cover the additional amount it will have to pay the investor who supplies a dollar of reserve capital that has a one in one thousand chance of being paid out in the form of claim payments. Because the insurer earns interest when it invests its reserve capital, not all, and generally not even a very large fraction, of the 10.1 percent nominal return needs to be added to the actuarially fair premium.[6] The only net cost on this score is the difference between what the firm earns as interest on the capital held as reserves and what it must pay to capital suppliers.

As a much more practical matter, firms do not attempt to amass that much capital. Rather, a firm insuring independent events needs relatively little capital in addition to the premiums it collects to cover the claims it will have to pay out. Even if the insured events are not independent but highly correlated – that is, even if one event triggers losses for many clients at the same time – the insurer generally can obtain sufficient capital to pay claims. But the supply arrangements and the resulting insurance supply curve become more complex, as we will discuss in Chapter 5.

In classical economics, if an insurer could obtain capital at the same cost to cover all eventualities, including simultaneous maximum losses by all policyholders, it would be expected to do so. Insurers do not hold reserves equal to the maximum possible total loss because the expenses associated with acquiring more funds rise as the amount of capital the insurer holds increases. More reluctant investors need to be convinced of the wisdom of tying up their resources for a period of time in an insurance company, which will require paying them a still higher interest rate on the capital they provide. At the same time, the expected benefit from adding each additional dollar of capital in advance to reserves decreases because of the smaller likelihood that it will be used to cover a large loss.

The benchmark supply model assumes free and costless entry and exit by insurers into the business of covering independent events. It predicts that actual premiums will not rise significantly above the sum of the actuarially fair premium and the net cost of capital plus administrative costs. In other words, in a competitive world, higher premiums would lead to excessive profits that would draw in more entrants.

One interesting implication of the competitive model is that, even if buyers of insurance would have been willing to pay much more than the cost of capital to cover their losses because they are very risk averse, the equilibrium market premium will still be close to the expected loss, because competition among existing insurers and free entry of new firms keeps premiums down even if buyers do not know their own loss probabilities. All buyers need do is to wait for offers for coverage and choose the cheapest one because new sellers will enter the market and charge lower premiums if existing sellers have set their prices sufficiently high that they are making especially large profits.

In the absence of regulation or insurer conspiracy, expected profits of insurers are likely to be close to the competitive level if there is free entry and a small chance of highly correlated losses. The price charged by insurers and the amount of coverage bought by consumers depends on the behavior of both parties involved in the transaction and on administrative costs. That is, the price would reflect expected costs of claims and administration, and sellers of insurance would be in competitive profit-maximizing equilibrium.

Obviously, circumstances exist that preclude the emergence of such a competitive market. One reason is that regulators limit entry to firms that can raise enough capital so they have adequate reserves. In addition, regulators may control the premium a firm may charge once it has entered the market. Another factor is that an insurer who has been selling policies in an area for some time may have a unique advantage, such as an agent who has many loyal customers who automatically renew their policies. Firms may conspire with one another to keep premiums high or keep other firms out. These conditions lead to behavior that differs from the benchmark competitive model of supply. If some insurance firms are not induced to enter the market by the possibility of earning a positive expected profit (because they are highly risk averse or have difficulty raising operating capital), then the benchmark model of supply will not adequately characterize the dynamics of the insurance market.

Our examples of insurers' behavior following the Florida hurricanes of 2004 and 2005 and after the terrorist attacks of 9/11 demonstrate other problems with the benchmark model of supply. When losses are highly correlated and the likelihood of the events occurring is highly uncertain, then insurers may be concerned about providing protection against these losses. In the case of natural disasters and terrorist attacks, insurers are concerned that they are not able to accurately estimate the premiums that they should charge. A very large loss may lead them to reconsider whether they believe the risk in question is an insurable one. We will discuss these and other types of behavior in actual markets in later chapters of the book and discuss ways that insurers' actions can more closely conform to the benchmark model of supply.

THE BENCHMARK MODEL OF DEMAND

The benchmark model of demand is based on the assumption that insurance buyers maximize their expected utility. Individuals purchase insurance because they are willing to pay a certain small premium to protect against an uncertain large loss. The explanation in classical economics as to when and why people view a sure thing as more desirable than an uncertain risk is based on expected utility theory. It has a long tradition in economics and policy analysis and it will serve as the benchmark model for analyses of demand-side anomalies.

Demand for Insurance using the Expected Utility Model

Expected utility theory tells us that risk-averse individuals are willing to purchase insurance at premiums that exceed their expected loss. A hypothetical example is the consumer who is willing to pay twelve dollars annually to insure against a loss of $100 that has a one in ten chance of occurring. The expected loss under that scenario is ten dollars. The additional two dollars – the risk premium, in expected utility parlance – reflects the extra amount above the expected loss the person is willing to pay for insurance. For the same expected loss, the risk premium will increase should the gamble involve a potentially larger loss and a smaller probability (for example, 1 in 100 chance of losing $1,000) because of the diminishing marginal utility of money – a way of characterizing their attitude toward financial risk.[7] In other words, the 1000th dollar of loss reduces utility more than the 100th dollar of loss for a risk-averse individual.

Insurance enables one to shift money from a high-income state (when one has not suffered a loss) to a low-income state (after experiencing a financial disaster). One dollar is, in a sense, less valuable to me when I have lots of money than when I have very little because I experience a decrease in wealth. Hence, purchasing insurance is a way of increasing a risk-averse person's expected utility unless the premium is unusually high or the potential losses in the future are relatively low.

Generally speaking, expected utility theory suggests that risk-averse individuals will be willing to pay a premium greater than their expected loss; this excess amount will depend on their level of risk aversion and the particulars of the risky prospect, notably the size of the loss relative to their wealth. Some individuals are highly averse to risk, others only moderately so. As an individual becomes more risk averse, the amount of risk premium he or she is willing to pay increases. Some individuals (though probably not many) are risk takers in the sense that they prefer taking a gamble in a risky situation rather than buying insurance to protect themselves against a large potential loss.

The previously cited example assumes that the consumer is considering a choice between purchasing insurance that will cover the entire loss should the untoward event occur, or remaining uninsured. A more realistic example would give the consumer a choice as to how much insurance to purchase, that is, whether to cover 100 percent of a possible loss or only 70 percent. The premiums for lower amounts of coverage obviously will be less than if one is fully protected. An individual decides how much insurance to purchase by trading off the higher expected loss for less than full coverage with the cost of paying higher premiums for more protection. As a means of clarifying the theory behind such a tradeoff, the next section discusses the decision to reduce coverage using a deductible..

Choosing Optimal Deductibles

Kenneth Arrow (1963) explained the classical theory for determining an optimal deductible. For our purposes, we assume that the consumer is risk averse and faces a single risk with a known probability and a specific loss. We assume a premium that takes into account the insurer's administrative costs, and that those administrative costs are proportional to the benefits paid out. That means a person pays a premium somewhat in excess of the expected loss.

Suppose that the consumer starts with insurance that covers the entire loss. But, on second thought, he wonders what would happen if he takes a deductible of one dollar of his loss. Although he understands that he will be one dollar poorer if the loss occurs than if it does not, he also knows that he can save on his premium since the expected insured loss and the insurer's costs of processing claims have been reduced. The net result is that, unless the person is extremely risk averse, he or she should feel better off by taking this deductible, thus self-insuring against the first dollar of loss.

Continue to run this thought experiment for several iterations by adding another dollar increase in the deductible each time. The consumer will have to incur more of the costs in case he or she suffers a loss, but the consumer will also save more on the premium. As the deductible gets larger and larger, however, there will come a point at which the consumer will not gain enough in lower premiums from increasing the deductible by another dollar to offset the increased pain from financial risk should he suffer a loss. That amount is the person's optimal or ideal deductible. The higher the cost of processing claims incurred by the insurer, the higher the optimal deductible, other things being equal. For risk-neutral individuals or risk takers, the strategy that maximizes expected utility is not to purchase any insurance at all (the largest possible deductible, in a sense) unless the premium is subsidized.

Using this logic, a consumer may have a good reason to take a relatively high deductible. Suppose the person is subject to losses of different sizes with different probabilities. Suppose also that the insurer's administrative cost depends in part on claims processing expenses and that it costs the same to process a small claim as a large one. When the consumer chooses a specific deductible, the insurer will need not pay any claims or incur any processing cost if the loss is small enough to be less than the deductible. When a claim for an amount larger than the deductible is filed, the insurer can conduct an investigation and pay the claim less the deductible. This will save the high processing costs that lead to a somewhat higher premium per dollar cost for small claims than for large claims, while still not exposing the person to a large amount of risk.

An additional reason an insurer wants a deductible on the policy is to promote safe behavior by the buyer of insurance. If the insured person knows that he or she will have to pay a portion of the losses, then there is an incentive to behave more carefully than if there were no deductible. In this sense, a deductible reduces the moral hazard problem – that is, the tendency for the insured to be less vigilant if he or she knows that losses will be fully covered.

In reality, consumers face a more complicated world than that implied by the expected utility model as illustrated by the two examples at the beginning of the chapter. Judy was uncertain as to the likelihood she had a genetic link to cancer and focused on ways to protect herself against this disease to alleviate her concerns without examining other alternatives. Doug did not know the risk of future accidents and the future potential premium costs associated with them and thus decided to avoid making a claim rather than make the tradeoffs implied by the expected utility model. In later chapters we will provide more insight into why individuals behave in the way Judy and Doug did and examine how to improve their decisions so they come closer to the benchmark model of demand.

SUMMARY

After presenting four examples of how consumers and insurers behave in practice, this chapter examined the world of insurance as it is characterized by classical economic theory. The benchmark model of supply in this ideal world assumes that insurers maximize long-run expected profits for their owners in a competitive market with free and costless entry and exit. The benchmark model of demand assumes that consumers purchase insurance because they can pay a small premium to avoid an uncertain large loss. The theoretical explanation as to why people should behave in this way is based on the expected utility model.

A fundamental principle that determines the supply of insurance is that insurers collectively pool risks facing individuals. In exchange for the payment of small premiums by many people against a specific risk, the insurer provides protection to the few who experience a large loss. If enough people purchase insurance and their losses are independent of each other, the law of large numbers comes into play, virtually assuring that the average loss within the group will be very close to what would be expected statistically.

In these simplified examples, the premiums people pay for insurance against a given loss represent each person's likelihood of the untoward event multiplied by the magnitude of the resulting loss, the so-called *actuarially fair premium*. In the real world, however, premiums are higher in order to cover administrative costs and to provide a profit to the insurer.

The expected utility model tells us that risk-averse individuals are willing to purchase insurance even at premiums that exceed their expected loss. How much risk premium a person is willing to pay depends upon how risk averse the person is and the particulars of the risky prospect.

Insurers are constrained by competitive market forces in the premiums they can charge; an insurer making excess profits will attract competitors that will offer lower premiums. While risk pooling and the law of large numbers make it unlikely that total losses will deviate from expected losses to any great extent, it still is possible that total claims in a given time period may exceed what was collected in premiums. Thus, insurers must maintain reserves to cover those unexpected losses and must raise that capital from investors.

To some extent, an insurer's administrative costs determine whether consumers will want to use deductibles – amounts that an insurer will not cover – in exchange for a lower premium. If the premium is much higher than the actuarially fair premium, only highly risk-averse individuals will select a low-deductible policy, while less risk-averse individuals will select a high-deductible policy. If the premiums were actuarially fair, no risk-averse person would want a deductible. Insurers can offer lower premiums for high-deductible policies because they pay out less in claims and because their administrative costs are lower. Insurers may also prefer policies with a high enough deductible level to reduce the likelihood that a person will behave in ways that increase claims if they are covered by insurance against the loss. Finally, if the loss is small relative to wealth, but the premium is high relative to the actuarially fair premium, even a risk-averse person may decide to purchase no coverage. Protection, in this case, may not be worth the price.

3

Anomalies and Rumors of Anomalies

The classical approach to economics tends to elegance and simplicity, as we saw in the benchmark models of supply and demand. The outcome of a competitive insurance market generally means resources are allocated efficiently and outputs are produced at lowest cost; consumer welfare is maximized, given the resources available to the economy. The only reason for intervention by the public sector is to correct any inequities from the resulting premiums, such as providing some type of subsidy to low-income residents currently residing in hazard-prone areas who cannot afford homeowners' insurance or to low-income households that might fail to buy health insurance without financial assistance.

But the real world is a considerably messier place. Individuals have difficulty understanding the purposes and concepts of insurance; firms often do not provide coverage at premiums that reflect risk. This chapter presents and analyzes anecdotal evidence of unusual insurance behavior reported by the media. Few of these journalistic examples use benchmark economic models to measure alleged mistakes by consumers considering buying insurance or insurers determining whether to offer coverage against a particular risk.

The chapter concludes by defining anomalies more formally. It will become evident that not everything that appears to be unusual behavior should be classified as such. In fact, as we show in the next chapter, we can find examples where insurance behavior is consistent with the benchmark models based on classical economic theory. However, many situations remain that deviate from these models.

INSURANCE IN THE MEDIA

Hints of anomalies appear regularly in the popular press, most often as discussions of "mistakes" that consumers make when they unwisely purchase insurance or when they do not buy a policy they should have. In our review of such news articles in recent years, we find that most of these reports do not explicitly characterize these choices as deviating from what expected utility theory would predict, but they do make value judgments that there is underpurchase or overpurchase of insurance. We use this anecdotal evidence as motivation for digging deeper into the rationale for actions by consumers and firms.

Many editorials and articles on insurance appeal to readers' desire to understand personal finance. One of the most common topics is the purchase of expensive, limited-coverage insurance. A good example, dating back to 1996, is the *New York Times* article entitled "When the Best Policy May Be No Policy at All" (Abelson 1996). It listed at least ten insurance policies that "offer little value for their money," among them cancer insurance, flight insurance, rental car insurance, and other specialty policies.[1]

The article focuses on the relatively low expected loss (either because the likelihood of the loss and/or the loss, if it occurred, is small) as compared to the relatively high price of these insurance products. It concludes that some insurance policies have low expected benefits relative to the cost of protection. In this sense, the argument presented against buying such policies is implicitly based on using the expected utility model that forms the basis for the benchmark model of demand.

There is no commentary as to why these overpriced policies are the ones the industry supplies – why competition does not seem to be working to bid premiums down closer to actual loss cost – other than the implicit suggestion that some insurers are trying to trap the unwary. In addition to being labeled overpriced, these insurance policies are also criticized because they target coverage for a single risk rather than offering protection against a larger class of risks. The discussion appropriately notes that the benefits from these policies are limited, because other similar risks are left uncovered. It is easy to understand the message: your money is better spent on comprehensive protection such as life, health,

Figure 3.1. Ernie (Piranha Club) © King Features Syndicate Inc.

auto, and homeowners' coverage rather than on specialty insurance policies, such as loss of life from a specific type of accident (like a plane crash) or getting a specific disease (like cancer).

These journalistic articles rarely indicate the number of individuals who actually purchase such policies. If only a few people buy this insurance, even if the costs of a policy are much greater than the expected benefits, such behavior would not constitute a serious anomaly. The articles may be giving good advice, but there may not be many people who need it.

The articles also tend to ignore the fundamental point that if the premium is low enough relative to the probability of a loss, some of these policies could still be worth their cost. That is, even a policy with limited coverage is a good buy if it is cheap enough and the possible losses are sufficiently high. The cartoon in Figure 3.1 illustrates this point, although some may argue that five cents is too much to pay for a policy given the extraordinarily low chance of this event occurring.

Since the article in the *New York Times* was written, some of these products have virtually disappeared from the market due to low demand. Many years ago, in one of the classic economic discussions of insurance, Robert Eisner and Robert Strotz (1961) wrote a paper arguing that no one should purchase flight insurance (coverage that pays benefits to your heirs if your plane crashes) since a life insurance policy was more comprehensive, covering death from all causes (except suicide) and a much better deal. In his 1982 book *The Invisible Bankers*, Andrew Tobias reinforces this point with a detailed discussion of why it is economically imprudent to purchase such coverage given the very low probability of a plane crashing. Today, few individuals purchase such coverage, and it is even hard to find flight insurance counters at the airport. You might find a charge added to your credit card bill, however, if you buy trip insurance. We discuss this example in more detail in Chapter 7, where we also treat a variety of other insurance offerings that cover damages from special risks.

Warnings in news media articles of underpurchase of insurance are somewhat less common than those of overpurchase. One frequently cited underinsured risk, however, is that of protecting lost income through disability insurance. A typical argument was made in a 2002 *CNN Money* piece entitled, "Ouch! Don't Forget Disability Insurance," that warns of a high probability of being disabled at some point during one's lifetime (Lobb 2002). In this case, the article contends that thirty percent of Americans will suffer a disability in which the person is unable to pursue normal activities for at least ninety days at some point in their lives. It also emphasizes the absence of disability benefits in many jobs, the provision of only limited benefits when employers do provide disability policies and sick leave provisions, and the difficulties of understanding the terms of the policies available in the individual market. Premiums and benefits are discussed in fairly broad terms, but the crux of the argument is that the high lifetime probability of becoming disabled and thus unable to earn income warrants purchasing this insurance.

Although the lifetime probability of a period of disability is relatively high, as indicated previously, these arguments fail to capture the relationship between the chance of being disabled, the expected cost of this condition, the likelihood that insurance benefits will be collected, and the annual premium. For example, if the likelihood of a person becoming disabled next year is one in 250, and the estimated covered loss should this occur is $180,000, then the expected loss is $720 ($1/250 \times \$180,000$), and it would not be unreasonable to pay a premium of about $800 or a little more for protection against this happening. But if the annual premium were $5,000, then one could argue that it would be financially unwise to purchase such a policy. In other words, if the disability insurance is highly overpriced, it might be rational to avoid buying coverage even against a serious risk.

The CNN piece also fails to take into account that many disabled individuals are physically or mentally handicapped from birth and are covered by Medicare or Social Security for their condition. The quoted statistic on lifetime disability, while technically correct, therefore seriously overstates the threat facing a person who has made it to working age without experiencing a disability.

Renters' insurance is another oft-cited example of underpurchased insurance. Most people who rent do not have it (Insurance Information Institute 2010). At around fifteen dollars per month, the affordability of renters' insurance is not in question. An article by a *Washington Post* financial writer, Michelle Singletary, highlights this point: "Skip just one movie a month (including the popcorn and soda) and you can afford renters' insurance" (Singletary 2003, 1). But affordability does not imply necessity or desirability. Information on the probability and typical amount of a loss is nowhere to be found in media arguments such as the *Washington Post* piece. Fifteen dollars a month (or $180 for the annual premium) may not be a good deal if there is a low chance you will claim benefits. We return to this and other examples in the following chapters, where we will provide a more formal analysis of how people might or should compare the premiums to the expected losses.

Evidence of anomalous behavior also encompasses concerns about complex types of coverage purchased. Return-of-premium life insurance policies have been denounced in many financial columns and newspaper articles because they cost more than a typical term-life policy. With this insurance, your heirs get death benefits if you die during the term of coverage, but the insurer refunds the total premiums paid if you are still alive at the end of the contract. Typically, the terms of these policies are from fifteen to thirty years, so that a thirty-year-old buying such a policy has a high likelihood of collecting this relatively large sum.[2]

The attraction of this feature is that, compared to term-life insurance, you are likely to get a rebate from paying premiums. Those who argue in favor of this type of insurance contend that with conventional term insurance, you are likely to pay premiums for years and get no return. In contrast, with return-of-premium coverage you probably will get something back at a time when you can still enjoy life. Of course, the cost of that additional benefit is built into the premium and the money is returned with little or no interest. Indeed, financial advisers question the decision to buy this type of policy because the extra premiums advanced to the insurer in anticipation of a rebate could be invested more wisely by the buyer (Bradford 2005).

Two additional forms of insurance that might be considered anomalous that have gained popular attention are policies with gaps in coverage and those with low deductibles to cover small losses but at the same time have low policy limits that provide little protection against a catastrophic loss. For example, mini-medical plans, which cover only a small number of doctor or hospital visits per year, are gaining popularity (Frase 2009). Some health insurers have been experimenting with gaps in coverage policies in the face of rapidly rising costs. The Medicare prescription drug benefit is an example of the so-called doughnut-hole format in which there is some initial coverage, followed by a gap in coverage, and finally some catastrophic coverage. These types of policies are potential demand-side anomalies – except that the doughnut-hole coverage was specified by Congress and was not triggered by buyer preferences. The political process thus contributes to anomalies as well as redressing them.

Supply-side anomalies are also covered in the popular press, but with much less frequency. We found no stories about insurers refusing to offer insurance against independent, small risks. The closest example is an article in the *Washington Post* asserting that health insurers refuse to cover high medical expenses, experimental treatments, or expenses of very high-risk people (Sun 2010). Most often, such risks or expenses are associated with an already present chronic condition, which would make the premium very costly. Insurers may be unwilling to seek approval for rates they know to be so high that almost no one will buy this coverage. Unless required to do so, they will not furnish coverage at premiums where they will be sure to lose money.

More discussion of supply anomalies occurs in settings where losses are highly correlated and coverage is not offered by insurers. A 2004 *Wall Street Journal* op-ed suggested that insurers excluded terrorism coverage from their policies for some time after the 9/11 attacks on the premise that forecasting future attacks was impossible (Jenkins 2004). The article argues instead that "terrorism is far from uninsurable" and that even in "high-risk" cities, "the odds of an attack that could jeopardize the conventional insurance industry's capital cushion are vastly lower than before 9/11." The *Journal* therefore criticized insurers as behaving in a nonoptimal fashion. The article asserted, but did not offer evidence indicating that the probability of a future attack is lower than insurers thought it to be. In fact, the article did not discuss how insurers would be able to estimate the likelihood of a future terrorist attack.

The opinion piece does not offer an explanation as to why insurers behaved in this way, other than by hinting that they held back from offering coverage in order to lobby for federal subsidies. It also makes the point that actuaries were slow to focus on the moderate terrorism risk and in so doing ignored a business opportunity. The implication of the article was that the insurance industry should have been able to profit from supplying such coverage at premiums attractive to buyers, given the supposedly low probability of truly catastrophic loss events. This, of course, has been the topic of much academic research and will be addressed in much more detail in Chapter 9.

Many additional contentions of overpriced or underpurchased insurance and the specification of unusual policy features can be found in print and online media. This suggests that there is general interest, in addition to considerable confusion, regarding the workings of the insurance industry and how it might be improved. As noted earlier, missing from these anecdotes is a thorough examination of what truly constitutes anomalous behavior with respect to economic theory.

Sensible insurance purchase decisions depend not only on how financially harmed you will be if the bad event occurs, but also on the likelihood that the event will occur. Both need to be considered when determining whether the premium is reasonable or too high. Simultaneous treatment of the likelihood of the event and the amount of the premium is often absent from these popular discussions of insurance. Even more striking, little consideration is given to risk aversion. How much insurance one should buy depends on an individual's own tolerance of risk, not on how other people might feel. Finally, discussions of supply gaps rarely offer any explanation for the absence of coverage. The media tend to blame insurers for being thick-headed or lacking vision. They normally do not mention that a potential reason for insurers' behavior is that regulators try to restrict them from charging premiums that they would want to charge in a competitive market setting, or that the administrative costs of some insurance might swamp the benefits from individuals wanting to purchase coverage.

There is voluminous academic literature outlining the reasons the benchmark expected utility model is inadequate as a description of how people think and behave with respect to a wide variety of financial decisions. There is also a growing body of evidence from controlled experiments (normally undertaken with college students) that when offered a set of risky options, people often make choices that cannot be explained by expected utility theory.[3] Sometimes the choices in these experiments are hypothetical and sometimes they involve moderate monetary prizes, but they do not occur in the context of fully functioning markets with profit-seeking firms supplying the insurance.

The evidence for demand anomalies usually consists of informal generalizations about behavior inconsistent with risk-averse consumers' purchasing decisions for a given premium offered by insurers. Some are extensions of pure theory. For example, Kenneth Arrow (1963) argues that a person should buy less than full coverage and sometimes remain uninsured if premiums greatly exceed the actuarially fair premium.

In some cases, insurance products that should be viewed as desirable based on the expected utility model are viewed as unattractive by consumers. In a series of thought experiments with realistic data, Peter Wakker, Richard Thaler, and Amos Tversky (1997) found that students, executives, and portfolio managers unanimously reject insurance that specifically allows for some positive probability of failing to pay promised benefits, even at a premium that ought to make it attractive according to standard theory. For example, they offered their subjects *probabilistic fire insurance* where there was a one percent chance that, in the event of a fire, the claim would not be paid. They found that people demand about a thirty percent reduction in the premium to compensate them for a one percent risk of not being paid, behavior reflecting risk aversion so great that it cannot be accommodated by any plausible utility function.

Other discussions of anomalies refer to actual behavior. For example, today, all property and most health insurance policies carry deductibles, but they generally seem to be *too small* relative to what individuals should take, given the size of the premium, if they were maximizing expected utility. People appear to be paying insurers a large amount for a combination of administrative expenses and profit to get protection against relatively small, manageable losses. In the 1970s, the insurance commissioner of Pennsylvania, Herbert Denenberg, mandated at least a $100 deductible (rather than a $50 deductible) for automobile collision policies. Although the plan purportedly saved consumers millions of dollars, it was opposed by the public and had to be rescinded (Cummins et al. 1974).

Some studies look carefully at demand-side anomalies in actual insurance markets. Items usually singled out are warranties, low-deductible insurance policies, or insurance against small losses where willingness to pay premiums far in excess of expected loss seems to reflect anomalous behavior. Using data on homeowners' insurance in Philadelphia and Orlando from one of the largest sellers of this coverage, David Cutler and Richard Zeckhauser (2004) provide evidence that consumers choose plans with deductibles that are too low. They found that sixty percent to ninety percent of the insured individuals had $500 deductibles. If the deductible were raised to $1,000, the premium savings would range from $220 to $270. Only if the probability of suffering a loss of more than $1,000 in the next year were greater than forty-four percent (i.e., $220/$500) could a person who was risk neutral justify taking this lower deductible. Some consumers may have had to take insurance to satisfy lenders, but such low deductibles would not make sense for those who owned their homes outright.

Sometimes anomalies arise because the benchmark theory unrealistically assumes that consumers are ever vigilant and ever calculating so that they can always select the most attractive policy given their degree of risk aversion, the cost of switching to other coverage, or choosing to be uninsured as soon as the price gets out of line. In reality, inertia and confusion mean that people often stick with overpriced, poorly designed policies (Liebman and Zeckhauser 2008).

Finally, a few studies identify large-scale behavior inconsistent with expected utility theory. For example, individuals in flood-prone areas of the United States fail to purchase flood insurance voluntarily even though premiums are highly subsidized by the federal government. Of those who do buy a policy, many cancel several years later when they have not experienced a flood. These individuals view their decision to purchase insurance as a bad investment rather than celebrating the fact that they have not suffered a loss during the past few years (Kunreuther et al. 1978; Michel-Kerjan, Lemoyne de Forges, and Kunreuther. 2011).

In addition to literature on improper purchasing, there has been some discussion of insurance instruments that seem desirable but have failed to emerge. Robert Shiller, in his 2003 book, *The New Financial Order: Risk in the 21st Century*, proposes several new types of coverage currently not on the market. These include *livelihood* or *career insurance*, which protects against long-term risks to individual paychecks. For example, when you embark on specialized training for a certain career, you should be able to buy insurance that will pay you should earnings in that career unexpectedly fall because of demand shifts or changes in technology, or for other reasons.

Shiller also proposes *home equity insurance* that would protect not just against risks such as fire, which is covered by homeowners' policies, but against losses in the values of homes from other causes. Such a policy was offered by the city of Oak Park, a suburb of Chicago, to attempt to stem the flight from mixed neighborhoods by whites who feared the value of their property would decrease due to racial change. Only a small percentage of the homeowners enrolled in the program, probably those particularly worried about this possibility. Others might have declined to purchase because they correctly anticipated what actually happened: homes in the neighborhood retained their values as racial change progressed.

The overall tenor of academic discussions of anomalies is that they do arise from common buyer behavior that differs from the benchmark model. The implicit value judgment emerging from these studies is that the behavior, or its consequences, should somehow be corrected. To our knowledge, there has been no attempt to determine how well insurance markets perform in general, or whether anomalous behavior is pervasive enough to cause major problems for the economy as a whole.

Given the less than satisfactory nature of advice consumers receive about insurance purchasing in the popular press, we now provide a realistic example of an insurance purchasing decision and how someone ought to think about it, according to economic theory. Joe Szechpach is a thirty-year-old, single Web designer who recently received a nice bonus to add to his $80,000 annual income. He rents a tasteful apartment for $2,000 a month and buys renters' insurance to cover his furniture and home electronics, but decides to use his bonus to buy a new Nissan 370Z roadster convertible with all the extras. The car has been his heart's desire for as long as he can remember. He purchases the $40,000 car using cash. Along with $30,000 in stocks and $40,000 in his retirement account (which he cannot access for at least thirty years without penalty), this constitutes all of his financial wealth. Beyond housing, he uses his income for living expenses and occasional travel abroad.

Although Joe is a careful driver, he realizes something could happen to his "baby." He is required to obtain liability insurance for his car at a premium of eighty dollars per month. He may also choose to buy collision insurance at an additional forty dollars per month. Based on the benchmark model of demand, is it rational for Joe to buy or forego collision insurance? What is the maximum he should be willing to pay to maximize his expected utility? And, conversely, what action on his part would represent anomalous behavior?

Let us begin by imagining that Joe knows there is some chance that he might crack up his new car and experience a partial or total loss. Based on what he has observed with respect to his own and his friends' driving behavior, he should be able to deduce a subjective probability of having an accident that damages his car in the next year. He may not have great confidence in his estimate, but he will come up with something between zero and one.

To decide whether to buy insurance, he will compute his expected insurance claims from accidents using his subjective probability estimate and compare this estimate with the premium per-dollar coverage charged by an insurer. If he thinks that the cost of buying coverage is less than the expected claims from an insurance policy (that is, the probability of experiencing a given amount of damage to the car multiplied by the amount of the claim, added up over each possible level of damage), purchasing insurance is an obvious good buy. He believes the odds are in his favor, and buying insurance when you expect to get back more than you put in is a no-brainer. If Joe is risk averse, he would be willing to pay a risk premium for insurance protection. But if the premium is too high relative to his perceived expected claims payments from insurance, he will decide to forego coverage, take a chance, and pay out of his own pocket if he causes damages to his car.

Joe might believe, rightly or wrongly, that he is a better driver than the insurance company considers him to be, and thus choose not to purchase any collision coverage at the market premium even if insurer administrative costs and profits are very low. Suppose he thinks the probability of his being in an accident is considerably less than the insurance company has calculated. Joe might be right, but he should remember that the insurance company is estimating his chances of an accident based on the company's claims experience of thousands of drivers, while Joe just has fourteen years of driving experience on which to base his risk estimates. Joe has only a fifty-fifty chance of being a better driver than the average person in the company's customer base. Still, if there is an anomaly here, it is not in Joe's behavior, but in his misperception of reality.

If a large proportion of people contemplating this (or any other insurance purchase) has opinions about the risk that differ from those of insurers, why don't the insurers – or analysts or even professors – try to convince them of the facts? If challenged, Joe might recognize that he is uncertain of his own probability estimate, and might therefore be willing to alter it if provided with new information on risks of automobile accidents. Buyers' willingness (or unwillingness) to revise their estimates of loss probabilities in the face of additional information, or whether they even consider the likelihood of certain events when making decisions, will be key factors in explaining their behavior.

Let us now pull these thoughts together. To simplify matters, assume that the only accident is one that destroys the car, so that the monetary loss is $40,000. Joe has in mind a subjective probability estimate that this might happen in any given year. Thus he thinks he knows the risk of totaling his car, which represents ten percent of his wealth. Should Joe's car be demolished, we assume that he will be made financially whole by receiving a claims payment large enough for him to buy another identical car. He has no affection for the particular vehicle that he currently drives, and would be willing to accept another 370Z (same color, same features, same mileage) as a perfect substitute for his current vehicle.

We now have the basis for a strong statement. We can say that if Joe is averse to risk, he should be willing to buy collision coverage on his car if he can obtain coverage at a premium per dollar that equals what he thinks the chances are that he will crash his car this year. In effect, such a premium would be actuarially fair from his perspective. If the actual premium is lower than his estimate of these expected benefits, he would want to buy even more than $40,000 of insurance if possible and gamble on the loss of his car because the price is so attractive. But we assume that insurers will not allow him to overinsure in this fashion because it creates a moral hazard, that is, an economic incentive for Joe to drive more carelessly than he normally would. Insurers diligently work against creating situations in which moral hazard is a potential problem.

What if the premium per dollar of coverage is greater than Joe's perception of the risk of a collision this year? If we assume his only choice is full coverage or no coverage, we can say that there is some *reservation premium* per dollar of coverage above which he will refuse coverage, because he perceives himself to be worse off paying for coverage than taking his chances that he won't have an accident. There will be a range between the lowest premium the insurer might offer and Joe's reservation premium. We will delve into the determination of these premiums for different kinds of insurance and different kinds of insurers and buyers later in the book.

Joe's story introduces an important difference between insurance and other consumer purchases such as food, clothing, and shelter, where there is an intrinsic demand for the products at some level. Joe does not have this same kind of need for collision insurance on his car. He could drive without it because he paid cash and hence no bank requires him to protect this asset. He will want insurance if he discovers that it is available at a price he finds attractive. If not, he will go without protection. Attractiveness, in turn, depends on how his subjective probability of a loss compares to the one the insurer is using.

If we have these data, we are in a position to say whether Joe will decide to purchase insurance and how much coverage he will want should he decide insurance is financially attractive. If the premium per dollar of coverage equaled his subjective estimate of the probability of an accident, we can say that he should buy coverage just equal to the amount of the loss, with no deductibles or limits if such a policy were available. If the premium per dollar is higher than the actuarially fair premium, Joe will probably choose not to buy full coverage, but rather a policy with a deductible to handle the small losses. If the premium is very high, above his reservation price for even a small amount of coverage, he will buy nothing. The amount of coverage he decides to purchase will be determined by his degree of risk aversion. Should he choose to take a policy with a deductible, he will be self-insuring for a portion of the loss should his car be involved in an accident in which he is at fault.[4]

DEFINING ANOMALIES

This hypothetical example allows us to define what we mean by demand-side and supply-side anomalies using the benchmark models of choice presented in Chapter 2. First, consider some obvious guidelines regarding behavior as defined by these benchmark models. Even if an event is risky, potential buyers should not purchase insurance if the premium is very high due to administrative costs or for other reasons. Conversely, if the price is sufficiently low relative to expected loss, one should always buy insurance, even if the person is not overly concerned about the risk.

There will almost always be a few consumers who, for various reasons, fail to buy the right insurance or purchase coverage that is inappropriate, such as taking the lowest deductible in exchange for lower limits so they are unprotected against potentially catastrophic losses. There will always be a few unscrupulous firms that seek to charge very high premiums just in case some naïve buyer comes along.

There are two key parameters characterizing an insurance market that would not be seriously subject to anomalous behavior: the premium charged and the proportion of individuals purchasing coverage.[5] We consider this market to be nonanomalous if the following conditions are satisfied:

- *Condition One*: the premium reflects the expected loss plus an appropriate loading (defined in Box 1) to cover administrative expenses and normal profits;
- *Condition Two*: a large majority of eligible consumers voluntarily purchase reasonable amounts of coverage at those premiums.

With respect to Condition One, we show in the accompanying sidebar (Box 1) that the key element in determining whether a premium is in a range considered nonanomalous is the *premium loading factor*. It is determined by the ratio of the expected loss to the premium charged by the insurer. We will use as our benchmark for nonanomalous premiums a premium loading factor of between **thirty percent and forty percent**, close to what is available in the market to a careful shopper. In doing so we recognize that the premium loading factor may be somewhat higher than this figure when insurers are concerned with the possibility of highly correlated losses that are large relative to the insurer's assets.

With respect to the proportion of consumers who buy coverage (Condition Two), we define the market penetration level as the ratio of actual buyers to eligible buyers. No real-world market ever hits a 100 percent penetration level due to differences in risk aversion among consumers and inattention to the task of buying insurance. Given the absence of data on what constitutes a meaningful penetration level, we use a benchmark value of **seventy percent** as a basis for characterizing a well-functioning insurance market.

TYPES OF ANOMALIES

Given these two parameters defining a well-functioning insurance market, we can characterize several possible types of anomalies on both the

Box 1. Defining Loading and Premium Loading Factor

The premium for an insurance policy covers two major costs: the *expected loss*, which is the claims incurred by the insurer during the year, and the *loading*, which is comprised of selling and administrative costs (e.g., marketing cost, salaries of employees, payment of the office buildings, utilities), costs associated with brokers and agents who market policies as well as expenses for those who determine and adjust claims following a loss. Premium taxes can also add to the loading.

There is another component of loading that is more difficult to understand – the cost of capital in the form of reserves to enable the insurer to pay unexpectedly high claims. The loading should thus include an amount that covers the transaction costs associated with making these assets available to an insurance company plus any higher tax cost to the investor associated with that investment. Often, one hears a call for insurance premiums that reflect actuarially fair rates without consideration of these other costs that the insurer incurs that make up the loading cost.

The loading is normally expressed as a percentage of the premium that the insurer is charging the consumer, which we designate as the premium loading factor. More specifically:

Premium = Expected Loss / (1 − Premium Loading Factor)

This translates into the following formula for Premium Loading Factor:

$$\text{Premium Loading Factor} = 1 - \frac{\text{Expected Loss}}{\text{Premium}}$$

To illustrate the determination of the premium loading factor, suppose that the annual expected loss from a homeowners' policy covering damage from fire and wind is $1,000, and that the loading is $500 so that the premium is $1500. Then the Premium Loading Factor = 1 −$1,000/$1,500 = .333 or 33.3 percent.

demand and supply side that will be discussed more extensively in later chapters.

Demand-Side Anomalies

Inadequate demand at reasonable premiums. When insurance is priced appropriately, an anomaly exists if demand is inadequate, that is, if the fraction purchasing coverage is below our seventy percent benchmark. If a small fraction fails to buy insurance we will lump that behavior into the set of inconsequential mistakes. In some cases, however, such as health insurance, where about twenty percent of people ineligible for public coverage do not obtain private coverage, we may still want to examine why this behavior may have occurred, but would not classify this failure to buy health insurance as anomalous.

The strongest form of this anomaly will be in markets in which the premium is below the expected loss because of subsidy or regulation, yet relatively many individuals do not voluntarily buy the coverage. The benchmark model of demand tells us that all risk-averse people should be willing to buy insurance if the premium is actuarially fair, so they certainly would want coverage if the price is subsidized to a level below the expected loss. Flood insurance sold through the National Flood Insurance Program is a good example of this anomaly, where a large number of homeowners in flood-prone regions have not voluntarily purchased subsidized flood insurance or retained their coverage even when banks required the policy in high-hazard areas.

Large demand at excessive premiums. Even though the premium has a loading factor above forty percent such that coverage is overpriced, an anomaly exists if there is considerable demand for coverage by those at risk. Some warranties fall into this category. About twenty percent to forty percent of purchasers of appliances or electronics buy warranties, even though their price is often considerably above expected repair costs over the length of the warranty (Huysentruyt and Read 2010). Based on a simple insurance model, this looks like an anomaly.

Purchasing the wrong amount or type of coverage. In some instances, the proportion of individuals purchasing insurance may be consistent with the case just described, but the amount or type of coverage many of them buy does not conform to the benchmark model. The strong preference for low-deductible policies is an example of this type of anomaly. There is empirical evidence that people stick with low deductibles for auto insurance and homeowners' coverage even though the premium reduction from increasing the deductible greatly exceeds the increased expected out of pocket payment (Cutler and Zeckhauser 2004; Sydnor 2010).

Supply-Side Anomalies

Coverage is not offered when it should be. Insurance that is not offered even though there would be sufficient demand at premium loading factors considerably greater than the thirty percent to forty percent benchmark falls into this category. Terrorism insurance after 9/11 is a prime example. The implied premium loading factor for the few companies that offered coverage was considerably greater than forty percent. For example, one firm bought $9 million worth of terrorism insurance to cover its building for one year at a price of $900,000. If this premium were considered actuarially fair, the likelihood of this event would be in the order of one in ten, an absurdly high annual probability.[6]

Coverage is priced below break-even premiums. Insurance is sometimes offered in a competitive market setting at premiums that would be below a premium loading factor of thirty percent and in some cases is below the expected loss. This supply anomaly will not be sustainable in a competitive setting, but it definitely occurs in regulated settings where insurers are forced to offer coverage at below the actuarially fair premium to high-risk consumers and then charge higher prices than they otherwise would to lower-risk individuals. In the late 1990s, insurers offering HMO health insurance coverage in a competitive market sustained substantial losses because they had set premiums considerably below the actuarially fair value (Pauly et al. 2002). Apparently, the insurers thought they were going to be more successful in containing health care costs than they actually were.[7] Eventually they took a more realistic view of costs, raised their premiums at double-digit annual growth rates, and returned to profitability.

SUMMARY

Contentions of overpriced or underpurchased insurance and the specification of unusual policy features can be found in the popular media.
These stories suggest a general interest in the workings of the insurance
industry and how it might be improved. Although some of the discussion is related to the question of whether the premiums are related to the
benefits, these anecdotes often do not provide a clear understanding or
explanation as to what truly constitutes anomalous behavior, so that the
advice offered to readers is wrong or misleading.

There is a general tendency by the media to conclude that if something
is risky it should be insured. This advice often does not consider the premium that would have to be paid and how it compares to the likelihood
of the event occurring and the resulting claim payments from having
insurance. We provide two conditions for characterizing nonanomalous
markets and then provide examples where both consumers and insurers
go astray. We also raise the possibility that the benchmark models of
supply and demand discussed in Chapter 2 may not always be the best
yardsticks against which to judge behavior in practice. In what follows,
we will track these differences and discuss their origins and meanings.

4

Behavior Consistent with Benchmark Models

Now that we have described the types of demand and supply anomalies relative to the benchmark models, we analyze several real-world insurance markets to illustrate when behavior would be classified as anomalous. At the heart of that determination are two questions:

- Do consumers make decisions regarding insurance purchases consistent with the expected utility model?
- Do insurers set premiums in competitive markets (without price regulation) so as to maximize expected profits?

RELEVANT ASSUMPTIONS FOR EXAMINING BEHAVIOR

Answers to these two questions are simplest in situations with well-specified and well-known loss probabilities and an insurance market that has the following characteristics:

- A substantial number of at-risk individuals whose losses are independent of one another;
- Loss amount per event that is large relative to buyers' wealth but small relative to insurers' capital;
- Low costs to consumers for becoming well informed about potential losses;
- Freedom of consumers to decide whether to buy insurance and, if so, how much coverage to purchase;[1]
- Free entry by insurers, with freedom to set premiums.

We will consider three markets that generally seem to possess these characteristics. On the demand side, we will examine whether the behavior of those at risk is consistent with the expected utility model. On the supply side, we will determine whether the premiums are consistent with incorporating administrative costs, competition, and the need to earn normal profits. We will consider a premium loading factor between thirty percent and forty percent of the premium as consistent with the benchmark model of supply. If, at such a price, we see roughly seventy percent or more eligible individuals voluntarily purchasing coverage, we will regard the market as consistent with the benchmark model of demand.

Automobile Collision Coverage

Individuals who have purchased automobile collision coverage can make claims if they suffer damage to their car not covered by payments from a negligent motorist. If another driver has caused the damage and has third-party liability coverage, then that person's insurer will cover the losses. Insurers generally consider collisions to be independent events so that the law of large numbers should apply when determining the level of premiums and reserves. Thousands of dollars of damage to a single vehicle will be a financial blow to the majority of households, but not to insurers with revenues and reserves in the millions (or billions) of dollars.

Insurers can estimate the expected collision damage to different kinds of vehicles with different kinds of drivers. Even optimistic drivers are aware that this kind of loss could happen to them, although they may underestimate its likelihood. We will reserve judgment on the consistency between insurer and driver loss estimates until we look at how this market operates today.

The typical benefit payment from collision insurance is the lesser of either the estimated cost to repair the damage or the market value of the vehicle before the accident. Owners of newer cars are likely to be paid the repair cost unless the car is destroyed. Drivers of older cars may find the cost of repairs exceeds the value of the vehicle. In that case, only the market value is paid.[2]

For the most part, the coverage from such policies is similar across insurers, although deductible levels may vary. Auto collision insurance thus looks like a strong candidate for designation as a well-functioning market due to the independence of individual losses, potential losses that are large relative to household wealth and low relative to insurer assets, and well-specified loss probabilities.

The total amount of incurred losses for collision coverage was $39 billion in 2008. Claim frequency for collision coverage hovered around five percent in each of the three most recent years of available data (2006–8). Average claim severity also remained relatively stable at approximately $3,000 in each of those years (Insurance Information Institute 2009a). As the frequency and severity of claims was relatively stable across these three years, insurers should be able to set premiums just high enough to cover claims and administration costs while earning profits consistent with those in a competitive market.

We can generate an estimate of the premium loading factor for this coverage with data on total premiums paid to insurers and claims paid out to clients. The *loss ratio* is calculated by adding the incurred losses and loss adjustment expenses and calculating the ratio of that sum to premiums earned. The premium loading factor is then calculated as (1 – loss ratio). In other words, the lower the loss ratio, the higher the premium loading factor.

The National Association of Insurance Commissioners releases an annual profitability report by line of business. Included in this report is a detailed breakdown of the premiums earned and related costs for all first-party damages, primarily collision, comprehensive (fire and theft), and physical damage coverage. The report for 2006 states that fifty-six percent of premiums were accounted for by incurred losses and another ten percent by loss adjustment expenses.[3] The remaining thirty-four percent of premiums were accounted for by administrative expenses including marketing costs and determining claims payments, taxes, and profits. Administrative expenses represent about twenty-two percent of premiums, with taxes and dividends at three percent, so the average realized profit would be about nine percent of premiums as shown in Table 4.1 (NAIC 2008). These aggregate data on the collision market indicate

Table 4.1. *Allocation of premiums for automobile collision insurance*

	Percent of Net Premiums Earned
Losses Incurred	56
Loss Adjustment Expenses	10
Administrative Expenses and taxes	25
Profits	9

Source: 2006 NAIC Profitability Report.

Table 4.2. *Collision premiums for a Honda Civic hatchback, by car value*

Model Year	Car Value	Annual Premium	Expected Benefit
1999	$4,910	$330	$218
1997	$3,705	$292	$193
1995	$2,680	$242	$160
1993	$2,190	$222	$147
1991	$1,615	$202	$133

Source: 2006 Esurance.com quotes and *Kelley Blue Book* values.

that the overall premium loading factor for collision coverage (thirty-four percent) is consistent with the benchmark model of supply.

In order to further examine how the collision market measures up to the benchmark supply model, we can determine how the price of insurance is related to the age and value of the car. Table 4.2 shows the online quotes (from the website Esurance.com) for annual premiums received for a $500 deductible policy on a Honda Civic hatchback with varying *Kelley Blue Book* values, depending on the model year. The expected benefits are calculated by using the loss ratio from the aggregate data presented above (1 – the premium loading factor of thirty-four percent = sixty-six percent) and multiplying it by the quoted premium.

The table shows that a sixty-seven percent drop in the value of the car, from $4,910 to $1,615, results in only a thirty-nine percent drop in both premiums and expected benefits. At first glance, this may appear puzzling. But that difference reflects what happens in real life: the loss distribution is concentrated at smaller claim levels, as would be expected given the much more common occurrence of minor accidents than totaling one's car. In other words, the cost of minor body damage repairs is likely to be approximately the same for an older car as for a newer car. Hence, a reduction in overall car value does not result in a proportionate reduction in expected benefit payments. Thus, the supply side of the collision market appears to function without marked anomalies.

On the demand side, two questions are of interest:

- Among those who buy new cars without bank financing, what proportion purchase collision coverage?
- As vehicles depreciate and car loans are paid off, how does the purchase of collision coverage change?

In 2007, seventy-two percent of insured drivers purchased collision coverage in addition to their liability coverage (Insurance Information Institute 2009a). This purchase rate slightly exceeds the seventy percent figure, characterizing behavior consistent with the benchmark model of demand. We know, however, that almost everyone buying a new car on credit or leasing a car is required to have collision coverage as a condition for their vehicle financing arrangement, and this could partially account for the high rate of purchase. Hence, we want to know the proportion buying voluntarily in order to determine if the market is in line with our benchmark model.

The best source of information on individual automobile insurance purchase decisions is the U.S. Department of Labor, Bureau of Labor Statistics' Consumer Expenditure Survey (CES).[4] But despite its relatively fine level of detail, the CES data are still not ideal for the purpose of measuring voluntary purchase decisions. The survey asks about household-level expenditures on automobile insurance in a given month as well as vehicle financing information. The latter should allow us to identify situations in which collision insurance is required. Unfortunately, the data do not provide a breakdown of auto insurance expenditures by type of coverage. For households without car loans, we do not know directly from the survey which households purchase only liability protection and which also buy collision coverage.

Despite these drawbacks, the CES provides an indirect estimate of the proportion of households voluntarily purchasing collision coverage on late-model vehicles. The structure of the data required several adjustments and imputations to obtain this estimate. The survey reports only the total insurance premiums a household pays for automobile insurance, not the premium per car. We therefore limited our sample to households with one car less than five years old. We then estimated a premium equation using a sample of cars purchased through financing, which thus required their owners to carry collision coverage. The equation is then used to predict the premium that would have included collision coverage for vehicles without financing. If the actual premium is more than seventy percent of the predicted premium, we assume collision coverage is present.

Using this methodology, we obtained an estimate of the voluntary purchase rate for collision coverage. Sixty-five percent of those who owned cars made in the last two years, who voluntarily purchased automobile insurance, had premiums greater than seventy percent of the predicted combined liability-collision premium (based on premium levels for those whose cars were financed). They were therefore assumed to have collision insurance. For owners of cars less than five years old, the estimated percentage of those having collision insurance was fifty-eight percent. One reason for this decrease in voluntary purchase of collision insurance is that the value of the car had decreased sufficiently when the vehicle was greater than two years old so that collision insurance was not a good buy.[5] For further information on these estimates, see the appendix of this chapter. As expected, we do see a decline in people choosing to have voluntary coverage as cars age and the potential size of the loss resulting from a collision falls.

We also obtained estimates from insurance industry analysts on the proportion of new car buyers who paid cash for their vehicles who purchase collision coverage. The analysts' strong impression was that virtually all of these buyers did so, especially when the territory was one with a low general-accident rate, so the premiums for coverage were low relative to income and the value of the car. Thus our data-based estimate of sixty-five percent of late model car owners having collision coverage certainly seems within the industry-accepted ballpark.

In summary, based on these data, the automobile collision insurance market seems consistent with benchmark behavior on both the supply and demand side. The thirty-four percent premium loading factor is within the acceptable range, and most individuals owning new cars purchase this competitively sold insurance against a moderately rare but costly event. We would therefore label the auto collision market as consistent with the benchmark models of supply and demand. People may still buy collision policies with deductibles that are too low even assuming actuarially based pricing. But this market does display a very large amount of appropriate purchasing behavior.

Renters' Insurance

Renters' insurance, also known as tenants' insurance, is a form of homeowners' coverage for those who do not own their residence. As we will show, it has about the same loading as collision coverage but often covers assets of lower value than that of a late-model car. It pays benefits equal to losses of or damage to the contents in the residence (less any deductible) with only a small number of causes of loss excluded, such as earthquake, landslide, nuclear hazard, and water damage from flooding. The maximum potential loss to a renter from such "all perils" coverage is much less than to a homeowner, because the renter is not at risk for the value of the structure.[6]

Renters' insurance is voluntary, whereas homeowners' insurance is required for those who have a mortgage. Although a landlord's policy will cover damage to the building resulting from an adverse event, that coverage does not provide protection for the loss of or damage to the contents of the apartments themselves unless landlord negligence can be proven. It is therefore up to the tenant to purchase a separate policy to protect the contents in the dwelling and provide liability protection.

Renters' insurance comes in two forms: actual cash value and replacement-cost value. The latter is more expensive, but for stolen or damaged items the insured receives a claims payment reflecting the cost of new products rather than the depreciated actual cash value of these items. Renters' insurance also typically includes liability coverage, which will protect the insured if someone slips in the bathroom or if Fido bites.

With more than 35 million occupied rental units in the United States, the market for such insurance is potentially large (U.S. Census Bureau

2008). Losses are expected to be uncorrelated across individuals. This should lead insurers to charge premiums with normal loading factors that reflect the risk. According to the Insurance Information Institute, claims on homeowners' insurance (of which renters' insurance is a subset) were fifty-eight percent of earned premiums in 2006 (a typical year with nominal catastrophic events) resulting in an average premium loading factor of forty-two percent, moderately above our benchmark range. Breaking down the forty-two percent, twenty-two percent went to sales expenses and six percent to general expenses with taxes (three percent) and underwriting profits (eleven percent) making up the remainder (Insurance Information Institute 2008). An almost identical breakdown of losses as a percent of premiums can also be found in the 2006 NAIC profitability report on homeowners' insurance (NAIC 2008).

Because renters' policies represent only a small subset of the more general homeowners' policies, however, the cost breakdown for renters' insurance could be quite different. Therefore, we will use additional data on renters' insurance to analyze the supply side of this market. The State Farm website provides individual quotes for a variety of renters' policies in West Philadelphia. A sample of these quotes and the associated policy details are included in Table 4.3.

The table shows that when a renter purchases the minimum coverage level of $10,000, he or she saves only eight dollars on premiums by raising the deductible from $500 to either $1,000 or $2,000. This very small saving implies that, in this case, taking the lowest deductible is the optimal strategy only if one believes that the annual likelihood of suffering a loss of $2,000 or more is at least 1/185 (i.e., the extra cost of eight dollars to obtain extra coverage of $2,000 − $500 = $1,500 or $8/$1,500). In effect, the loading is especially high when a person buys small amounts of coverage. The more normal deductible–premium relationship emerges for the other levels of coverage. Moving from a $500 to a $1,000 deductible generates a premium savings of at least fifteen dollars for contents coverage at or above $20,000. The savings from choosing a $2,000 versus a $1,000 deductible is nine dollars or more for the more generous coverage amounts.

Without additional information on the likelihood and level of claims, it is difficult to estimate a premium loading factor, but the data suggest

Table 4.3. *Sample premiums for renters' insurance, 2008*

Deductible	Contents Coverage	Quote
$500	$10,000	$108
	$20,000	$141
	$30,000	$175
	$40,000	$204
$1,000	$10,000	$100
	$20,000	$125
	$30,000	$156
	$40,000	$182
$2,000	$10,000	$100
	$20,000	$116
	$30,000	$143
	$40,000	$167

Source: Quotes from www.statefarm.com, December 2008.

that the expected losses for renters' insurance are fairly low. Hence, the fixed costs of marketing the policy can cause the premium charged to exceed the actuarially fair premium by a larger magnitude for policies with low levels of coverage. If this is the case, these premiums will reflect an abnormally high premium loading factor.[7] At higher levels of coverage, we expect to see a more typical relationship between premiums, deductibles, and coverage amounts.

Putting the pieces together, we see that in the renters' insurance market, the premium loading factor is relatively high on average, the amount of wealth to be protected is often small, and the loading is especially high when the amount of coverage is low. The benchmark model would then indicate that we would not expect to find many renters purchasing this insurance. But to confidently label this market as consistent with the benchmark supply model we would like additional information on the expected losses and on the value consumers attach to protection against those losses.

Although not available for Pennsylvania, a study by Epic Consulting showed that the average renter's claim in Michigan was around $2,500 with a frequency of four percent, resulting in an expected loss of $100 (i.e., .04[$2,500]) (Miller and Southwood 2004). This does confirm that expected losses are relatively low and lends support to the conclusion previously stated. In Michigan, the average premium was $184, which implies a premium loading factor of forty-six percent (1 − [$100/$184]). In Pennsylvania, for which the State Farm estimates were obtained, the average premium was $145. If the claim frequency and severity in Pennsylvania is similar to that in Michigan, this would imply an average premium loading factor of approximately thirty-one percent (1 − $100/$145). These analyses, taken together with an estimate of forty-two percent loading for the homeowners' market more generally, imply that renters' insurance is at or a little above the upper end of our standards for the benchmark premium loading factor of thirty percent to forty percent. Also, with the exception of the lowest coverage level, the premium schedule reflects the risks of the policies with respect to contents and deductibles.

We now discuss whether the demand-side behavior of buyers of renters' insurance is consistent with the benchmark model. Despite being on the high end in terms of loading, the annual premium for renters' insurance is relatively low compared to renters' income. The nationwide average annual premium for a renter's policy in 2006 was $189 (Insurance Information Institute 2008). Except for those in the lowest income brackets, everyone should be able to afford coverage, but that does not necessarily mean that all will buy policies. Renters may judge the premiums to be too high relative to their perceived expected losses, or they may not think about purchasing such coverage or even know about its availability.

A key issue is the relationship of the value of the contents at risk to the person's wealth. Under the expected utility model, a renter heavily invested in antiques or expensive electronic equipment should be more likely to buy coverage than an ascetic with relatively few possessions. As we noted in our discussion of the benchmark model, when the amount of loss is low and the implied premium loading factor is high, it is reasonable for most people to decline coverage.

The Independent Insurance Agents and Brokers of America had this to say about renters' insurance following a survey that found sixty-five percent of renters do *not* purchase this insurance:

Renters who make up this group fail to realize that for an affordable monthly cost, they can insure all possessions in their apartments or rented homes. Such coverage is essential, given the fact that a fire, theft, acts of vandalism, lightning, tornado, hurricane or other catastrophe could leave them on the hook for the replacement of possessions worth tens of thousands of dollars. (Steele 2003, 1)

That statement is true, however, only for those renters who have tens of thousands of dollars of possessions at risk. It is highly unlikely that most renters have jewelry and electronics worth much more than $10,000, and burglars seldom steal furniture.

Additional estimates of the proportion of renters purchasing coverage vary widely. A 2006 study by the Insurance Research Council found that forty-three percent of renters responding to a voluntary survey reported that they purchased insurance, while estimates from the government's 2003 American Housing Survey (administered to a random sample of all households) suggest a number closer to twenty-two percent (U.S. Census Bureau 2004). According to the AHS study, renters with incomes above the overall median annual household income of $41,000 purchase renters' insurance at a higher, but still modest, rate of thirty-four percent. In addition, as expected, those renters who purchase renters' insurance have an average annual income of $50,000 compared to an average annual income of $32,000 for those who do not purchase coverage.

None of these estimates come close to meeting the seventy percent purchase rate set by the benchmark model of demand for large, low-probability losses. But expected losses in this market are very low, so a decision not to purchase these policies is likely to be sensible. Those renters with more at risk who would find a policy attractive appear to be the population purchasing coverage. Assuming this to be the case, the renters' market appears to function fairly well on the demand side, given that the expected loss many consumers are facing in this case is just not that large and the premium loading factor on their policy is relatively high so they would not want to purchase coverage if they were maximizing expected utility.

Term-Life Insurance

Life insurance comes in many forms, all of which provide funds to the beneficiary upon the death of the insured person. A household can be greatly affected by the death of a family member whose income was vital.

Term-life insurance protects against this risk by promising to pay a pre-specified dollar amount if the policyholder dies during the term of coverage. Death of a breadwinner obviously involves much more than just a financial loss, but we will continue to evaluate the decision to sell or buy life insurance using the benchmark models of supply and demand.

We first consider whether pricing of term-life insurance aligns with the benchmark model. Unlike collision coverage and renters' insurance, both of which charge an annual premium in exchange for a single year of coverage with the possibility of a change in premium next year, term-life insurance typically charges a fixed annual premium for the length of the policy, which could be as long as twenty or thirty years. For example, a forty-year-old male with a twenty-five-year term insurance policy could be charged an annual premium of $825 for $500,000 coverage, and this premium would remain the same for each of the next twenty-five years if the person lived that long and maintained coverage. There is no charge for canceling term insurance by failing to continue to pay the premiums. The benefit upon the death of a beneficiary is a fixed dollar amount.

In 2007, benefit payments for life insurance policies of all types were eighty-five percent of the premiums earned in that year (American Council of Life Insurers 2008). This implies a premium loading factor of fifteen percent. It is not surprising to find a lower premium loading factor for life insurance than collision or renters' insurance because the marketing costs for this coverage are much less than the other two examples given that the typical policy is a multiyear one.

To further explore the life insurance market, Table 4.4 displays quoted premiums, from the website term4sale.com, for males and females of varying ages for a twenty-year policy, along with the implied and actual probabilities of death. The actual probabilities of death are obtained from the 2001 Commissioners Standard Ordinary Mortality Table in the 2008 *American Council of Life Insurers Fact Book*, while the implied probabilities that would make the quoted premium actuarially fair are calculated by dividing the premium by the coverage amount. All quotes are for average risks and a $500,000 ($250,000) policy from American General Life Insurance Company. American General had an excellent rating from the A.M. Best Company with available premium data for all of the age/sex combinations of interest.

Table 4.4. *Term-life insurance premiums and death rates, by age and sex*

	Premium for $500,000 ($250,000)	Implied death rate per 100,000 individuals for $500,000 ($250,000) coverage	Actual death rate per 100,000 individuals
MALES			
30-year-old	$530 ($290)	106 (116)	110
40-year-old	$825 ($438)	165 (175)	170
50-year-old	$1,985 ($1,018)	397 (407)	380
FEMALES			
30-year-old	$410 ($230)	82 (92)	70
40-year-old	$685 ($368)	137 (147)	130
50-year-old	$1,475 ($763)	295 (305)	310

Source: 2006 premium quotes for twenty-year term policies from Term4Sale.com.

The most striking thing about these data is how close the actual death rates are to the death rates implied by the structure of the premiums under the assumption that the loading cost is zero. This implies that premiums are close to being actuarially fair. This would be consistent with a highly competitive term-life insurance market and low premium loading factors as suggested by the aggregate 2007 data. It is also likely that underwriting guidelines exclude buyers with high-risk conditions, in which case the actual mortality rate for purchasers will be lower than the mortality rate of the U.S. population. When the actual death rate is less than the implied death rate, this means that the insurer is charging premiums above the actuarially fair rate. This is true for men of all ages for the $250,000 policy and for thirty- and forty-year-old women for the $250,000 policy and for the $500,000 policy. In all cases, however, the actual death rate will increase over the course of the term so that the premiums (which do not change over time) will be closer to, or even below, their actuarially fair values. The main point is that term-life insurance premiums are closely related to risk so that pricing is consistent with the benchmark model of supply.

The structure of the premiums also indicates that there may be modest cross-subsidization among the age/sex combinations. For example, insured females in the thirty- and forty-year-old brackets will help pay for the claims of insured males in the same age brackets who die. The insurer will also recoup some of its entire deficit through interest earned on the investments of premiums paid at the beginning of the annual contract.

On the whole, it appears that pricing of term-life insurance is in line with the benchmark model and may be a good example of how competition drives the price closer to its actuarially fair value. With the ability to sell policies online, there may be substantially reduced overhead costs that allow this to occur. As Jeffrey Brown and Austan Goolsbee (2002) show, the growth of the Internet has reduced term-life prices by eight percent to fifteen percent and increased consumer surplus by $115 million to $215 million per year and perhaps more.

Given that the supply side of the market appears to be performing well, we now ask whether consumer behavior is consistent with the benchmark model for term-life insurance.

To decide whether people who should demand life insurance based on the benchmark model actually buy it, we need to define the population at risk. The simplest specification would be working adults in households of two or more who earn an income (in money or in kind) that is a meaningful part of total household income. According to the life insurance research institute, LIMRA International, the proportion of households with two adults having some type of life insurance (not limited to term life) in 2004 was close to ninety percent.

The proportion of households with life insurance is thus in the range of the benchmark model. Moreover, the kinds of households that buy coverage are also consistent with that model. The data show that seventy-two percent of households whose head is between thirty-five years and forty-four years old have a term policy. This percentage steadily declines with age because their needs for providing for dependents fall as their children grow up and both husband and wife are more likely to be income earners (Retzloff 2005a). LIMRA data show that eighty-five percent of husbands and seventy-two percent of wives have some life insurance and the respective proportions increase with personal income as expected (Retzloff 2005b). The evidence suggests that most of those who need life insurance do carry some coverage.

SUMMARY

This chapter examined three markets that perform closely in line with the benchmark models of supply and demand. Automobile collision insurance and term-life insurance have reasonable premium loading factors, and consumers purchase coverage in an appropriate manner. Renters' insurance has a high premium loading factor for coverage of a loss that is often small relative to wealth, and here consumers appropriately choose not to purchase coverage. These markets are characterized by independence of losses, a comparatively high frequency of loss, and reasonably high average claims. The fact that some insurance markets function reasonably well is all the more reason to identify the characteristics of situations where anomalies exist.

APPENDIX TO CHAPTER 4

Estimate of Voluntary Collision Purchase Using Consumer Expenditure Survey Data

Step One: Estimate a premium equation using those individuals with financing.

Premiums. The premiums that are reported are not specifically associated with a particular car. This presents a challenge when a consumer unit (CU) has more than one car. About eighty percent of cars are in a CU with more than one car. We therefore limited our analysis to those with only one car.

We calculate a monthly premium for each CU in each quarter by dividing the reported premium by the number of months in the premium term (e.g., annual, semi-annual, quarterly). We then calculate the average monthly premium for the CU across all quarters with reported premiums.

- The mean premium for those with financing is $93/month.
- The mean premium for those without financing is $80/month.

Independent variables. The independent variables used to predict premiums for those with financing should include measures of the CU's location, income, and value of the car, as this determines collision costs.

The best proxy for value of the car is the purchase price and the vehicle year. The purchase price is available for a limited number of vehicles purchased without financing if they were purchased in the reference periods for the survey – cars that are five years old or newer. We derive an estimate of the purchase price for various makes/models of vehicles by taking the median purchase price for each make/model and attaching this value to all vehicles of that make/model missing a purchase price or not purchased new.

- The mean purchase price for all new vehicles is $23,921.
- The mean purchase price for financed vehicles is $24,165.
- The mean purchase price for unfinanced vehicles is $23,801.

We end up with 758 observations of financed vehicles with all the necessary information to estimate the premium.

Step Two: Use the model to predict premiums for those purchasing cars without financing.
- The mean predicted monthly premium for those with financing is $93.
- The mean predicted monthly premium for those without financing is $90.

Step Three: Compare actual and predicted premiums to infer the percentage purchasing collision coverage.
Using a threshold of seventy percent, such that if the actual premium is greater than seventy percent of the predicted premium for those without financing, we assume they are purchasing collision. The proportion of those without financing with premiums above seventy percent of the predicted premium (who we assume are purchasing collision coverage), is seventy-three percent for cars less than a year old, sixty-five percent for cars less than two years old (based on eighty-five observations) and fifty-eight percent for cars less than five years old (based on 427 observations).

PART II

UNDERSTANDING CONSUMER AND INSURER BEHAVIOR

5

Real-World Complications

So far, we have offered a view of what the supply and demand for insurance look like in three markets in which consumers and insurers behave much as classical economics predicts. The conditions we set for the benchmark models of demand and supply assumed that consumers have good information on the likelihood of a loss and its consequences, so they can determine how much insurance to purchase so as to maximize their expected utility. From an insurer perspective, all risks were assumed to be independent so that, according to the law of large numbers, providers of coverage could price on the basis of expected losses without fear of being driven into bankruptcy by massive total claims.

Although these assumptions present a picture of how an insurance market should work and sometimes is approximated in reality, as exemplified by the three markets highlighted in Chapter 4, the untidy truth is that they are often violated in other markets. In this chapter, we delve into some of the complications that arise when information is imperfect, consumers do not maximize expected utility (EU), and losses are not independent. These modifications to the benchmark models of demand and supply lead us to address the question as to whether the formal approaches that incorporate these features can explain the actual functioning of insurance markets, or whether anomalies still exist that require other models of choice.

The benchmark models presented in Chapter 2 tell us that people decide whether to buy insurance by comparing their own subjective estimates of expected benefits from insurance – that is, the likelihood of obtaining compensation for a loss – against the cost of the policy. The premium set by the insurer reflects its judgments about the likelihood of losses of different magnitudes occurring and projected claims within its customer base. The benchmark models assumed that these estimates were the same for consumers and insurers and could be calculated (by both parties) from a large sample of data on frequency of losses in a stable environment.

Actual buyer behavior may deviate from the benchmark models of choice for several reasons. We first turn to a situation in which the consumer does not have accurate information about the risk and is either unclear or misinformed as to what coverage is available and/or what premiums are being charged. We then look at the case in which the consumer has relevant information on the risk that the insurer does *not* possess. This is followed by two sections focusing on the effects of correlated losses on the pricing and supply of insurance. Finally, we describe what a reasonably well-functioning insurance and reinsurance market might look like when there are correlated losses.

SEARCH COSTS

When people want insurance to protect themselves against a specific event, they should carefully consider the options open to them. An obstacle arises at the outset: search costs associated with obtaining information on loss probabilities and insurance premiums. If these costs are high relative to the potential gains from collecting additional data, some individuals will be deterred from gathering the information needed to purchase coverage. To introduce search costs into the model, we can think of an individual comparing two situations:

- *Situation One*: Do not search for information on the characteristics of the risks, premiums, or available coverage. This means the person will remain uninsured.
- *Situation Two*: Incur some search cost, either by paying an agent or using one's own time to obtain information, and then determine how much coverage, if any, to purchase. The person then decides whether or not to purchase insurance.

If the search cost is high enough and if the difference in expected utility from searching compared to not searching and not buying insurance is small enough, the person will not search and will remain uninsured (Situation One). The intuition here is that if the person believes that a given risk is small enough that his or her overall expected utility will not be much affected regardless of how much coverage is purchased (including being uninsured), then it is not worth the time and effort to even think about or to search for data on the premium – even if that premium might be close to actuarially fair. The key issue is whether the difference in expected utility with and without insurance is sufficiently large that a person will want to search for data needed to determine what coverage (if any) should be purchased.

This simple model, described in more detail by Howard Kunreuther and Mark Pauly (2004), may help to explain the lack of interest in insurance against low-probability, high-loss events such as a storm-of-the-century deluge for a property not located in a flood plain, or catastrophic health insurance coverage, even if policies are offered at premiums that reflect the risk. Life is just too short to worry about everything that might go wrong.

In these cases, insurance that bundles together independent rare events into an umbrella or all-perils policy is likely to make a great deal of sense. For example, flood coverage could be incorporated into an all-hazards policy, and losses against catastrophic health care costs could be part of a comprehensive health insurance policy. From a social welfare perspective, when the perilous events that many consider not worth bothering about actually do occur, there may be a call for the government to step in. For this reason, unless bundling works to get buyers' attention, there may be a case for requiring individuals to purchase coverage against these very low-probability, high-consequence events.

MISTAKES AND ANOMALOUS BEHAVIOR

These observations extend to decision-making costs other than search costs. Making the ideal EU-maximizing choice about insurance is a complicated and arduous task that involves fairly sophisticated understanding of probability theory and good estimates of actual parameters of the problem. Given this characterization, it should not be surprising that people sometimes make mistakes when it comes to insurance even though they may want to maximize their expected utility (Liebman and

Zeckhauser 2008). If one adds in the disutility associated with gathering information and thinking hard about making choices, it may be rational to be mildly irrational. The insight from the Kunreuther and Pauly 2004 study is that it is desirable to incur search costs when there is a lot at stake. This assumes that people would want to follow the EU model if they could do so easily. That may not be right!

We begin by noting that there are a number of settings in which people seem to make mistakes. In our discussion of "rumors of anomalies" we noted how common it is for buyers to be advised to pay attention to the premium and the loss without suggesting that they take account of the probability (or the loading on the insurance). In empirical research, Jason Abaluck and Jonathan Gruber (2011) found that buyers of Medicare prescription drug coverage overemphasized the magnitude of the premium rather than the expected benefits (or impact on their expected out of pocket payments) from different plans.

Presumably, a way of distinguishing mistakes with respect to the benchmark model of individuals making an effort to maximize expected utility is to see if people change their minds when presented with better information or decision aids. Indeed, Robin Hogarth and Howard Kunreuther (1995) found that when asked to specify what factors influenced decisions to purchase a warranty, few individuals mentioned the likelihood of a loss when they were not given data on the probability of a product failure. Only when provided with information on the probability of a product failure did it become important in the decision-making process for many of them.

Another example of the impact of new information on behavior is whether people update probability information based on their past experience. Consumers may not know if there is a reason to think that last period's event implies a significant change in probability. People have a hard time incorporating statistical concepts into their thinking. We regret past decisions that turned out poorly. We use case-based decision making (Gilboa and Schmeidler 1995) or other heuristics that overweight recent events.

We forget about low-probability events – even if they produced serious consequences – as our recollection of past experiences fades. And we continue to feel uncomfortable about uncertainty, particularly when the likelihood of an event is highly ambiguous or unknown. These behaviors may reflect mistakes with respect to trying to maximize expected utility, or they may be regular enough and persistent enough even in the face of information and advice to suggest a different model.

A final kind of mistake is inconsistency. There are many different threats to a person's wealth, and different insurance products are sold for each. The fully informed and competent expected utility maximizer would, for each event, choose appropriate coverage (for example, the size of the deductible) by focusing on a utility function that treats any reduction in wealth, regardless of cause, the same. But the differences across insurances in loading and the possibility that the impact of insurance on precautions (moral hazard) varies across types of losses, makes it difficult to choose the portfolio of insurance policies that is consistent with expected utility maximization.

Levon Barseghyan, Jeffrey Prince, and Joshua Teitelbaum (2011) provide evidence to suggest that individuals are inconsistent with respect to their preferences by choosing more protection against losses on homeowners' policies than on auto collision policies. If insurance affects the care with which someone drives to avoid a small accident more than the care taken to prevent a small loss at home, the observed pattern could still be rational: you are willing to expose yourself to a larger loss for collision coverage in order to hold down premiums by providing a stronger incentive to drive carefully – but otherwise this is a flaw in decision making. On the other hand, Liran Einav and colleagues (2010) found consistency in consumer choices across a range of health-related insurance policies.

INFORMATION IMPERFECTIONS AND ASYMMETRY

Much of the success of insurance for consumers and insurers rests on having sufficient information to assess risk and being able to weigh the price of purchasing or selling coverage against that risk. But there often are instances in which one or the other side of a transaction, and sometimes both sides, either do not have enough information, or have the wrong information, with which to make good decisions. Such *information asymmetries* or *imperfect information* complicates insurance, leading to poor decisions by both buyers and sellers.

IMPERFECT INFORMATION ABOUT RISK

Consider the situation in which those at risk do not know their loss probability. Perhaps the risk stems from a new and valuable, but potentially dangerous, product, say a hydrogen-fueled automobile. Buyers know the product might create a loss to them and would want insurance to cover the cost of damage if such an adverse event occurs. Because the product is a new one, consumers may not have a good idea of the likelihood of such occurrences and the resulting loss.[1] Hence, there are likely to be misperceptions associated with the likelihood or consequences of a disaster that may lead individuals to purchase too little insurance or no insurance at all.

Usually, there is some basis for estimating a probability – the results of small-scale trials, calculations based on engineering data, or loss probabilities for more familiar situations thought to be analogous to this one. Still, when there are ambiguous or poorly understood probabilities, buyers and sellers of insurance face a challenge. At a minimum, they both will need to estimate the loss probability in some subjective fashion.

In other cases, the insurer may have good information on the likelihood of the event occurring but the consumer may perceive the probability or the magnitude of a loss as much lower than analysts estimate it to be. In these situations the buyer may not have an economic incentive to purchase insurance even at an actuarially fair premium. Consumers will view insurance as overpriced and will be unlikely to want coverage unless they are highly risk averse. If such views are widespread, an insurance market may not exist. Of course, a person could perceive the risks to be higher than the scientific estimates, in which case full insurance coverage is likely to be an attractive option if an individual maximizes expected utility.

Insurers might be expected to try to convince buyers of the loss probability by providing them with scientific information in the form of the actuarial estimates that are the foundation of the company's pricing decision. The trouble is, the more resources and compensation to perform this task of explanation and persuasion, the higher the administrative costs and therefore the higher the premium. Moreover, one insurer's education campaign or information-filled sales pitch may benefit another insurer who spends less on informing the public but charges lower premiums, thus discouraging all insurers from incurring these costs. More fundamentally, there is a kind of Catch-22: buyers who underestimate the probability of experiencing a loss will not be willing to pay premiums close to the expected loss. Insurers' efforts to persuade buyers that the company's loss probability estimates are correct can be costly and may push the break-even premium even higher than the now better informed buyers would be willing to pay.

Individual health insurance markets are a good example of this phenomenon. These policies typically carry loadings twice as high as the average in group insurance. Those extra costs primarily go for sales expenses to persuade people one by one of their need for insurance. As a result, the proportion purchasing individual coverage is on the order of twenty-five percent to thirty-five percent compared to a sixty-five percent to ninety-five percent purchase rate for people with access to group coverage (Pauly and Nichols 2002). Insurance provided to individuals cannot be purchased with tax-free income as can group coverage. In addition, the high administrative cost of selling policies to individuals makes a difference in the purchase rate.

INFORMATION ASYMMETRY AND ADVERSE SELECTION

Now suppose that there are two risk types, good and poor, with different probabilities of experiencing a given loss, and that potential insurance customers know what their risk type is. Further assume that the informational shoe is on the other foot – the insurer may be unable to distinguish between the good risks and the poor ones. If the insurer sets a premium based on the average probability of a loss using the entire population as a basis for this estimate, it is possible that only the poor risk types will buy coverage. This situation is referred to as *adverse selection* and the challenges it poses for insurers is highlighted in the classic paper by Michael Rothschild and Joseph Stiglitz (1976). In theory, good risks will underpurchase coverage or buy no coverage at all. There may even fail to be a competitive equilibrium.

In this case, the resulting expected losses will be higher than if both good and poor risks purchased insurance. Either the insurer will lose money or it will be forced to increase the premium until it covers the losses of those poor risks who will still want to buy coverage. That, of course, will make the insurance even less attractive to the good risks who might then not buy complete coverage or any coverage at all. The assumption underlying adverse selection is that buyers of insurance have an informational advantage because they know their *risk type*. Insurers, on the other hand, must invest considerable expense even to collect incomplete information to distinguish between risks, and sometimes such information is not available at any cost.

In addition to the assumption of informational asymmetry, the standard models of adverse selection make two other assumptions that may not be realistic. One is that risk aversion is distributed independently of risk; high risks are on average no less risk averse than low risks. The other is that insurance buyers do choose insurance that maximizes their expected utility. That is, high risks seeing a bargain in insurance seize on the opportunity to buy more coverage, and low risks respond to the ever-increasing premiums by buying lower amounts of coverage or dropping out of the market. In effect, the observation that insurance could be characterized by adverse selection is itself testimony to the relevance of the traditional EU model. Indeed, it can be shown in theory that if enough high risks are not aware of or do not choose to take advantage of their inside information, the standard model of adverse selection (and its policy implications) does not apply (Sandroni and Squintani 2007). However, the interpretation of an empirical finding that there is little or no adverse selection is much more nuanced and ambiguous in terms of implications for demand anomalies.

To illustrate, suppose some homes have a low probability of suffering windstorm damage (the good risks), and others have a higher probability (the poor risks), but insurers have no way of telling which loss probability is associated with which property. Such a situation could occur if insurers did not inspect individual homes to determine how well they are constructed. The good risks stand a one in ten annual probability of loss and the poor risks stand a three in ten annual probability. For simplicity, assume that the loss is $100 for both groups and that there are an equal number of potentially insurable individuals in each risk class. Since there is an equal number in both risk classes, the expected loss for a random buyer in the population is $20.

If the insurer charges an actuarially fair premium across the entire population, the poor-risk class would almost surely purchase coverage, because their expected annual loss is thirty dollars (.3 x $100), and they would be pleased to pay only twenty dollars for the insurance. But the good risks have an expected annual loss of ten dollars (.1 x $100), so they would have to be extremely risk averse to be interested in paying a premium of twenty dollars. If only the poor risks purchase coverage, the insurer initially will suffer an average annual loss of ten dollars (twenty dollars minus thirty dollars) on every policy it sells, due to its inability to distinguish good from poor risks.

Once insurers realize that they are only catering to the poor risks, they will raise their premium to thirty dollars. This new market equilibrium may be inefficient because the good risks are not willing to purchase insurance at any premium that will cover the insurers' costs for all risks, even though they would have been willing to purchase insurance if they were charged a premium that reflected their expected losses.

But is this market anomalous? It clearly is inefficient relative to a fully informed insurance market equilibrium in which premiums reflected the expected loss for each group. In that case, the poor risks would obtain their desired level of coverage at a high premium, and the good risks would purchase coverage at a lower premium. This kind of inefficiency has many parallels in other markets where there is information asymmetry, such as the market for used cars.[2] But the inefficiency of this market is not due to irrational behavior by buyers or sellers but to the inability of insurers to distinguish good risks from bad ones due to information imperfections.

This is not the end of the story. New insurers may offer less generous policies at low enough premiums that appeal to the good risks but not to the poor risks, and then offer full coverage and a much higher cost-per-dollar coverage that appeals to the poor risks, but not to the good ones. As shown by Michael Rothschild and Joseph Stiglitz (1976), this may or may not lead to a stable equilibrium depending on the relative differences between good and bad risks and the number of individuals in each risk class. If there is an equilibrium, because it will involve under-purchase of insurance by the lower risks, a mandate for some minimum amount of insurance purchase by everyone may improve efficiency.

In short, there may still be a case for government intervention to improve efficiency, although the reason is not anomalous behavior but rather an environment in which information asymmetry prevents insurers from offering coverage against specific risks at competitive prices that all buyers find attractive.

ADVERSE SELECTION IN PRACTICE

Does adverse selection, which involves profit-maximizing behavior by insurers and expected utility maximization by potential demanders, actually occur in practice? There will always be relevant information that the consumer will know but the insurer will have a difficult time uncovering. Do I occasionally step on the accelerator to see how my new "baby" will handle at excessive speeds? Are we planning on having another child next year? The relevant question is whether these differences are large enough to matter in terms of affecting either premiums or patterns of insurance purchasing.

The answer is that there are some examples of adverse selection that researchers have identified, but also many cases where it cannot be shown to exist, even though on a priori grounds it looks like the circumstances that would lead to adverse selection are present. In the first category of good evidence for adverse selection are studies of auto insurance in some countries and for some kinds of coverage. In one of the best known studies, Alma Cohen (2005) found convincing evidence for adverse selection in auto insurance in Israel by showing that drivers who chose lower deductible tended to be higher risks. But in a study of French drivers, Pierre–Andre Chiappori and Bernard Salanie (2000) did not find adverse selection and in a recent study using data from a German subsidiary of a French insurance company, Martin Spindler (2011) detected adverse selection for comprehensive automobile coverage (protection against theft and collision with wildlife) but, suprisingly, not for collision coverage.

In the United States, as we have noted in Chapter 4, the purchase rate for collision coverage is high enough to suggest that adverse selection is not a problem. Perhaps some careful drivers are underpurchasing collision coverage, but no one has alleged this to be a problem.

Where adverse selection does potentially occur, and to a serious degree, is in markets where regulation prevents insurers from taking into account risk information they surely could have. This "artificial" or "non-essential" adverse selection seems to be most characteristic of health insurance and property insurance markets where "risk rating" is prohibited by law (as in some states in the United States and in all group health insurance) or regulators depress premiums for high-risk exposures for political reasons (as in hurricane insurance in Florida). These cases will be discussed in more detail later, but here we note that there is some evidence of fairly severe adverse selection in large group health insurance (Bundorf, Herring, and Pauly 2010) and reluctance of insurers to remain in property insurance markets where premiums are highly regulated. In contrast, in individual health insurance markets in the United States where risk rating is permitted, adverse selection is absent; if anything, it is the higher risks who go without coverage (Bundorf, Herring, and Pauly 2010; Pauly and Herring 2007).

Even when rate regulation creates a golden opportunity for adverse selection, some populations of buyers have characteristics that inhibit its emergence. The most studied example is "Medigap" insurance in the United States, voluntarily purchased but heavily regulated insurance to cover the many gaps in traditional Medicare insurance. David Cutler, Amy Finkelstein, and Kathleen McGarry (2008) discovered that it is the lower risks, not the higher risks, who are most likely to take Medigap coverage. They attribute this phenomenon to "preferred or advantageous risk selection" where people who attach high values to insurance protection because they are risk averse are also lower risks, perhaps because they take steps to keep themselves healthy. In addition, Hanming Fang, Michael P. Keane, and Dan Silverman (2008) note that the higher risks may be cognitively less capable of making rational insurance purchase decisions that require them to compare the benefits and costs of specific types of coverage than the (healthier) lower risks, which further inhibits adverse selection.

Even in the largely unregulated long-term care insurance market, Amy Finkelstein and Kathleen McGarry (2006) find evidence of preferred risk selection. Failure to find adverse selection, as in the Fang et al. Medigap study, may be consistent with the hypothesis that some buyers are not EU maximizers, but it is also consistent with the hypothesis that little serious information asymmetry exists. In a well-known paper, John Cawley and Tomas Philipson (1999) come to this conclusion about term-life insurance; they find little evidence that people with lower life expectancies are more likely to buy life insurance than those who have higher odds of survival. The risk categories insurers create based on information they collect when they underwrite and sell policies (usually information about family history and recent health care use) picks up almost all of the risk variation in the market. Their conclusion has been challenged to some extent by Daifeng He (2009), who found that, within rating categories, elderly and near elderly who bought new life insurance policies were more likely to die sooner. However, this is an unusual sample of buyers (most people who buy life insurance are young), and the rating categories still picked up a great deal of the risk variation.

In summary, adverse selection does occur, especially where regulation does not allow insurers to use information they have in hand, but it is far from ubiquitous. At present, it seems impossible to draw strong conclusions about adverse selection, which should suggest caution in advocating policy interventions in insurance markets on these grounds.

INFORMATION IMPERFECTION AND MORAL HAZARD

Suppose insured individuals facing equal loss prospects behave in a manner that increases the expected loss from what it was prior to their purchase of insurance (Pauly 1968; Zeckhauser 1970). Furthermore, suppose that the insurer cannot determine that the policyholder's behavior has changed in this way.

This behavior – termed *moral hazard* – poses a problem for the insurer. By moral hazard, we mean the tendency for an insured individual to incur larger losses, take less care, and/or take additional risks than if

"It doesn't look good. Leave it with us
overnight and hope it gets stolen."

Figure 5.1. © CartoonStock Ltd.

the person had no coverage. Premiums will then be raised to reflect the
higher risk.

There are good reasons to expect moral hazard in many insurance situations. The insured individual has less incentive to take the same amount
of care as when he or she was uninsured, knowing that if there is an accident or disaster, he or she now has protection. This careless behavior
increases the probability of a loss. The insurer may not be able to detect
such behavior because it is costly and often extremely difficult to monitor
and control a person's actions and determine whether the insured behaves
differently after purchasing insurance. Similarly, it may not be possible for
the insurer to determine if a person will decide to claim more on a policy
than the actual loss by inflating the damage or by increasing the estimate
of loss as illustrated by the cartoon in Figure 5.1.[3]

The numerical example used to illustrate adverse selection can also
demonstrate moral hazard. Suppose there were only good risks who

face a loss probability of one in ten *before* they purchase insurance coverage. Once insured, they behave more carelessly and the loss probability rises to three in ten. If the insurance company does not know that moral hazard exists, it will sell policies at a price of ten dollars to reflect the estimated actuarial loss. But the real loss will be thirty dollars because of the individuals' careless behavior. Therefore, the firm will lose twenty dollars on each policy it sells. If it decides to renew the insurance policy after determining that the insured behaved carelessly, then the firm will want to raise the premium to reflect the higher probability of a claim. In that case, some people will buy less coverage.

There is another kind of moral hazard illustrated by the behavior of individuals who have health insurance. Even if I cannot change the probability of getting a cold, I may be more likely to visit a doctor and seek a prescription if I have coverage than if I do not. Because my insurer pays claims based on my use of medical care rather than on how sick I really am, there is an economic incentive for an insured person to take advantage of being financially protected by using medical care that produces positive but low benefits for two reasons: the insurance covers the cost of care, and making a claim on my policy does not affect my future premiums.

One phenomenon that can create a true anomaly in the case of moral hazard is the apparent reluctance of some people to buy insurance that contains provisions intended to limit or restrict the extent of moral hazard. In the case of health insurance, for example, either moderately high levels of patient cost sharing of their losses or more direct constraints on utilization (as is the case with managed care policies) can control moral hazard. Yet many consumers (and public policy makers) regard this kind of insurance as undesirable. That is, they fail to select insurance with high cost sharing or managed care that could control moral hazard and, at the same time lower their premiums.

To illustrate this point, there has been rapid growth in the use of diagnostic scans of various types, most notably CT scans, MRI scans, and bone density scans. At least some of this use of costly equipment is in response to patients' desires for reassurance that they are healthy, combined with little or no patient cost sharing. Some selective increases in cost-sharing levels for procedures known to be overused would be in consumers' best interests, but has not been generally popular. Other factors unrelated to moral hazard, such as tax subsidies and imperfect knowledge of what really constitutes overuse, contribute to this reluctance to curtail procedures that are not cost-effective. In other words, there clearly is a residual desire for generous coverage by some consumers as long as the premium does not become unbearable. If consumers utilize different decision rules than those implied by expected utility, we would classify this behavior as an anomaly on the demand side. We will address this and related issues in Chapter 6.

In general, moral hazard produces an anomaly but not because individuals are deviating from the expected utility-maximization rule. Rather, the problem exists because of imperfect insurer information: the insurer does not know if the buyer of health insurance is doing everything possible to stay healthy or to be treated appropriately, or if the buyer of a homeowners' policy is really taking precautions to avoid damage to the home from fire or other events covered by insurance.

EFFECTS OF CORRELATED RISKS ON INSURANCE SUPPLY

We now turn to a broader range of assumptions on the supply side to see how these might affect insurers' motivations to offer coverage. Although the law of large numbers is applicable to many risks, there are situations in which it does not hold. This is especially true when losses are correlated rather than independent. When losses across individuals are perfectly correlated – if Person A suffers a loss, then Person B will suffer the same loss – it becomes impossible to pool risks using the law of large numbers.

Even if there is a positive but not perfect correlation between risks, there is still a high probability that aggregate losses will be more substantial than for the case of a given number of independent risks of the same expected loss. The question facing insurers seeking to maximize expected profits is the size of their reserves needed to prevent ruin from a large loss if the insured risks are correlated. Here we present a simple model and draw some conclusions from it.

As pointed out in Chapter 2, an insurer could guarantee that all poli-cyholders will be paid for their losses and avoid bankruptcy if it held reserves equal to the difference between the premium revenues it collects and the maximum total loss on all its contracts. That is, if it collects premiums totaling $1,000,000 for policies for aggregate coverage of $100,000,000, the insurer's reserves would have to be $99,000,000 to be absolutely certain that all claims would be paid in full. In fact, no insurer holds reserves that even come close to this amount, because they weigh the cost of adding capital to their reserves against the expected benefits they could obtain from increasing their reserves.

The cost of obtaining additional reserves reflects the higher transaction costs to acquire more capital due to the need of convincing suppliers of capital that they will achieve as high an expected return as they would if their funds were utilized in other investments given a possible large loss due to correlated risks.[4] The benefit of holding reserves is that it reduces the chances that correlated losses will bankrupt the insurer.

As we have already seen, for a large insurer covering many independent events, the chances of losses exceeding premiums by any appreciable amount are extremely small, so reserves can be modest relative to premiums. But in the case of correlated losses, the probability of ruin or insolvency becomes much higher for any given level of reserves. But obtaining higher reserves may mean higher transaction costs to obtain capital, thus leading to higher premiums per dollar of benefits. In a perfect capital market, this sequence of events would not occur since insurers could get as much capital as they want at the going price after suffering a severe loss. Even in a market with some theoretical imperfections, the share of global capital committed to a particular line of insurance (or even to all insurance) is quite small, so there should be ample supplies of capital to meet the additional need for reserves. When there is a relatively small pool of capital associated with investing in insurance, as often occurs following large-scale catastrophes, an unexpected surge in the demand for additional funds drives up the transactions costs of replenishing depleted reserves.

Recapping, the insurance supply works best when the insured events are independent and the size of the maximum loss per event is small relative to the insurer's total premium revenue or reserves. Thus we should expect that insurance markets are more likely to exist and function well for independent risks than for ones with highly correlated losses.

ROLE OF RESERVES IN DEALING WITH CORRELATED LOSSES

The previous section explained the relevant tradeoffs profit-driven insurers face in determining the level of reserves for covering large claims payments, and how this desired level affects the supply curve of insurance. Here we provide a more in-depth discussion of insurer and capital market behavior when losses are correlated.

To what extent can the benchmark model predict that insurers will supply coverage at premiums consumers are willing to pay? If there is a possibility of a large loss relative to the typical insurance firm's premiums and reserves, there is a greater likelihood that the insurer will be unable to pay its claims in full and may, if necessary, declare insolvency or ruin. In such a case, the policyholders may receive less than the contractually specified claims payments.

One way to think about this problem is to consider investor McDuck, who already owns a financial asset that is low risk and liquid and that pays a return in the form of interest. Suppose McDuck were approached by an insurance company and asked, in effect, to pledge or transfer some of his assets to the company to use as reserves in return for an ownership share in the company. The expected return from funds held as insurance firm reserves will be lower than the interest rate McDuck can earn in his own portfolio for three reasons.

For one thing there is a chance that some or all of these assets will be needed to pay for the insured losses so that McDuck's expected return is reduced by the expected claims payments. The second is that McDuck will have to incur transaction costs to make the transfer of his funds to the insurer. This cost surely includes the time it will take to match McDuck with a suitable insurance investment and the cost of drawing up contracts. Finally, there would be a cost from any reduction McDuck expects in the return on the asset if it is managed by the insurance company's staff rather than by McDuck himself.

Let us call the settings in which the extreme event does not occur the *good times*. So the good-times return on the stock McDuck received must balance the lower or even negative return on that stock when the extreme event occurs. How much higher it needs to be depends on McDuck's attitude toward risk as it relates to the earnings on his new insurance company stock. If he is risk averse and that stock is a large proportion of his wealth, he will require a *good-times* return in excess of the expected value of the reduced return from large losses that would occur after an extreme event. To achieve this objective, the insurer would have to raise premiums over what they would be if it were risk neutral when its objective is maximizing expected profits.

But we should not be too quick to jump to this conclusion, because there is another real possibility: McDuck (and suppliers of capital in general) may own diversified portfolios of assets in which the value of the insurance company's stock (or its return) is only a tiny fraction of the total value of the portfolio. In this case, an extreme event that creates significant claims payments relative to a large insurance company's assets or revenues will have a very small negative impact on the wealth of any investor for whom the insurance firms' stock is a small part of his or her diversified portfolio.

More generally, if a very large loss experienced by an insurer or the insurance industry is small relative to the entire capital market, and if all investors own diversified portfolios, the only significant cost to additional reserves is the additional return on capital (related to transactions costs and limitations on the range of investments) that an investor requires for transferring the management of his or her assets to the insurance company rather than having direct control of these resources.

A problem with the diversified portfolio model is that, although the insolvency of one of many insurance companies in McDuck's portfolio might not matter to him, it might matter to the managers of the insurance company that gets into financial difficulties. Thus the managers might behave in a more risk-averse fashion than McDuck or other investors would like them to act. This will shift the composition of investors in insurance firms toward those who are also cautious, but the match may be imperfect. In other words, there may be a divergence between what stockholders want and what insurance firm managers want in terms of the level of protection against ruin.

Suppose McDuck wants the firm in which he invested to operate so as to maximize expected profits and incur the risk of bankruptcy that may be associated with these decisions. The managers of his company may feel differently, and they are likely in a position to make their preferences count. David Mayers and Clifford Smith (1990) contend that the transaction costs associated with bankruptcy can make it rational for managers to be risk averse, and may be why property/liability companies purchase reinsurance.

Bruce Greenwald and Joseph Stiglitz (1990) argue that managers suffer grave damage to their personal career prospects when their companies become insolvent and they cannot diversify this risk in the same way that stockholders can. Of course, if the transactions costs of adding reserves are low enough, both stockholders and managers will want virtually complete protection. But managers may choose a level of reserves that is higher than what stockholders would have chosen but that requires them to increase premiums.

Problems of interdependencies complicate this situation for both the company and the investor. For large corporations, a failure in one part of the world or one division, such as the release of deadly methyl isocyanate gas in 1984 at Union Carbide's pesticide plant in Bhopal, India, can lead to disruption or bankruptcy of the entire firm nationwide or even worldwide. An ownership group such as Lloyd's, which controls a number of semi-autonomous syndicates, can fail if one syndicate experiences a severe enough loss. In February 1995, Barings Bank was destroyed by the actions of a single trader in its Singapore unit, and in 2002 Arthur Andersen was sent into bankruptcy by the actions of its Houston branch working with Enron. Similar events have happened to other financial services units in recent years, most notably the near collapse of the American International Group, the world's largest insurer, as a result of a 377-person London unit known as AIG Financial Products that was run with almost complete autonomy from the parent company (Kunreuther 2009).

When firms have managers who pursue objectives that differ from those of investors, it does not fit the benchmark model of efficient capital markets and in that sense is anomalous. As noted, however, there are reasons these divergences may occur that involve imperfect information and transactions costs, so this anomalous behavior does not necessarily imply that agents are using a different decision model than the one posited by classical economics. What would be anomalous is a situation in which one of the parties – say, the managers – sets reserves not to maximize their utility by protecting their jobs but even higher in order to avoid feelings of anxiety or stress, or because they assumed the worst will always happen. We do not have evidence on this.

EQUILIBRIUM OF INSURANCE FIRMS AND CAPITAL MARKETS

The last example dealt with insurance firm behavior related to the objectives and behavior of an individual investor. Now we turn to the deeper problem of optimal and equilibrium arrangements for insurers relative to the entire capital market worldwide. We assume that there is a chance that total losses for a major portion of insurers' portfolios may be so large that it affects others, as illustrated by the financial crisis that reared up during the second quarter of 2008. Although firms may still want to maximize expected profits, the concerns of investors now come into play. If we assume that investors are trying to maximize their own expected utility, what arrangements should emerge to cover situations such as the financial crisis and what would be the resulting outcomes?

We first need to describe risk transfer instruments available to insurers or investors to deal with the possibility of a total loss much larger or smaller than average. One commonly used vehicle is reinsurance. If a single insurer has accepted some portfolio of risks, it has the option of transferring a portion of its obligation to pay claims, should there be a severe loss, to another firm called a reinsurer. A reinsurer provides protection to an insurer in the same way that an insurer provides protection to a consumer facing a specific risk. The insurer transfers a portion of the premium it has collected from its policyholders to the reinsurer as compensation for the reinsurer accepting some of the losses from a specific event. The reinsurance industry then faces the problem of how best to spread the risk associated with the portfolio of exposures it has accepted.

The theoretical problem of equilibrium in a reinsurance market with risk-averse agents has been addressed and solved by actuary-economist Karl Borch (1962). We first give the intuition behind Borch's results, and then further relate them to possible detailed real-world applications of this theory. Borch showed that, in a world without transaction costs, every economic agent (called an investor) will agree to accept a tiny part of the risk associated with insurance of every asset so that it bears some of the risk associated with the total loss experienced by the world capital market. Although the proof of this proposition is complex, the intuition is straightforward: such an arrangement permits the maximum amount of risk spreading through portfolio diversification by investors.

But there is a nonintuitive implication of this obvious proposition. An insurance buyer who suffers a loss may have most of his or her share of the total world loss compensated by an insurance claims payment. Other investors who have not experienced the peril may share in the total loss by receiving a smaller return from their insurance investment than they could have obtained if they had invested their funds elsewhere. The insured individuals might not receive complete protection against a given loss, however, because there will always be some chance, however small, that the firm or policyholder will suffer a large loss at a time when the total loss in the world is also very large. In that case, the policyholder will have to bear some portion of the loss.

Given the enormous size of the modern global capital market relative to any extreme event to date, and given the existence of an efficient capital market, it would seem that broad risk spreading should be possible, so that the chances of incomplete payment for the reasons just discussed should be very low. Even a set of highly correlated risks could be reinsured at a net premium that contains very little add-on as compensation for this risk, as long as the total loss is still small relative to the total value of the world's capital stock.

There could still be some risks that cannot be pooled across portfolios because they are large and all-encompassing, such as a global market collapse or a collision with an asteroid. But the kinds of risks that insurance normally covers do not include these cataclysmic events that would swamp investors' capital. Thus these models predict that insurance markets should be able to handle large correlated losses (such as terrorism or hurricanes) rather well. In reality, imperfect information on the risk and other real-world constraints prevents this from occurring. We will also show that investors may not behave as if they maximize expected utility as postulated by the benchmark model because they have other goals and objectives that are not normally considered in the model that Borch has formulated.

RELATIONSHIP TO MUTUAL INSURANCE

An institutional arrangement exists in real life that is consistent with the benchmark model of supply and is in the spirit of Borch's theory – mutual insurance. A mutual insurer is an insurance firm that has no stockholders or investors, but instead spreads losses among the people it insures. Each member pays a premium in each time period that reflects the actuarially fair premium.

If the risk adheres to the law of large numbers, aggregate premiums will be close to the actual total losses (plus administrative costs and premium taxes) as long as there are many people willing to become members. In the rare event that actual losses fall appreciably short of the total premiums collected, the mutual insurer returns the residual to policyholders; if the losses exceed the premiums and any upfront reserves the members might have provided to get the insurer off the ground, the members are assessed an additional charge to cover these losses.

This story works even if the number of customers is small or their losses are large or are highly correlated, as long as all members of the pool abide by the stated rules. Those who do not happen to experience a loss still pay premiums and get nothing in return. All members of the mutual insurance firm pay a premium even if they have suffered a loss in much the same way that consumers pay premiums to protect themselves against a loss. In a mutual insurer, which is a special case of Borch's model, the premiums and any additional assessments to each individual are determined by the expected insured loss. That means that if you are part of a mutual fire insurance arrangement and your house has an expected loss twice what mine is, you will pay twice the premium and have to bear twice my share of total losses in excess of premiums and reserves should this unlikely situation occur. Of course, if expected losses differ in ways that cannot be measured and related to premiums, or if the mutual insurer chooses to charge the same premiums to people who actually differ in their expected loss, then the members with the lower expected loss will likely leave to form their own mutual insurance firm. The Borch model and the associated model of mutual insurance are actually at the heart of the traditional conceptualization of insurance markets. Although mutual firms do exist, some with quite long histories, most insurers today are joint stock companies with shareholders as well as policyholders. One good reason for this arrangement is obvious: there is more flexibility in choosing how to distribute a risk among people than in the mutual world where every risk bearer is a customer and vice versa.

IMPLICATIONS FOR INSURER SUPPLY BEHAVIOR

We now link these ideas of insurer behavior to characterize the insurance market supply curve, which shows how the price of insurance may change as insurers are called upon to make more coverage available. We want to determine both the average level of premiums relative to the expected insured loss and the shape of the supply curve as it relates to buyers' demand for more coverage.

We assume that the insurance market is competitive, so each insurer in the very short run supplies different amounts of coverage to different people at a given market price or premium. The insurer's decision on how much to supply and the level of the price that will prevail in such a market depend on the costs of making the product available, the costs of the expected loss, the administrative cost, and expected profits.

What would the supply curve of insurance look like if there is free entry and exit into the insurance market, no industry-specific resources in short supply that causes its price to increase with volume, and no capital market imperfections? The price of insurance should be constant no matter how much insurance is demanded.

Is this conclusion realistic? For insurance against correlated events or events whose losses are very large, there may be a problem obtaining sufficient risk capital to keep reserves above the regulatory threshold.

If there is insurance industry-specific risk capital – in the form of reinsurance, specialized financial risk transfer instruments like catastrophe bonds, or apprehension about investing – the required return on capital may increase as insurers' portfolios expand and, therefore, their need for reserve capital grows.

The total collapse of an insurance market after correlated losses, when insurers refuse to supply any coverage, is not consistent with the benchmark model of insurance behavior or capital supply, as we discuss in more detail in Chapter 8. So, at this point, we will conclude that models based on the benchmark assumptions about the objectives of insurance buyers, insurance firms, and investors should yield a supply curve of insurance (even for insurance of large losses) that is stable – no sudden shortages – and, at most, mildly upward sloping for really large changes in demand for insurance against correlated losses. As we show later, actual insurer behavior does not match this model due to regulatory constraints as well as features of insurer behavior that do not conform to the assumptions in the benchmark model and the extensions discussed in this chapter.

SUMMARY

Insurance markets may not work as expected when information is imperfect and losses are correlated. Consumers seeking insurance are confronted with search costs associated with obtaining information on risks and available coverage. If search costs are perceived to be high relative to the expected gains from collecting this information, some individuals may be deterred from purchasing insurance.

There is *information asymmetry* when either the consumer or insurer has information about a risk that the other does not possess. Risks may be poorly understood, leading to bad decisions by purchasers, and/ or companies may make mistakes about whom they choose to insure. *Adverse selection* occurs when only poor risks buy insurance priced for average risks. In that case, the resulting expected insured losses will be higher than if both good and poor risks purchased coverage. Either the insurer will lose money or it will be forced to increase the premium until it covers the losses of those poor risks who buy coverage. That, in turn, will make the insurance even less attractive to the good risks.

Another result of information imperfection may be *moral hazard*. This occurs when an individual behaves differently after purchasing insurance than he or she did prior to having coverage. The insured individual has less incentive to take the same amount of care as when he or she was uninsured, knowing that if there is an accident or disaster, he or she has protection. This less careful behavior increases the probability of a loss from what it was at the time that the individual purchased a policy.

The insurer may not be able to detect such behavior. It is costly and often extremely difficult to monitor and control a person's actions and determine whether that person is behaving differently after purchasing insurance. Similarly, it may not be possible for the insurer to determine if a person will decide to claim more on a policy than the actual loss by inflating the damage either by fraud or by seeking more extensive repairs.

While the law of large numbers is applicable to many risks, there are situations in which it does not hold. That is especially true when losses are correlated rather than independent. When correlation of losses is perfect – if Person A suffers a loss, Person B suffers the same loss – it becomes impossible to pool risks in that market using the law of large numbers. Even if correlation is imperfect, there is still a high probability that losses will be much more substantial than for the case of a given number of independent risks of the same expected value. Correlated losses raise the probability of an insurer's ruin unless the insurer has sufficient reserves. Some of that risk of ruin can be reduced by diversification through risk transfer instruments such as reinsurance.

If investors advancing reserves to an insurer have well-diversified portfolios, they will not be overly concerned about the risks the insurer takes because the consequences of failure will not severely impair their portfolios. But the insurer's managers, whose careers are inextricably tied to the company's fate, may fear the consequences of risk and thus manage the company in a more risk-averse (and less profitable) manner than investors would prefer.

In all these cases, insurance markets may not work well, but the behavior of buyers and sellers should still correspond to a (modified) version of the benchmark models of demand and supply. In the next chapters, we provide empirical evidence as to why these benchmark models, even modified to include imperfect information and imperfect stockholder control, do not characterize the actual behavior of most buyers and sellers of insurance.

6

Why People Do or Do Not Demand Insurance

The benchmark model of demand developed in Chapter 2, based on expected utility theory, postulates a world in which the collection and processing of relevant information is costless to consumers, risk is perceived accurately, and the individual is assumed capable of choosing the amount of insurance that maximizes his or her expected utility. As long as people are risk averse, they are willing to pay a premium greater than the expected value of losses from a set of prespecified risky events. The maximum amount an individual is willing to pay for a given level of coverage depends on that individual's degree of risk aversion. The optimal amount of coverage is determined by comparing the benefits of more financial protection should a disaster occur with the additional premiums for purchasing this additional coverage.

In the last chapter, we explored extensions to the benchmark model of demand that introduced imperfect information and search costs, but maintained the assumption that individuals choose options that maximize their expected utility. This chapter further relaxes some of the benchmark model assumptions and explores different theories of choice and behavior under risk. As we will show, commonly observed behaviors inconsistent with expected utility maximization can be explained by other theories supported by data from experiments, field studies, and consumers' actual insurance-related decisions.

The first theory we examine is *prospect theory*, developed by Daniel Kahneman and Amos Tversky (1979). It is the descriptive choice model that social scientists commonly use today as an alternative to the expected utility model. We describe some insurance situations in which prospect theory predicts actual behavior better than expected utility theory, but also show when prospect theory fails to explain choices. We then outline a theory of *goals and plans* that provides a framework for highlighting the decision process for specifying actions that cannot be explained by either expected utility theory or prospect theory. We will also discuss other less formal descriptive models that provide insight into factors considered by individuals demanding insurance. In Chapter 7, we will undertake a more extended discussion of certain behaviors that can be explained by these ad hoc models of choice.

PROSPECT THEORY AND THE DEMAND FOR INSURANCE

Kahneman and Tversky (1979) developed prospect theory as a model to describe how individuals make choices in the face of uncertainty. One of its central features is the concept of a reference point that normally reflects the individual's current status when approaching a specific decision. Insurance decisions usually are made when an individual is considering whether or not to purchase coverage, as when a homeowner buys a house in California and is considering whether to purchase earthquake insurance, or when a policy expires and one has to decide whether to renew it. In either case, the reference point is likely to be the status quo at the time one makes the decision. Those currently without coverage must decide whether to buy coverage or remain uninsured. Those currently with insurance must decide whether to renew their current policy, change the amount of coverage they now have, or cancel a policy. In both situations, the individual has to decide whether to pay a certain premium to protect against an uncertain but possible loss. The size of the premium will depend on how much coverage the consumer buys.

The Value Function

In analyzing the decision to buy insurance, prospect theory emphasizes the changes in wealth from a given reference point rather than the final wealth level that forms the basis for choices using the benchmark expected utility model. Prospect theory also values losses differently than it values gains, as shown by the value function in Figure 6.1.

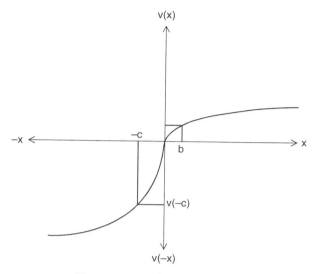

Figure 6.1. Sample value function.

The x-axis depicts the magnitude of the gain or loss and v(x) and v(−x) represent the value associated with a gain of x or loss of −x. Note that the value function is steeper in the loss domain than in the gain domain. Empirical investigations show that individuals tend to experience the pain of a loss approximately twice as strongly as they enjoy gains of the same magnitude (Tversky and Kahneman 1991). In other words, a certain loss of twenty dollars will be viewed as considerably more painful than the positive feeling from a gain of twenty dollars. Stated simply, people tend to be loss averse relative to their reference point, which may not reflect their current wealth that is the basis for expected utility.

In a controlled experiment, Zur Shapira and Itzhak Venezia (2008) found that both students and practicing managers evaluate the prices of policies with and without deductibles by anchoring on the value of the lower deductible rather than calculating the expected benefit of taking the additional coverage. In other words, they viewed having a $100 deductible rather than a $500 deductible as providing them with $400 in additional benefits rather than incorporating the chances of experiencing a loss into their evaluation process. Low deductibles thus were viewed as being much more attractive than they should have been.

In contrast, expected utility theory views the insurance decision in the context of a person's wealth level and assumes that individuals are averse to risk. Just how risk averse they are varies with the person's wealth level. As a person's wealth increases, he or she is likely to be less risk averse with respect to a loss of a given dollar amount. Person A with a net worth of $1 million can afford to lose $10,000 with much less financial pain than Person B whose net worth is only $100,000. Hence, Person A is more willing to take risks and forego costly insurance than Person B.

According to expected utility theory, people are supposed to buy insurance even if the premium is slightly higher than the expected loss. In prospect theory, in contrast, the shape of the value function implies that the desire to avoid losses drives consumers to treat the risk of experiencing a loss differently than obtaining a positive return. In the gain domain, the value function implies that a person will be averse to risky gambles involving positive outcomes, while in the loss domain an individual is assumed to be risk taking and averse to insurance when it comes to uncertain losses.

Prospect theory thus implies that an individual confronted with the certainty of a gain of twenty dollars versus a twenty percent chance of gaining $100 will prefer the sure thing, foregoing the one in five chance that he or she might collect five times more. But an individual confronted with the choice between a twenty percent chance of losing $100 or the certainty of losing twenty dollars will avoid the certain loss and take on the (fair) gamble of the twenty percent chance of losing $100. This implies that if people accurately estimated the probabilities of different outcomes occurring, they would have no interest in purchasing insurance even if the premiums were actuarially fair.

The Weighting Function

To explain consumer interest in purchasing insurance with prospect theory, we need to turn instead to the use of the *weighting function* characterizing how individuals perceive probabilities. Empirical studies suggest that individuals overweight the chances of low-probability events where the likelihood is below thirty percent to forty percent: risks that are most relevant to insurance and underweight the chances of higher-probability events occurring (Camerer and Ho 1994; Wu and Gonzalez 1996). According to prospect theory, highly unlikely events are either ignored or overweighted.

For a low-probability event that is not ignored, a person who is risk taking in the loss domain may still be willing to purchase insurance if the decision weight implied by the weighting function reflects an over-estimation of the probability of a loss. In other words, a high enough perceived chance of incurring a loss makes insurance attractive, even with premiums that reflect a thirty percent to forty percent premium loading factor. This explanation has some intuitive psychological plausibility: people worry (sometimes excessively) about low-probability, high-negative-impact events, and hence assign them high weights when considering their likelihood.

There is a fundamental empirical difficulty with prospect theory's account of insurance purchase using decision weights that also applies to the expected utility model. Empirical research suggests that the loss probability often does not play a role in people's decision processes (Camerer and Kunreuther 1989; Hogarth and Kunreuther 1995; Huber, Wider, and Huber 1997). When loss probability is in fact considered, it is derived from experience, not from actuarial tables. Ralph Hertwig and his colleagues showed that when the individual's probabilities are based on experience, rather than on statistical summaries, he or she will under-weight low probabilities in making risky decisions except when there has been a very recent occurrence of the event class in question (Hertwig et al. 2004). Hence, the hypothesis of overweighting of low probabilities postulated by prospect theory may not be relevant for many insurance decisions.

Nevertheless, one of the best examples of how prospect theory can explain actual insurance behavior better than the benchmark model of demand is the choice of low deductibles and the purchase of insurance policies that offer rebates if one doesn't suffer a loss, even though such policies are generally not as financially attractive as those without such dividends. When faced with the prospect of a loss, the consumer may experience both the cost of the accumulated insurance premiums and the additional out-of-pocket cost of the deductible. As shown in Figure 6.2[1], the negative value of the additional premium caused by eliminating the

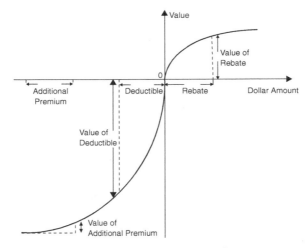

Figure 6.2. Deductible and rebate frames.

deductible is very small relative to the very large reduction in negative value caused by reducing the deductible to zero.

Because people are more sensitive to losses than to gains, a better inducement for an insurer to encourage individuals to avoid making claims would be to offer them a rebate from which claims are deducted, rather than a deductible. Figure 6.2 demonstrates that insurance with a rebate should be more attractive than an equivalent but less expensive policy with a deductible, since the negative value of the deductible is perceived as much greater than the positive value of the rebate. Insurance policies with rebates may satisfy a person's need to collect something on an insurance policy when they have not suffered a loss.

Explaining Insurance Anomalies by Myopic Loss Aversion

Individuals often make decisions one at a time, focusing on their impact on changes in their wealth rather than the level of wealth. A tendency to assess risks in isolation and treat loss as more painful than the pleasure of gains is termed by Shlomo Benartzi and Richard Thaler (1995) as *myopic loss aversion*. A similar failure to consider lifetime wealth explains an individual's reluctance to buy insurance with large deductibles. Matthew Rabin and Richard Thaler (2001) suggest that due to these behavioral characteristics, individuals would not choose to buy an insurance policy that packaged many risks together.

While we agree that individuals are generally myopic and loss averse, their decision process with respect to purchasing insurance is likely to reflect a number of other factors in addition to these behavioral characteristics. A "bundled" insurance policy, such as homeowners' coverage, that provides coverage against many risks is attractive because it reduces search and transaction costs. Furthermore, a comprehensive policy addresses the concern that individuals may have about not being covered for some event.

The history of property-casualty insurance is interesting in this regard. The first versions of such insurance distinguished specific perils from the standard fire coverage, such as tornado, explosion, riot, and hail. An extended coverage (EC) policy was developed in the 1930s to combine property protection against these and other perils. When first introduced, the policy was purchased by few individuals and was even viewed as a luxury. However, after the 1938 hurricane in the Northeast, the first to hit New England in a century, many individuals wanted to purchase the EC endorsement; this bundled policy eventually predominated in the market. That change was assisted by a requirement from many banks that it be added to fire insurance as a condition for a mortgage. The EC policy eventually became part of a standard homeowners' policy. Even when not required by a lender, many homeowners purchase standard homeowners' coverage to protect their investment against losses from fire, theft, and wind with loadings on the order of thirty percent or more of the premium (Kunreuther and Pauly 2004). Things are still not perfectly consistent with the theory, however; coverage for losses from floods and earthquakes is still separate, is not required by many banks, and is often declined by homeowners. As we shall see, however, there may be supply-side reasons for this as well.

A GOAL-BASED MODEL OF CHOICE

The *goal-based model of choice* developed by David Krantz and Howard Kunreuther (2007) is another theory of decision making in which preferences are constructed based on the decision context and a decision maker focuses on preset goals rather than on maximizing utility or value.[2] We show that this approach leads to new explanations of how people make choices and raises novel questions with respect to descriptive theories of behavior and prescriptive guidelines for aiding the decision maker and improving choices.

Role of Goals and Plans

Both expected utility theory and prospect theory assume that financial considerations determine a person's decisions regarding insurance purchase. But people often construct or select insurance plans designed to achieve multiple goals, not all of which are purely financial.

The concept that goals and context have a strong influence on decision making can be traced to Aristotle's *Ethics* (circa 350 BCE), in which he highlighted the importance of multiple goals as a basis for making choices and stated that the importance of different goals vary with the occasion. This concept is consistent with a theory of choice by Paul Slovic (1995) in which preferences are constructed based on context and a decision maker focuses on goals rather than on maximizing happiness or utility.

A plan to purchase a particular amount of fire and theft insurance on a home or on the contents of a rented apartment may be based on satisfying the following six goals (and perhaps others) simultaneously:

- *Goal One*: reduce the chances of a catastrophic financial loss.
- *Goal Two*: satisfy mortgage requirements by a bank or conditions specified by a landlord.
- *Goal Three*: reduce anxiety about risks of a loss.
- *Goal Four*: avoid regret and/or provide consolation in case a loss occurs.
- *Goal Five*: present the appearance of prudence to others who will learn about the insurance purchase.
- *Goal Six*: maintain a relationship with an insurance agent.

These positive reasons for purchasing coverage will then be pitted against other goals such as "Avoid highly burdensome insurance premium payments" and "I don't think the disaster will happen to me so insurance is not a good investment."

The relative importance of these goals varies with the decision maker as well as the context in which the decision may be triggered, such as a specific thought or concern. For example, an insurance purchaser may think chiefly about the goals of satisfying the requirements of the bank that holds the mortgage loan (Goal Two). But when that same person reflects on protecting valuable works of art, he or she may think chiefly about reducing anxiety (Goal Three) and avoiding regret (Goal Four).

To illustrate how the plan/goal representation captures the insurance decision-making process, consider behavior that is often observed: people often purchase flood insurance after suffering damage in a flood, but then many cancel their policies when several consecutive years pass with no flood.[3] One explanation is that avoiding anxiety and feeling justified are both important goals. Following flood damage, anxiety is high, and reducing it is a salient goal; it is also easy to justify buying the insurance, because a flood has just occurred and the experience is deeply etched in the purchaser's recent memory. But a couple of years later, many people may find that the prospect of a flood no longer intrudes on their peace of mind, so anxiety avoidance (Goal Three) takes on less importance.

A similar phenomenon is the tendency to rebuild on sites that have been devastated by flood. An example is Pass Christian, Mississippi, which was inundated by Hurricane Katrina in 2005. The storm wiped out all structures on the coast. Ironically, this was not the first time that apartments had been rebuilt in this area after a disaster. Hurricane Camille destroyed the coastal buildings in Pass Christian in 1969. But apparently no lessons were learned: an apartment complex was rebuilt in 2007 – on the same vulnerable site (Figure 6.3). Note that it is the same swimming pool in both photos.

In a similar spirit, insured individuals do not feel justified in continuing to pay premiums if they do not collect on their policy. The differential weighting of these goals at the time one suffered a flood and after several years without experiencing another loss can lead individuals to decide to allow the existing policy to lapse. These individuals view insurance as a poor investment rather than celebrating the fact that they have not suffered any losses for the past few years.

A decision adviser can explain that the rationale for insurance is to avoid catastrophic losses and avoid regret if one does not have a policy.

Figure 6.3. 1515 East Beach Blvd., Pass Christian, MS, after Katrina (left) and today (right).

The goal/plan theory of behavior predicts that a decision maker who puts heavy weight on these two factors will likely continue to purchase flood insurance year after year if the cost is fair. If the cost increases significantly (because flood maps are redrawn, for example, to indicate an increase in risk), the consumer may decide to drop coverage unless knowledge of the new maps is communicated in a way that raises anxiety about the flood that rarely happens but could occur. Conversely, the consumer may decide not to drop coverage if the redrawn maps imply a reduced risk and premiums are lowered to reflect this change (Sulzberger 2011).

Taxonomy of Insurance-Related Goals

We now discuss four of the main goal categories that may influence insurance purchase using the plans/goals model: investment goals, satisfying legal or other official requirements, worry or regret, and satisfying social and/or cognitive norms. Two other goals – maintaining a relationship with a trusted agent/adviser and affording premiums – may also play a role. These goal categories do not themselves constitute a complete theory of demand for insurance, but do seem to capture some aspects of behavior inconsistent with expected utility theory.

Investment goals. Many homeowners view insurance through an investment lens rather than as a protective measure. These individuals purchase coverage with the expectation that they will collect on their policy often enough so that it is considered a worthwhile expenditure. It is difficult for them to appreciate the maxim that "the best return on one's insurance policy is no return at all," meaning that one was spared damage from an event for which one was insured. At one level, everyone agrees that a person is better off not suffering a loss than experiencing one. But for those who treat insurance as an investment, each year that they do not collect on their policy they regret having bought coverage.

Satisfying requirements. Coverage is often mandatory: Automobile liability insurance is required by most states; homeowners' insurance is normally required by mortgage lenders; flood insurance must be purchased as a condition for a federally insured mortgage in special flood hazard areas; and malpractice insurance is needed for several different professions. In these cases, purchase of insurance may be viewed as a sub-goal for meeting end goals, such as owning a car or a home or practicing one's profession. The amount of coverage and size of the deductible are often discretionary so that the relative importance of specific goals will play a key role in these decisions.

Emotion-related goals: Worry or regret. There is a growing literature on how affect and emotional goals influence an individual's decisions under risk (Finucane et al. 2000; Loewenstein et al. 2001). Three goals in this category with relevance to insurance are reduction of anxiety (i.e., peace of mind), avoidance of anticipated regret, and consolation. Because emotions – even anticipation of anxiety or regret – have considerable immediate presence, individuals sometimes purchase an insurance policy that has a high loading cost in order to satisfy emotional goals, even if it leads to a shortage of funds with which to pursue other goals in the more distant future. Long-term care insurance is a good example. Elderly households of modest means can more frequently become financially stressed by trying to keep up high nursing home insurance payments than by paying for nursing home care – which will eventually be covered by Medicaid. But still, eight percent of nursing home expenditures is paid by private insurance, which means that some people have bought private coverage.

For low-probability, high-impact events, individuals may buy coverage to reduce their anxiety about experiencing a large financial loss. It is important to separate the following two goals: financial protection from the loss and reduction of anxiety about the loss. Situations vary in the degree to which financial losses are made vivid and to which they provoke or relieve anxiety. Hence, the relative importance of these goals may change over time.

One may also anticipate anxiety and take measures to avoid it. For example, some people claim that they refuse to fly, not because they fear a crash, but because they anticipate and dislike feeling anxious about a crash while they are on the plane. But if one cannot avoid anxiety about a loss, one may still find opportunities to reduce this emotion by taking protective measures, including insurance, where appropriate. This feeling may partially explain the demand by the few who purchase flight insurance. Similarly, one might expect an individual to pay more for insurance if he or she feared a specific event (e.g., a car or painting being stolen; a house being damaged from an earthquake) than if he or she was not very concerned about the event occurring even if the actual expected losses were the same.

Regret (Bell 1982; Braun and Muermann 2004; Loomes and Sugden 1982) and disappointment (Bell 1985) are quite different from anxiety, in that they are primarily experienced after a loss occurs rather than before. Consider the example of mailing a package worth fifty dollars. If you do not purchase insurance, and if the package is lost or badly damaged, you likely wish that you had purchased the coverage. Sometimes, the emotion of regret or disappointment accompanying such a wish is quite unpleasant. If, at the time of mailing, you anticipate unpleasant regret or disappointment if an uninsured loss occurs, then you may decide to purchase insurance as a way of avoiding the possibility of such emotions.

Individuals may also purchase insurance as a form of consolation should they suffer a loss. In particular, if you had special affection for an item, such as a piece of art, then the knowledge that you can make a claim should the item be destroyed or stolen has special meaning. Christopher Hsee and Howard Kunreuther (2000) attribute the need for consolation to individuals' willingness to pay higher premiums for the same amount of coverage for objects they love than for those for which they have no special feeling. This behavior is consistent with Adam Smith's observation about human nature in *The Theory of Moral Sentiments*, first published in 1759. Smith writes:

A man grows fond of a snuff-box, of a pen-knife, of a staff which he has long made use of, and conceives something like real love and affection for them. If he breaks or loses them, he is vexed all out of proportion to the value of the damage. The house which we have long lived in, the tree whose verdure and shade we have long enjoyed, are both looked upon with a sort of respect that seems due to such benefactors. The decay of the one, or the ruin of the other, affects us with a kind of melancholy though we should sustain no loss by it. (1759/1966, 136–7)

Usually, a strong positive attachment to an object either has no effect on the probability of damage or loss or it may reduce this probability if extra care is taken. Indeed, in a study of willingness to purchase warranties (Piao and Kunreuther 2006), subjects believed that loving an object made it seem less likely that the object would need repair than if one was neutral or disappointed with the object. This was true whether or not statistical information about repair frequencies was given. But this same study also showed that love did not, on average, produce a significant change in the anticipated cost of repair. If anything, anticipated cost decreases for objects that one loves because of the extra care one takes with these items. People should thus be less willing to purchase warranties at a particular price for loved objects than for ones for which they have no special affection. In fact, they appear to be more willing to do so.

With respect to negative feelings about a situation, experimental findings of Yuval Rottenstreich and Christopher Hsee (2001) and Cass Sunstein (2003) indicate that people focus on how severe the outcome will be rather than on its probability when they have strong emotional feelings attached to the event. Christian Schade and colleagues (2011) show that consumers demanding insurance coverage are those who are most concerned about the negative outcome. This concern may be generated by past experience, as shown by empirical studies on purchasing flood or earthquake insurance only after the disaster occurs (Kunreuther et al. 1978; Palm 1995). In the case of terrorism, a national field survey conducted in November 2001 revealed that Americans living within 100 miles of the World Trade Center felt a greater personal risk from terror than if they lived farther away (Fischhoff et al. 2003). This may explain the large New York area demand for terrorism insurance coverage immediately after 9/11 even at extremely high premiums (U.S. Government Accountability Office 2002; Wharton Risk Management and Decision Processes Center 2005).

Satisfying social and/or cognitive norms. Many insurance decisions are based on what other people are doing or on what those who one respects believe is an appropriate action to take. For example, a new parent may purchase life insurance mainly because his or her parent, partner, or financial adviser thinks that it is important to provide protection for the spouse and child. The amount purchased might follow some standard guideline (e.g., three times annual income) regardless of the loading on the insurance or the buyer's risk aversion. Once again, multiple goals may come into play: the new parent may be trying to achieve the goal of financial protection for the family against a low-probability, high-impact event, but trying as well to satisfy what others expect or wish him or her to do.

There is also empirical evidence that purchase of insurance, like adoption of new products, is based on knowledge of what friends and neighbors have done. Here one should distinguish between nonextraneous social influence – those actions and opinions of other people that provide useful information to a decision maker about the probability of a catastrophic event, about the likely consequences of such an event, or about the nature of insurance plans – and social influence that seems extraneous to making a decision as to whether to purchase insurance and, if so, how much coverage to take.

A clear-cut demonstration of extraneous social influence would show an associated change in the likelihood of selecting a particular plan involving insurance that is unaccompanied by changes in beliefs about the probabilities or consequences of a loss event. An illustration of this behavior came from pretesting an earthquake questionnaire in San Francisco, CA. A homeowner, hearing that his neighbor had purchased earthquake insurance, indicated that he would want to buy such coverage himself without changing his beliefs about the risk he was facing or knowing about the actual cost of coverage (Kunreuther et al. 1978).

Numerous other examples can be cited. Someone who purchases insurance soon after suffering damage from a disaster may do so in part because it is easy to justify the expenditure by pointing to the event that just occurred. Cancellation of insurance coverage after being protected for some years may occur because it is hard to justify an expenditure that has not paid off. The importance of justification as part of the decision process has been demonstrated in experiments that suggest the importance of social norms as an important determinant of choice (Shafir, Simonson, and Tversky 1993). In the process, people often use arguments that have little to do with the tradeoffs between the cost of insurance and the expected loss that forms the basis of economic analyses of insurance or warranty transactions (Hogarth and Kunreuther 1995).

Other Behavioral Explanations

In addition to the factors characterizing behavior, individuals may not process information in ways that are assumed in the benchmark model. Some examples of this misprocessing behavior include a bias toward maintaining the status quo and hence a reluctance to consider new alternatives, an availability bias which leads to an overweighting of recent events in the decision process, and budget constraints.

Status quo bias. There is considerable empirical evidence that some individuals are reluctant to depart from the status quo even though there may be substantial benefits to them from doing so (Samuelson and Zeckhauser 1988). This behavior can be partially explained by loss aversion associated with the value function in Figure 6.1 where the disadvantages of moving from the status quo loom larger than the advantages of doing so (Tversky and Kahneman 1991).

There is also empirical evidence that shows that people are more sensitive to the increased probability of a loss than the decreased probability of a loss. One of the most dramatic examples of this effect was a field study conducted by W. Kip Viscusi, Wesley A. Magat, and Joel Huber (1987). Respondents in a shopping mall were shown a fictitious can of insecticide (priced at ten dollars) and were told to assume that they currently used the product and that the current risk level was fifteen injuries per ten thousand bottles sold. On average they were willing to pay an additional $3.78 per bottle to eliminate the risk. When asked what price reduction they would require if instead the risk were increased by an additional 1/10,000 (to 16/10,000), over seventy-five percent of the respondents indicated they would then refuse to buy the product at any price.

These responses indicate that individuals are much less interested in reducing risks through investment in protective measures than making sure that the risk does not increase from its current level. These findings could be used to persuade homeowners in hazard-prone areas to undertake preventive measures. For example, if those residing in flood-prone regions were informed that global warming is very likely to cause sea level rise and that the potential damage will be much worse if they maintain the status quo, they may decide to undertake adaptive measures such as making property more flood resistant or elevating their structures.

Availability bias. There are situations in which people assess the probability of an event by the ease with which instances of occurrence can be brought to mind. For example, one might assess the likelihood of a future flood by recalling recent occurrences of these disasters. Hence a resident in a hazard-prone location is likely to estimate the chances of a future flood as much higher right after experiencing water damage from an event than four or five years later should there not have been another disaster during this interval. This judgmental heuristic is called the *availability bias* to highlight the importance of available information in estimating the likelihood of an event occurring (Kahneman and Tversky 1973).

Short-run budget constraints. Another reason that some individuals may not purchase insurance is that they believe they are constrained by their current income flow or available liquidity and that they do not have easy access to funds for investment in protection against low-probability events. In focus group interviews to determine factors influencing decisions on whether to buy flood or earthquake coverage, one uninsured worker answered the question "How does one decide on how much to pay for insurance?" as follows:

A blue-collar worker doesn't just run up there with $200 [the insurance premium] and buy a policy. The world knows that 90 percent of us live from payday to payday.... He can't come up with that much cash all of a sudden and turn around and meet all his other obligations. (Kunreuther et al. 1978, p. 113)

Of course, if the loss (or the asset at risk) is only monetary, it is irrational to say that "I cannot afford insurance" to protect myself financially against the loss of the asset. If I cannot afford insurance, I cannot afford to hold the asset at its current level and in its current form. I would be better off using some of the value of the asset to pay for insurance rather than run the risk of losing the asset entirely. And I should plan ahead to put aside the money needed to pay the premium rather than face the need to pay all of a sudden. But, if the asset is illiquid (like a home), the person may not be willing to incur the transactions cost of borrowing against the value of the asset in order to pay for insurance. More generally, the phenomenon of unaffordability may arise when the asset in question is more than just a part of the person's wealth. In addition, people may think that a decision on insurance against a risk that has been and will be around a long time does not have to be made immediately but can be delayed.

Individuals may not buy insurance because they mentally allocate their planned expenditures of income into different accounts so that they feel constrained in what they are willing to spend on certain activities (Thaler 1985). If a family has an account labeled "expenditures on protective activities" and is already committed to spending considerable funds on required insurance (e.g., homeowners', automobile, life, medical), it may feel that it has exhausted its insurance budget and will not want to buy coverage for events such as earthquakes or floods. Or people may respond to an increase in insurance premiums caused by higher expected losses by seeking to reduce coverage in order to keep the premium within the bounds of the mental account.

The idea of borrowing small amounts today to expand one's budget in order to pay the annual premium for an insurance that will avoid a large loss tomorrow may not be part of some consumers' mental accounting procedures. For example, many people who do not have health insurance appear to have sufficient income and assets that they could buy insurance and still have enough left over to pay other expenses (Bundorf and Pauly 2006). They may be using this budgeting heuristic as the basis for not purchasing insurance.

SUMMARY

This chapter examined alternative theories with respect to the demand for insurance that may help explain behavior by individuals that does not conform to the expected utility model. Prospect theory is the most widely used descriptive model of choice and can explain some anomalous behavior such as the purchase of low deductibles. It can also provide one explanation as to why people choose to be uninsured; they do not want to suffer the certain loss of shelling out money for insurance premiums on which they may never collect. To explain why people do buy coverage, prospect theory relies on a weighting function that overestimates low probabilities – but there is empirical evidence that individuals do not explicitly consider probabilities when making insurance purchase decisions.

An alternative theory contends that individuals purchase insurance to satisfy a set of goals that include financial considerations, emotional needs such as peace of mind, and satisfying social norms. The weights on these goals are context dependent and can change over time as illustrated by the decisions of individuals to purchase insurance immediately after a disaster and cancel their coverage a few years later if they have not experienced any losses. Other factors that need to be considered in characterizing insurance purchase decisions are the status quo bias, availability bias, and budget constraints.

7

Demand Anomalies

This chapter discusses significant anomalies in the demand for insurance using the benchmark model of demand as a reference point. It then explains many (but not all) of these anomalies by invoking the theories of choice and behavior outlined in Chapter 6. The unexplained anomalies remain puzzles for the reader to reflect on. The chapter includes a discussion of several general demand-side anomalies followed by a detailed analysis of a few specific insurance markets likely to be affected by these anomalies. It is worth restating here the three broad types of demand-side anomalies explained in Chapter 3:

- Inadequate demand at reasonable premiums (underpurchase);
- Large demand at excessive premiums (overpurchase);
- Purchasing the wrong amount or type of coverage.

SEVEN ANOMALIES

The following examples of anomalies can occur across a variety of insurance markets.

Failure to Protect against Low-Probability, High-Consequence Events

Many people fail to purchase protection against relatively rare but serious losses offered at market premiums unless they are required to do so by stipulations in lending agreements such as buying homeowners' insurance as a condition for a mortgage. Although the probability of an individual incurring a loss is low, the pool of individuals at risk for such events is large. For victims, the financial protection from insurance can make the difference between recovery of their normal pattern of consumption and deep and continuing difficulties.

Given the large number of individuals subject to a particular loss, the risk can be spread widely. The small probability of its occurrence implies that the cost of insurance for each person will be relatively low in relation to the resulting loss. The failure to purchase insurance in such circumstances by a substantial proportion of at-risk individuals is an example of the first type of demand-side anomaly noted earlier.

One possible explanation for such behavior is that people at risk assume that someone else will pay for the costs associated with a sufficiently large event. The federal government normally provides public disaster relief if there is a declaration of a state of emergency following a natural disaster. The U.S. Small Business Administration provides low-interest loans to homeowners and businesses that suffer losses in order to aid the recovery process. For example, following the severe Tennessee floods of April 2010, homeowners who could not obtain credit elsewhere were able to receive loans for up to $200,000 at an interest rate of 2.75 percent to repair or rebuild their damaged or destroyed property. If they had access to credit elsewhere, the annual interest rate on the loan was four percent.[1]

Federal disaster assistance may create a type of Samaritan's Dilemma: providing assistance after the hardship reduces parties' incentives to manage risk or obtain insurance before it occurs. But the governmental payments to any given individual are not guaranteed, and often cover only a small portion of a person's loss. So individuals likely will bear considerable residual risk. Still, because they must use any insurance benefits before receiving relief, they may assume, sometimes incorrectly, that much of their insurance premium would go for coverage that just substitutes for disaster relief. This explanation is not really based on anomalous behavior, but represents an individually rational (if socially inefficient) response to economic incentives.

What makes nonpurchase of insurance an anomaly is the empirical evidence of buyers' perception of what will transpire when large-scale disasters occur. Data on factors influencing the insurance decisions of those subject to hazards strongly suggest that they do not focus on the expectation of future public assistance when deciding on insurance. Most homeowners in earthquake- and hurricane-prone areas did not expect to receive aid from the federal government following a disaster, and yet still did not buy coverage if they could avoid doing so (Kunreuther et al. 1978). To our knowledge, there are no empirical studies suggesting that people have modified their decision process in recent years. It is unclear whether those residing in hazard-prone areas today have greater expectations of the federal government coming to their rescue, given that it assisted companies during the financial crisis of 2008–9. Does the bailout of Wall Street mean that Main Street (or even Rural Route) can expect the same kind of help, or did that form of assistance lead the government to tighten its belt with respect to other forms of future financial aid?

Many of the other ideas discussed previously can be used to explain this general lack of insurance purchase. Search costs or a general misperception of individual risk may prevent purchase. The value function of prospect theory, which describes individuals as willing to take a risk rather than suffer a certain loss in the form of a premium payment, can make even actuarially fair insurance unattractive. Furthermore, the goal of reducing overly burdensome premium payments and the related concepts of budget constraints and mental accounting may explain this anomalous behavior.

Purchasing Insurance after a Disaster Occurs

Individuals are often more interested in buying insurance coverage after a disaster occurs rather than prior to the event. This is true even though premiums usually increase after the catastrophe. A prime example of this behavior is the purchase of earthquake insurance following a major seismic event. Surveys of owner-occupied homes in California counties affected by the 1989 Loma Prieta earthquake showed a significant increase in coverage. Just prior to the disaster, only 22.4 percent of homeowners had earthquake coverage. Four years later, 36.6 percent had purchased earthquake insurance – a seventy-two percent increase in coverage (Palm 1995).

There are at least two explanations for this second type of demand-side anomaly. The event may have been more salient in people's minds due to the availability bias, so residents in quake-prone areas perceived the likelihood of a loss from a future disaster to be much higher than before the quake occurred, even though seismologists point out that the likelihood of another severe quake is lower after one has been experienced because the stress on the fault has been relieved. People may also focus on emotion-related goals due to their concern about the consequences of a future disaster. They then would decide to purchase insurance to gain peace of mind. This latter form of behavior is consistent with the studies in California following the 1989 earthquake in which "worry that an earthquake will destroy my house or cause major damage in the future" was the most important determinant in a homeowner's decision to buy earthquake insurance (Palm 1995).

Cancelling Insurance if There Has Been No Loss

After maintaining insurance coverage for several years and never submitting a claim, many individuals choose to cancel their policy. This anomaly exists in the market for flood insurance, for example, when homeowners who have purchased flood insurance and not collected on their policy after a few years do not renew their policy. This finding is particularly striking because the National Flood Insurance Program (NFIP) requires that homes located in high-risk special flood hazard areas (SFHAs) purchase and maintain insurance as a condition for federally backed mortgages. Failure to continue to obtain flood insurance can be classified as an underpurchase demand-side anomaly (inadequate demand at reasonable premiums).

To further analyze the cancellation of NFIP policies, researchers examined the number of new policies issued by the NFIP and their respective durations through 2009 for those residing in SFHAs and non-SFHAs (Michel-Kerjan, Lemoyne de Forges, and Kunreuther 2011). Their results, presented in Table 7.1, can be interpreted as follows: of the 841,000 new policies in 2001, only seventy-three percent were still in force one year later. After two years, only forty-nine percent of the original 2001 policies were still in place. Eight years later, in 2009, only twenty

Table 7.1. *Tenure results: duration of new NFIP policies by year after purchase, 2001-2009*

	2001	2002	2003	2004	2005	2006	2007	2008	2009
New flood policies-in-force ('000s)									
All	841	876	1,186	986	849	1,299	974	894	1,051
SFHA/Non-SFHA	542 | 299	613 | 264	880 | 306	696 | 291	529 | 320	635 | 664	542 | 432	487 | 407	595 | 456
Tenure longer than:									
1 year	73%	67%	77%	78%	76%	73%	74%	73%	
SFHA/Non-SFHA	74% | 71%	67% | 67%	78% | 76%	77% | 80%	75% | 78%	74% | 72%	74% | 74%	75% | 70%	
2 years	49%	52%	65%	65%	63%	59%	58%		
SFHA/Non-SFHA	48% | 52%	52% | 50%	66% | 64%	64% | 67%	62% | 64%	59% | 60%	58% | 59%		
3 years	39%	44%	57%	55%	53%	48%			
SFHA/Non-SFHA	37% | 41%	44% | 43%	57% | 56%	54% | 57%	53% | 54%	47% | 49%			
4 years	33%	38%	50%	48%	44%				
SFHA/Non-SFHA	32% | 36%	39% | 38%	50% | 48%	47% | 49%	43% | 44%				
5 years	29%	33%	44%	38%					
SFHA/Non-SFHA	28% | 31%	34% | 33%	44% | 42%	38% | 38%					
6 years	25%	30%	33%						
SFHA/Non-SFHA	24% | 28%	30% | 29%	34% | 32%						
7 years	22%	26%							
SFHA/Non-SFHA	21% | 25%	26% | 25%							
8 years	20%								
SFHA/Non-SFHA	18% | 22%								

Source: Michel-Kerjan, Lemoyne de Forges, and Kunreuther 2011 (original data from NFIP).

percent of them were still in place. Similar patterns were found for each of the other years between 2002 and 2008 in which a flood insurance policy was first purchased.

Although some of these individuals may have sold their homes and hence cancelled their policies because they moved, the large percentage decrease in the insured policies in force over time can only be partially explained by migration patterns. Data from the annual American Community Survey over the period covered by the flood insurance dataset revealed that the median length of residence was between five and six years – somewhat higher than the two year to four year median tenure of flood insurance. All new homeowners in SFHAs are required to purchase flood insurance as a condition for obtaining a federally insured mortgage; however, some must have let their policy lapse when the financial institution holding their mortgage did not enforce that requirement.

Such failure to maintain coverage is consistent with the hypothesis that consumers treat insurance as a short-term investment (Kunreuther et al. 1978). In this case, flood insurance was judged by individuals to be an unattractive use of funds rather than a hedge against a financial loss. More specifically, if you have not collected on your policy over several years, you are likely to feel that the premiums paid have been wasted. Some people may still buy in order to reduce their worry and use this rationale to justify their actions to themselves and their peers. But others may balk at continuing to pay for insurance if they are now unconcerned with the consequences of a future flood. Finally, some individuals may treat a string of flood-free years as evidence that the probability of a future flood in their area is now lower than immediately after a flood occurred. But this view is fallacious because, in reality, the risk of damage remains the same as before the flood occurred, and may even increase if there are new building developments that turn grasslands to concrete, thus increasing runoff of water into rivers, lakes, and streams.

Preferences for Policies with Rebates

As discussed in Chapter 6, controlled experiments suggest that individuals prefer policies with rebates even if the value of such a policy is lower than one in which there is no cash return at the end of the policy period.

Consider the following two comprehensive and collision automobile insurance policies that cover accidents during the coming year:

- *Policy One* costs $1,000 and has a $600 annual deductible which will be subtracted from the total annual claims against the policy.
- *Policy Two* costs $1,600 and has no deductible. It will give you a rebate of $600 at the end of the year minus any claims paid by the insurer. Should your claims exceed $600, the insurer will give you *no* rebate but will pay the claims.

It should be clear that Policy One is always more attractive under the benchmark model of demand than is Policy Two, due to the time value of money. Under Policy Two, the buyer in effect makes a loan of $600 to the insurance company at the beginning of the year by paying the extra premium to qualify for a rebate. The loan is repaid without interest at the end of the year, but only in full if no claim is made. If a claim is greater than $600, then the buyer effectively forgives the loan that it made to the insurer at the beginning of the year. Yet when 187 subjects at the University of Pennsylvania were asked whether they would purchase Policy One, only forty-four percent said "Yes." When the same individuals were asked whether they would purchase Policy Two, sixty-eight percent said "Yes" (Johnson et al. 1993).

Note that Policy Two with a rebate is less financially attractive than Policy One with a deductible since the rebate is in essence a $600 interest-free loan to the insurance company. Given any positive discount rate for money, the consumer is worse off choosing Policy Two. However, respondents were more likely to take the rebate policy than the deductible one and the difference was statistically significant at $p<.001$. This is an example of the third type of anomaly in which preferring this policy type is not consistent with expected utility theory. It can be explained by the value function of prospect theory depicted in Figure 6.2 in Chapter 6. The perceived benefits of the $600 rebate exceed the perceived cost of the extra $600 premium that lowers the deductible to zero.

Preference for Low Deductibles

Many insurance policies offer the option of choosing a higher deductible at a lower premium. Deductibles exclude relatively small losses that would be paid if a person had full coverage. Automobile collision coverage will usually have several possible deductible values at different premiums. Sometimes deductibles are defined per time period, as in the case of Medicare in which if a person makes a series of claims during the year, he or she is only personally responsible for a single deductible. For other policies, the deductible is associated with each loss-producing event, as with collision insurance under which deductibles have to be paid for each accident that causes damage to your own car – a contract more costly to the policyholder.

The premium reduction associated with the higher deductible reflects both a lower expected benefit and lower administrative expenses associated with processing claims. Suppose you have a one-in-ten chance of incurring a deductible of $100. Eliminating the deductible would increase premiums by $20 if the loading is fifty percent. Taking this step is not a very wise choice according to the expected utility model, unless the person is extremely risk averse.

People who purchase low deductibles appear to overpay to buy protection against losses that are quite small that they could easily cover with payments out of pocket. This is another example of the third type of demand-side anomaly – purchasing the wrong amount of coverage. Nonetheless, low-deductibles are popular, with a commonly used strategy of purchasing the lowest possible deductible offered by the insurer. Researchers who examined decisions with respect to auto insurance (in Boston and Miami) and homeowners' insurance (in Philadelphia and Orlando) found that between sixty percent and ninety percent of the individuals in each of these cities selected a $500 deductible when they could have purchased insurance with somewhat larger deductibles and generated substantial savings in premiums (Cutler and Zeckhauser 2004). It is hard to believe that adding another $500 of exposure would make a serious dent in the wealth of someone who owns a home worth hundreds of thousands of dollars. Unless the lender required a policy with a low deductible, this behavior is not consistent with the expected utility model.

Justin Sydnor's 2010 study of deductible choices by fifty thousand homeowners using a data set provided by an insurance company found that eighty-three percent of customers chose a deductible lower than the maximum available one, even though the increased premium for this additional coverage would be hard to justify on cost-benefit grounds (Sydnor 2010). In Sydnor's example, a prototypical homeowner paid $100 to reduce the deductible from $1,000 to $500. With claim rates less than five percent, the expected benefit from the additional coverage was worth less than twenty-five dollars (i.e., .05 x $500). Thus the loading on this part of the coverage was seventy-five percent of the premium, an enormous cost.[2] That would also mean that low-deductible policies were extremely profitable for insurers, implying that they had some degree of monopoly power with respect to their clients. If the market was perfectly competitive then insurers would lower the cost of a smaller deductible so that profits from selling such a policy would not be abnormally high.

Similarly, another study found that of the more than one million flood insurance policies in force in 2005, 98.3 percent of customers chose a deductible lower than the maximum of $5,000. Further, almost eighty percent of policyholders chose the lowest possible deductible, $500, and around eighteen percent chose the second lowest deductible available, $1,000 (Michel-Kerjan and Kousky 2010). Levon Barseghyan, Jeffrey Prince, and Joshua Teitelbaum (2011) found that households made inconsistent choices in selecting deductibles for homeowners' and auto insurance, exhibiting more risk aversion in the former case than in the latter, but was unable to provide an explanation for these inconsistencies.[3]

There is an alternative interpretation of a preference for low or zero deductibles consistent with expected utility theory, suggested by Neil Doherty and Harris Schlesinger (1983). The consumer may correctly estimate that some of the utility loss suffered from an adverse event may not be covered by insurance. The actual loss in utility from a car crash, for example, is more than just the reduction in the value of the car or the cost of repairs (whichever is less). In addition to the psychological distress of having a really bad day, the consumer may count the time cost of taking his car around for estimates, dropping it off for repairs and being without it for some period of time, and the all-around hassle of dealing with insurers. But insurance will not explicitly cover those kinds of costs. They represent a kind of uninsurable deductible. After having experienced the pain associated with these transaction costs, the consumer may then reasonably judge that he does not want to add to his uninsured loss by having a large deductible. In fact, he may want full coverage of the insured loss if a policy with no deductible were offered by the insurer. Perhaps this rationale explains why people chose lower deductibles for homeowners' insurance than auto insurance: it is harder to make living adjustments while the damage to your kitchen from a fire is being repaired compared to obtaining a loaner car when your own vehicle is being repaired after a collision.

Unwillingness to Make Small Claims above the Deductible

After purchasing a policy, people are sometimes unwilling to make small claims above their deductible level. One reason for having this higher *pseudodeductible* is a fear, whether justified or not, that their insurance premium will increase as a result of filing a claim. This is most pronounced in automobile insurance but is also true for homeowners' insurance.

The goals and plans model of David Krantz and Howard Kunreuther (2007) provides insight into why individuals behave in this way. At the time buyers purchase a policy, they are likely to focus on the *insurance as an investment* goal and therefore seek the lowest deductible. After the event occurs, they turn their attention to the *financial protection* goal, then realize that collecting a small amount hardly matters to their wealth and worry more about what might happen to their future premiums. This behavior suggests that these individuals do not properly consider the time dimension associated with their insurance decisions – what they do today has an impact on their expenditures tomorrow. Of course, if it is correct that future premiums will increase substantially if one makes even a small claim, then it may make economic sense to hold off. However, if a person knew in advance that insurers would behave in this manner, then he or she should have chosen a higher deductible rather than paying for a lower deductible that is very likely to be left unused.

Data on homeowners' insurance claims from a large personal-lines insurance company support this hypothesis (Braun et al. 2006). The

"I know you haven't had an accident in 15 years.
That's why we're raising your rates - because
you're about due one."

Figure 7.1. © Visual Humour.

researchers estimated that fifty-two percent of households with at least one claim (eighty percent of all households) could have saved money by taking a higher policy deductible than they actually did with no change in their actual decisions on filing a claim. To illustrate, a sample household with a $500 deductible would not file a claim on a loss below $3,000. It could have saved money on premiums by taking a deductible of $1,000 or $2,000.[4] Of course, some consumers may explicitly inquire about the extent to which future premiums depend on claims experience. In contrast to the cartoon shown in Figure 7.1, auto insurance premiums are experience rated so that past claims do play a role in what insurers will charge the policyholder in the future, but this is not generally true for homeowners' coverage.

There is a rational explanation for this behavior. Suppose I believe that my insurer's experience rating rule is to raise premiums based in part on *any* claim, not just on the dollar amount of the claim, or to cancel coverage if there are many claims, even if they are small. Then if my deductible is $500 and my claim is $600, I won't file if I think doing so will add more than $100 to the future premiums I will have to pay. Yet I may prefer a $500 deductible to a $1,000 deductible if I total the car and decide to make a claim.

Of course, one may wonder why people buy coverage from insurers who they think will punish them for making claims. Today, some insurers offer policies at slightly higher premiums than the competition and explicitly promise that one accident will not increase premiums for a given future time period.[5] Is purchase of such a policy anomalous? In large part, the answer depends on the price: How much does one have to pay for such a guarantee, and how does it compare with the expected cost from an event that would otherwise have caused the premium to take a big jump? Unless it is priced favorably, it is unlikely that avoiding such premium fluctuations will much matter for a person's wealth from a lifetime perspective; however, it may be of concern to people who desire stable premiums over time for budgetary planning. It also seems plausible to attribute such purchase decisions to a desire to avoid the bad feeling of having one's premium increase because of one's own negligence. Both interfamily dynamics and self-criticism may cause the person to want to avoid the appearance of having done something careless for which punishment is now being meted out.

Status Quo Bias: A Natural Insurance Experiment

Changes in the insurance laws in New Jersey in 1988 and in Pennsylvania in 1990 provided an opportunity to examine the impact of the status quo bias on the choice of auto insurance policies. Both states introduced a limited tort option (i.e., one has a limited right to sue the other driver), with accompanying lower insurance rates, but the insurance policies for drivers varied by state. In New Jersey, motorists had to actively choose the full right to sue at a more expensive price. In Pennsylvania, however, the status quo was the full right to sue, with motorists now having an opportunity to reduce their insurance costs by giving up some of their right to sue.

When offered the choice, only about twenty percent of New Jersey drivers chose to acquire the full right to sue with eighty percent maintaining the status quo of no right to sue. In Pennsylvania, seventy-five percent of the insured population retained the full right to sue. Similar results were obtained in a hypothetical study of 136 university employees. The effect was even larger in the real world than in the controlled experiment (Johnson et al. 1993).

INSURANCE MARKETS IN WHICH DEMAND DIFFERS
FROM THE BENCHMARK MODEL

We now discuss several markets in which demand behavior appears to differ from the benchmark model. In the process, we will examine the extent of the anomaly and alternative explanations for the behavior.

Flight Insurance: Insuring Specific Risks

In the past, flight insurance was available for purchase at most airports because many individuals bought this coverage, even though its price relative to expected benefits was high. Benefits are paid only in the event that the insured is killed, or in some cases suffers a loss of limb or eyesight, on the particular flight for which the insurance is purchased. Although the policies are inexpensive (a $500,000 policy sells for fifty dollars),[6] the probability of making a claim is extraordinarily low.

Although the purchase of flight insurance is considered an anomaly, the limited market for flight insurance suggests it is not an important one today. We discuss it here to illustrate why flight insurance coverage may have been very popular in past years and why few people buy it today. In a *New York Times* article on air safety, Massachusetts Institute of Technology professor Arnold Barnett mentions that there are so few commercial airline crashes that a person could travel on a plane every day for twenty-six thousand years without being involved in a crash (Kolata 1994).[7] In other words, the likelihood of a crash in the 1990s was less than one in 9.5 million and is most likely somewhat lower than that today. This microscopic probability of collecting on such a policy makes even the low premiums for such insurance absurdly overpriced.

A general accidental death insurance policy that offers $250,000 for death in any accident (including commercial airplane flights) plus many other benefits (injury, automobile accident, etc.) can be obtained for about ten dollars per month for one person (Insure.com 2010). Thus, flight insurance coverage for $500,000 for a single airplane flight is much more expensive than if one bought the general insurance policy with a full month of coverage that includes death or injury from an airplane crash. The very high loading on such a policy indicates that a substantial demand for this product would represent a demand-side anomaly. As in the case of low-deductible policies, however, such a high premium relative to benefits is inconsistent with competitive insurance markets.

Although expected utility theory cannot explain this behavior, there are several possible reasons for the demand for flight insurance. The presence of flight insurance counters at many airports reduced the transaction costs of purchasing a policy. Purchasing flight insurance at the airport may, for some people, have provided peace of mind. For the purpose of such anxiety reduction, spending money to buy such coverage may be preferred to ordering a drink at an airport bar. There may also be a heightened concern in providing financial security for loved ones at the time one flies. Flight insurance offers an opportunity to take specific action to relieve this additional anxiety. These extrafinancial goals might make flight insurance worth the cost. Note, however, that flight insurance usually is purchased because these extrafinancial goals are especially salient in the airport context. Such coverage would probably be much less popular if flight insurance were sold at grocery stores.[8]

Individuals may also focus on the coverage amounts of an insurance policy if the plane crashed, rather than on the probability of such an event. The high ratio of coverage level to premium (i.e., ten thousand to one for $500,000 in coverage which costs fifty dollars) makes this insurance appear attractive, even though this ratio implies that the probability of a plane crash that would make this coverage actuarially fair is 1/10,000. Given the twenty-eight thousand or so scheduled domestic and international flights each day by U.S. airlines, a probability that high would imply 2.8 crashes roughly every two days, a daunting statistic indeed.

Today, the fraction of travelers who buy this insurance is very small. Perhaps the falloff in demand for flight insurance is associated with greater experience with air travel by the population. Alternatively, people may just have come to their senses about what a bad deal it is. Perhaps the popularization of Robert Eisner and Robert Strotz's argument by Andrew Tobias in his book *The Invisible Bankers* (1982), which has a whole chapter on flight insurance, had an impact.

Rental Car Insurance

One of the many hassles of planning a trip is renting a car and navigating through the various insurance clauses that one has to initial when signing the contract at the car rental counter. In most cases, the rental agreement includes the minimum level of third-party liability coverage required by law in a given jurisdiction at no extra charge. On top of this, however, rental companies offer a variety of supplemental insurance products. Among these are additional liability insurance, eliminating the deductible, personal accident insurance, personal effects coverage, and the collision-damage waiver. The last item is intended to protect the consumer if the rental car is damaged or stolen while in his or her possession.

Rental car companies may hold the driver responsible for the full value of such damages if no other coverage applies and the waiver is not purchased. Other sources of coverage may include a personal auto insurance policy or the credit card used for purchase. Given the number of travel columnists who discuss the decision to purchase the waiver, it is clearly one with which consumers struggle (Insurance Information Institute 2009b). A fairly typical example of the content of such sites was found at the Insurance Information Network of California (2008):

If you aren't covered under your own insurance or credit card then you may consider purchasing the collision damage waiver. It's a better option to pay about $8 to $11 a day than $15,000 to $20,000 to replace the rental car.

But is this really sound advice according to expected utility theory? The statistics suggest otherwise. Paying eight dollars per day for rental car insurance for a year would cost about $3,000. This cost, with a car valued at $30,000, implies an annual probability of totaling the car at one in ten if the insurance premium was actuarially fair. The National Highway Traffic Safety Administration, however, reports an annual probability of one in twenty of being involved in any crash, so the chance of a total loss would be much lower (NHTSA 2007). Unless you are very risk averse, you would be much better off taking a chance than paying such a high premium.

Perhaps the more relevant risk is that of damaging the car. According to U.S. collision coverage data for recent model vehicles, there is a one in fourteen annual probability of a collision claim (Insurance Information Institute 2009a). Divided by fifty-two, this figure gives us a probability of a claim in a week of less than 1 in 700. The average loss per claim was given as $4,000. This would then suggest an actuarially fair premium of $5.71 for the week, compared with the rental car insurance premium of $56 per week, approximately ten times higher. The actual car rental insurance fee translates into a premium loading factor of almost ninety percent. Purchasing any insurance at this kind of loading is inconsistent with the expected utility model and would represent an overpurchase demand-side anomaly if a substantial proportion of those renting cars did so.[9]

A number of explanations for choosing this generally high-priced option may be found by focusing on the goals suggested in Chapter 6. Anxiety over the prospect of driving an unfamiliar car in foreign territory may be a factor, as may be the anticipated regret one would feel without insurance should one be involved in a collision that ruined a dream vacation. Additionally, budget constraints may be a very important factor in many cases. Rental car companies typically allow individuals to forego buying the collision damage waiver if they have their own auto policy that will cover the costs or use a credit card that provides such coverage. But if neither of these options exist, drivers will be liable for all damages. Without a credit card, they will normally not be permitted to rent the car without taking the insurance. For these individuals, what looks like an insurance anomaly may be better thought of as just an addition to the price for the car rental.[10]

Cancer Insurance

Cancer insurance, billed as supplemental health insurance, is usually sold as individual insurance in the United States, but recently has been marketed through the workplace as a group benefit for which employees pay 100 percent of the premium, but with tax breaks because the premium can be shielded from income taxation. This insurance is also quite common in Japan, where a quarter of the population has cancer insurance (despite universal national health insurance) that pays cash benefits upon diagnosis, treatment, and death from cancer (Bennett, Weinberg, and Lieberman 1998).

The Aflac duck has been pitched to television viewers only since 2000, but the company has offered cancer insurance for many years. The cancer policies offered by Aflac and other insurers are designed to provide additional, more flexible coverage than comprehensive health insurance. While conventional health insurance just pays to cover actual medical costs incurred, Aflac offers insurance that pays additional cash in excess of actual medical costs.

Here, we concentrate on Aflac's cancer-only coverage. The policies have an indemnity structure in which policyholders are reimbursed at specified rates for particular services when cancer – and only cancer – occurs. Most policies contain an upfront cash benefit upon diagnosis (which is treated as taxable income) and additional payments at specified rates for hospital days, chemotherapy, and radiation, and some nonmedical costs such as transportation or childcare. Such payments are received in addition to any reimbursement from conventional health insurance. There is no formal monetary deductible, but sometimes the payments do not kick in until after some days in the hospital.

Sellers of cancer insurance stress the high lifetime probability of being diagnosed with cancer (three in ten individuals will receive such a diagnosis) and the high direct and indirect costs of the disease (National Association of Insurance Commissioners 2006).[11] Despite these contentions, the insurance has frequently come under attack as overpriced, and consumer advocates tend to discourage its purchase (Silverman 2005). And, indeed, the great majority of people do not buy this kind of insurance, clever marketing notwithstanding. The remainder of this section will determine the value of such policies according to the expected utility model and explain whether consumer behavior is anomalous or not.

A sample Aflac cancer plan offered to employees of the State of Florida pays $300 per day for every day in the hospital associated with cancer and costs $408 per year (Capital Insurance Agency 2008); this money can be used for any purpose, regardless of what the person's regular health insurance pays. The insurance premiums are deducted from an employee's paycheck biweekly, which makes the purchase of such coverage relatively painless as the employee does not make any payments directly. Despite the high probability of a cancer diagnosis over one's lifetime, the probability of contracting this disease in any one year is only 1 in 250 (NAIC 2006).

Although no data provides a precise estimate of the loading on this policy, it appears to be substantially above the benchmark level (see the appendix to this chapter). However, even if such insurance were sold at a reasonable loading, its purchase would be an anomaly. The purpose of insurance is to try to help people protect against unexpected reductions in their wealth from all causes; ordinary health insurance does this for almost all illnesses. This cancer insurance adds payments on top of what medical insurance pays; it may very possibly result in a final wealth level that is higher after the person is hospitalized for cancer. In effect, this insurance causes people to gamble that they will make money if they get cancer. Aflac argues that you may need the money for other costs not covered by health insurance, but even if such costs exist and are substantial, they do not depend on whether your serious illness is cancer or something else.

Although the purchase of comprehensive health insurance and disability insurance is recommended by experts (and the expected utility model) as a more rational way to insure against the risks of health expenses and lost income associated with all illnesses, some people still find cancer insurance to be attractive. Aflac had more than four hundred thousand payroll accounts in the United States in 2008, but it is unclear how many policies this translates to, or the extent of purchase outside the employment setting (Aflac 2008).[12]

The arguments frequently given by purchasers for such insurance revolve around reduction of anxiety. A few representative comments include "I can feel a little more secure with it" and "I want the peace of mind that I'll have additional funds in the event that someone develops cancer" (Luhby 2004). Perhaps left unsaid is the sentiment "I dread cancer most of all." Buying high-priced insurance based on "relative dread" for different illnesses is not part of the expected utility model.

Extended Warranties

Purchasing anything from a toaster to a Lamborghini will likely include a decision regarding an optional extended warranty or service contract that will extend the manufacturer's warranty by a specified number of years. By most accounts, these contracts are thought to be huge profit drivers because the price paid by the consumer for the warranty substantially exceeds the expected loss to the firm selling the warranty. An extreme example is an electronics store warranty costing $49.99 for a DVD player that costs only $39.99 to purchase. Of course, if the warranty pays for repairs multiple times and if the cost of those repairs can exceed the purchase price, the warranty may make sense. But usually the seller reserves the right to replace rather than repair. Still, as long as an annual warranty covers the original purchase and the replacement for the whole year, there may be a case for rational purchase by a highly risk-averse person who believes that he or she has a fairly high probability of using the warranty more than once.

In reality, however, the numbers do not add up. The United Kingdom's Office of Fair Trading did a study of extended warranties and reported on the details for washing machines among other things (Office of Fair Trading 2002). They found that the price for a warranty on such a machine ranged in equivalent U.S. $200 to $300, and that the average cost of repair was eighty dollars. The repair cost estimate was based on a survey of independent repair shops.

The likelihood that a washing machine will need a repair in its first three years is twenty-two percent according to Consumer Reports (2005). Assuming that U.S. and UK machines are roughly equivalent in their repair rates, this would suggest that an actuarially fair premium for a three-year warranty would be $17.60. Even if the true repair cost was double or triple that reported in the survey, this insurance should not be attractive to someone who undertook any type of expected benefit-cost calculation. Additionally, the first year in the three-year period is already covered by the manufacturer's warranty. The prices quoted for washing machine warranties in the UK study were for a five-year extended warranty, but this does little to make them financially attractive. According to the repair shops, forty-five percent of washing machines repaired are older than five years.

Despite all this evidence against purchasing such an extended warranty, thirty-two percent of British washing machine purchasers bought one (Office of Fair Trading 2002). Why? One study argues that the seller has a monopoly over information about the loss probability, so some individuals buy the product because they have overestimated the probability of needing repairs and collecting on it (Cutler and Zeckhauser 2004). A related argument is that the seller may underprice the product and use an overpriced warranty to collect more from buyers who value the product highly.

Another reason for warranties is that they provide a signal to the buyer about product quality; a seller willing to offer a warranty must have some confidence in the durability of its product. The puzzle here is that an over-priced warranty signals a rate of repairs higher than what really prevails, and so should discourage purchase of the appliance. (Perhaps that is the reason salespeople wait to discuss the warranty until after the person agrees to buy the appliance.) But maybe the implied defect rate is lower than what the consumer might otherwise assume; at least offering the warranty shows that the product is unlikely to be a lemon. It is hard to distinguish the "overestimate of repair probability" theory – which is consistent with expected utility – from some alternative unspecified theory to explain why people buy warranties. That is, imperfect buyer information, as a result of strategic behavior by a seller with market power and secret information, would signal a poorly functioning market rather than a behavioral anomaly.

Although most buyers do not purchase warranties, the fraction who do purchase them is not negligible. A recent study showed that people were more likely to buy a warranty on a product they really liked or one on which they got a good deal (Chen, Kalra, and Sun 2009). Buyer ignorance about the probability of needing repairs can probably explain much of this purchase, although the high price of some warranties relative to the purchase price should alert even ignorant buyers. Purchasing warranties can also be explained by the value function of prospect theory. Adding the cost of the warranty to the cost of the product adds very little in percentage terms. We conclude that demand for warranties by most individuals is inconsistent with the expected utility model and should be considered an overpurchase demand-side anomaly.

Life Insurance

In Chapter 4, we concluded that life insurance purchase behavior is fairly rational in that most eligible individuals purchase some coverage.

Although the proportion voluntarily buying insurance is high enough so it conforms to the benchmark demand model, the amount and type of coverage purchased may not be. Many buyers purchase whole-life coverage. It pays a death benefit at the time a person dies but also a cash value to the insured at a designated age (e.g., sixty-five years old) based on the total premiums paid and the interest returned on the investment by the insurer of this fund. The anomaly is that they prefer a whole-life policy to the more financially attractive term-life coverage.

More generally, in the analysis of whole-life insurance, buyers are urged to solve for the implicit return on the savings portion of the policy and compare it to an interest rate that reflects what they could obtain if they invested this money in a relatively safe interest-bearing security. Unless the insurer has special skills at investing, the return from the insurance must be lower than the market rate because loading costs must be paid. Hence whole life is generally thought to be a poor buy and people are advised to "buy term and invest the difference" at a presumably higher return than would be yielded by whole-life coverage (*SmartMoney* 2005).

Although whole-life insurance continues to sell, it is losing ground to the more efficient term products. The percent of adults with whole-life policies fell from forty-eight percent in 1998 to forty-four percent in 2004 (Retzloff 2005b). Those who maintain only whole-life insurance coverage may reflect the belief that insurance is an investment where they will get some type of rebate if they live to a prespecified age (e.g., sixty-five years old). Of course, whole life typically pays the entire death benefit if you live to be 100 – but you will have been paying premiums for years and years if you are lucky enough to reach the century mark. If they use this type of reasoning they would be unlikely to "invest" their money in a term policy for which there is a high probability that they will see no return.

Individuals also typically choose levels of coverage for term life lower than what analysts advise to protect against fluctuations in family consumption (Retzloff 2005a). It would seem that this is evidence of anomalous behavior, based not only on the rule-of-thumb advice used by the industry but also on the more formal models of optimal purchasing for optimal consumption smoothing developed by some economists

(Kotlikoff and Gokhale 2002). The typical format of such a planning model instructs the breadwinner to estimate how much money his or her family would need to replace his or her lost income, less consumption, should the buyer die prematurely.

The problem with household financial planning models offered by consultants is that they do not take into account the probability of collecting benefits or the implied loading costs. The amount of lost income one would want to replace depends on the loading one would have to pay. With low premium loading factors, it makes sense to assure heirs of a higher standard of living, but not if the loading is substantial. Sellers of life insurance will frequently point with pride to falling premiums, failing to note that the decline is due to a decrease in death rates. Insurance is now cheaper, but only because heirs are less likely to collect. Hence, the premium loading factor could be even larger than before given the increased longevity of the population. If coverage amounts are still low after accounting for loading costs, there may be a behavioral explanation, in that many individuals may purchase term insurance when they are young and incomes are low, and fail to appropriately update their coverage. This is another example of the presence of the status quo bias in decision making.

ANNUITIES[13]

Why Take an Annuity?

People live to varying ages after they retire. If they have only a limited private nest egg in addition to Social Security, they ought to seek insurance that will assure them of an acceptable level of consumption (or income) for as long as they live. If a person is rich enough to sustain high consumption until age 100, there is no need for such insurance. On the other hand, even people of moderately high means rarely have enough to reasonably assure high enough income to sustain their desired level of consumption if they should live for many years. So how should they plan?

Those who want to determine how to invest and spend down their financial assets to protect their consumption during their retirement years could turn to an investment adviser who could estimate the annual return on their financial assets. The adviser might also have a formula that forecasts how much one could reasonably expect to consume over time before death at different ages.[14] The person could then plan how much of the return to safely consume – but would inevitably risk leaving unplanned levels of assets behind upon early death or run the risk of very low consumption if he or she lived to a ripe old age.

A better alternative to this somewhat complicated planning process is to use some of your wealth to buy an *immediate annuity* whereby you pay a lump sum amount for an insurance policy that promises to make predetermined annual payments from that point onward for as long as you live. Such an annuity provides protection against outliving your assets. With an annuity, you face the possibility that your estate loses money if you die soon after retirement but, in return, you gain the assurance that income will always be there to meet your consumption needs while you are alive. Compared to the investment strategy, the person could have a higher level of consumption every year. Of course, there is a risk whatever one does: the portfolio recommended by an adviser could tank, or the annuity company could go broke. The likelihood of either of these adverse events can be reduced by choosing safer assets or a safer annuity company in exchange for a lower expected return on the annuity.[15] Indeed, many companies offer annuities that have the highest ratings for financial security, so the insolvency risk can be made very small if one is willing to pay the price.

And yet very few people take immediate annuities. Among all retirees, only one percent bought an annuity (Lieber 2010). In a study of a subset of retirees with 401(k) plans in a convenience sample of 500 medium to large firms, only two percent to six percent took immediate annuities (Schaus 2005). Those consumers who do have annuities tend to choose small ones that replace only a fraction of their desired consumption, a much smaller share than one would think reasonable, even if they plan to leave some wealth to heirs and even if they wish to retain some wealth in a liquid form in case of emergencies.

In theory, people should divide their wealth when they retire into a part they will leave to their heirs and a moderate and moderately liquid contingency fund for uninsured risks (the house needs a new roof;

you have health-related expenses like nursing home care that Medicare doesn't cover). They should then annuitize the rest (Yaari 1965). In practice, they might plan by selecting some annual consumption level as the minimum they want to see secured and annuitize enough of their wealth to get that. Either way, those approaching retirement age should take an annuity of some significant amount, but few do. As we will see, people whose only retirement provision is Social Security and possibly ownership of a modest home are not likely to buy annuities because they have few financial resources; however, even among the minority of seniors with upper-middle-class incomes and nontrivial liquid financial wealth, annuity purchase is rare. Does this reflect anomalous behavior on their part?

Tradeoffs

To explore this question, we begin with an example of the choice a person might face as he or she nears retirement. The numbers are hypothetical but intended to highlight the potential tradeoffs. Suppose someone at age sixty-five is assured some income from Social Security and from a defined-benefit pension plan. Let's say that the annual income from these two sources amounts to $40,000 per year. The person also has $500,000 in financial wealth (not including the value of the home). Consider the following two options.

In Option One the person could invest his or her wealth in a reasonably safe portfolio in such a way as to generate an expected additional income of $30,000 per year for the next thirty-five years, eventually drawing down the portfolio so that it would become zero at age 100. If the person lives to be 100, he or she gets to consume that amount each year. If the person dies anytime between before he or she reaches age 100, any remaining investment portfolio goes to heirs. If he or she lives past 100, then he or she will have to rely on other forms of assistance to survive, perhaps from family members.

Option Two uses the $500,000 to buy an immediate annuity that promises the person an additional income of $50,000 per year as long as he or she lives. Of course, this higher income comes with a catch; the income stops when the person dies and none of the investment is returned to the estate. So if the person is killed in an accident right after signing the annuity papers, the person's heirs get nothing; they lose the entire $500,000. What would the expected utility model tell a risk-averse person to do?

Let us begin with the case that the person does not care at all about heirs. Option Two, which provides $50,000 for as long as he or she lives, seems preferable to Option One, where one expects to get $30,000 until the age of 100 or to leave a big estate behind if one dies early. The annuity provides a higher certain income when the person needs it the most. In real life, the firm managing the annuity will probably do a better job of protecting the portfolio against market fluctuations, so the annuity income is probably surer than had this individual personally invested his or her portfolio in stocks and bonds. A $50,000 annual income is not absolutely guaranteed since annuity firms have been known to go under, but this return is as certain as one can reasonably expect because annuity firms invest the money in very safe securities. For these reasons, according to the expected utility model, a risk-averse person who does not care a great deal about heirs should want to buy an immediate annuity.

Suppose a person cares as much about income for heirs as for himself or herself. In this case, there may be a preference for investing funds on one's own (Option One) rather than purchasing an immediate annuity where one runs the risk of losing income for heirs if one dies and the income stream dries up. If he or she were only concerned about heirs, he or she would *not* have an annuity and would put any extra money into term-life insurance. But assuming there are not that many elderly family altruists, we would expect most people with wealth that could be annuitized to do so for these reasons. But do such people buy annuities in the way the expected utility model would suggest?

If one looks only at actual annuities (either purchased or in force for retirees) the answer seems to be that many people do not do what the benchmark model of demand implies they should. Only about two percent of retirees are covered by immediate annuities. But these statistics may be somewhat misleading because there are other ways to assure income in retirement. The most obvious and the most prevalent is Social Security, which (along with Railroad Retirement) covers virtually all American workers. If the income furnished by Social Security satisfied one's consumption needs, there would be no need to enhance it with an annuity. Whole-life insurance plans generally have some cash value that can be used directly or converted to an annuity upon retirement.

In addition, about 50 million workers have a guaranteed pension plan, either defined benefit (DB) from an employer or defined contribution (DC), the latter usually in the form of a 401(k) account. Technically, only DB plans guarantee income (and even that guarantee is only as good as an employer's survival).[16] DC plans generally provide assurance of some positive gross payout, but with the precise amount subject to fluctuations in the market. Many DC plans have an option to convert to an immediate annuity after retirement, but few people do so (James Poterba, personal communication in July 2010).

An Anomaly in Annuities?

Still, a very large proportion of people who enter retirement with sizeable assets choose not to convert even a portion of their portfolio into an annuity. If the purpose of accumulating assets is to facilitate postretirement consumption, it appears that the great majority of these people are not using annuities as they should, in terms of the benchmark model. An article in *Forbes* concluded that "Immediate annuities make sense for a lot more people than the number who buy them" (Barrett 2010). Is this true, and if so, why?

One possibility is that people are behaving according to the expected utility model, but the loading on annuities is too high to make this insurance an attractive option. This seems not to be the case. Indeed, the cost of annuity insurance relative to what could have been earned by investing the amount of insurance premium implied a premium loading factor of twenty percent for a population with average life expectancy (Mitchell et al. 1999). Because those who bought annuities live longer than average, the premium loading factor of an annuity for them is more likely to be in the range of ten percent. Even those who live less than the average life expectancy would likely have a premium loading factor below our benchmark percentage unless they died within a few years after purchasing the annuity. From this vantage point, an annuity should be very attractive to a risk-averse person.[17]

Indeed, the estimated utility gain from using annuities relative to using the best financial planning model more than compensates for this loading when using reasonable estimates of risk aversion (Mitchell et al. 1999). One does sacrifice some expected income by choosing an annuity, both because of administrative costs and because the annuity firm will invest in safer but lower-yielding securities than in a typical investor's portfolio.[18]

Another possibility is that adverse selection exists that drives lower risks out of the market. There is evidence for adverse selection in annuity markets. In a series of studies examining compulsory and voluntary annuity markets in the United Kingdom, Amy Finkelstein and James Poterba (2004) find that those with shorter life expectancies are less likely to take annuities voluntarily or, if they do take them, select options with larger payouts earlier in the retirement period. Nevertheless, the Mitchell et al. calculations show much lower take-up than would be rational even after adjusting for adverse selection, and even while focusing on those who have longer life expectancies. Adverse selection would predict a smaller market than in its absence, but not as small a market as exists.

Sources of Anomalies

The low take-up for annuities may imply that people are not presently trying to assure themselves of high consumption at very old ages or gain peace of mind in case they outlive their retirement assets. But then what are they thinking? The alternative informal model of people ignoring low-probability events seems less plausible here as well. No one would reasonably say that living into your nineties is something that could never happen to them. In fact, most people hope that they will live to a ripe old age and beat the odds. If you continue to feel, as you did in your twenties, that you will live forever, it is all the more reason to buy an annuity. Because the annuity purchase decision is usually made upon retirement, when the adequacy of any pension or Social Security is also at issue, it should be a salient option with respect to planning for future income and its expenditures.

Low levels of annuity purchasing might be consistent with the expected utility model if the person has other resources and constraints or has objectives other than smoothing lifetime consumption opportunities. Someone with modest financial wealth expecting to go on Social Security or receive exogenously determined pensions might see little additional benefit from annuitizing that wealth. If administrative loadings have a fixed cost component, a tiny annuity might not be worth the cost. At the other extreme, if the person has a generous defined benefit pension or a very high level of wealth, and is not terribly risk averse, the need for an annuity to secure a reasonable level of consumption might be small.

In addition to Social Security crowding out annuities, Medicaid may also do so. Of course, a person with high assets would not be eligible for Medicaid. But if the person does not annuitize but considers the possibility of using up those assets late in life, the protection provided by Medicaid at that point may discourage both annuities and long-term care insurance. Paradoxically, the availability of lower-quality welfare-based Medicaid may encourage retention of assets to avoid "public care" early in retirement (Ameriks et al. 2011) and discourage the purchase of long-term care insurance later as assets fall (Brown and Finkelstein 2007, 2008).

As indicated previously, if people value bequests, some of the value of the annuity is lost if one dies early. A strong enough bequest motive therefore could explain low take-up of annuities. An annuity may also interfere with an intrafamily bargain about providing care when one is old that takes the following form: I agree to retain my assets and so promise to bequeath wealth upon my death to my heirs if they promise to take care of me should I have exhausted my assets by living into my nineties. If instead I provide for my heirs in the more rational model suggested by Menahem E. Yaari (1965), by buying life insurance or making a transfer early in retirement, I lose my leverage later on in life when I may most need it.

Alternative Explanations

People may forego annuities because they believe they can invest their nest egg better than the annuity firm. Excessive optimism regarding their own investment ability might be a contributing factor to the non-purchase of annuities for those people who actively manage their own wealth portfolios. Moreover, the idea that I will walk into the annuity firm office a near-millionaire and exit with much less in liquid wealth may be hard for people to accept (despite the theory that views wealth and income streams as equivalent).

A related explanation, with some support in terms of surveys of buyer opinions (Brown et al. 2008), views the main adverse consequence of buying an annuity as the potential loss of all wealth invested in the annuity because one believes one may die shortly after the purchase is concluded. The person, according to this view, looks at the purchase of an annuity as a gamble: He or she feels that it will have been a good bet if he or she lives long, but worries that, if he or she dies early, it will have been a poor investment.

There have been some attempts to probe this behavior more deeply. On the one hand, research shows that the *pattern* of annuity purchases is rational: they are more likely to be bought by those one would expect to have a higher demand for them – people who do not expect to die soon (Schulze and Post 2010) or who have more wealth, are more financially sophisticated, or who have high pension income (Inkmann, Lopes, and Michaelides 2011). So behavior is not random, but in the United States at least, the average level of purchase still seems irrationally low. Research does also indicate that buyers' intentions about annuities can be affected by framing and default options (Benartzi, Previtero, and Thaler 2011; Brown et al. 2008). Given the competitive market in financial planning for the middle class, however, it is puzzling why those marketing annuities choose to frame the problem in terms of an investment option rather than highlighting the consumption consequences of purchasing an annuity.

At this point, the safest conclusion is that behavior of demanders for annuities is likely to be anomalous for a reason similar to the reluctance of individuals to invest in mitigation measures to reduce their losses from natural disasters. Individuals are highly myopic in their decisions to invest in protective measures and perceive the up-front costs to be much greater than the expected returns over the next few years. To illustrate, a person is not willing to part with a large portion of his or her wealth when retiring at sixty-five years old because he or she is considering only the returns should he or she live for the next few years. He does not consider living into his seventies, eighties, or nineties, and thus perceives this investment in protection to have an expected benefit-cost ratio less than one. This type of myopia would be inconsistent with our benchmark model of expected utility. There is evidence (Brown 2001) that people who report having a short time horizon are less likely than average to take annuities.

Overcoming Anomalies in Buying Annuities

Most people do not buy annuities. This behavior seems to reflect a mix of these features of the market:

- Those approaching retirement are not provided with and do not seek detailed information on the advantages of the product so, despite the plethora of financial planning talk shows, websites, and presentations, they do little thinking about this product.
- Individuals are often myopic and loss averse, as well as likely to overestimate their own ability to invest wisely, and so may not want to give up control of their nest egg for lifetime investing. Although they do think about the chances of dying tomorrow and losing the annuity premium, they do not think about the chances of living for a very long time and needing resources for consumption.

If these are the principal reasons individuals do not buy annuities, the most obvious solution is to provide better and more convincing information on the attractive properties of annuities and the very high return you get on your annuity investment if you live to a ripe old age. Planners need to construct more persuasive scenarios than they currently offer if people are going to be induced to change. More specifically, these scenarios could show their clients that they will have to curtail their consumption considerably if they live longer than expected and are not financially protected.

SUMMARY

Demand-side anomalies fall into three different categories:

- *Category One*: inadequate demand at reasonable premiums (underpurchase). For example, homeowners often do not buy coverage voluntarily against natural disasters until after experiencing a catastrophe. When they do buy insurance, they often cancel their policy if they have not suffered a loss after a few years. This occurs even if premiums are subsidized, and even if the potential loss from the disaster is large relative to their wealth.

- *Category Two*: large demand at excessive premiums (overpurchase). This applies to the purchase of insurance against damage to rental cars, warranties on appliances and electronics, and other consumer durables. A significant number of individuals buy insurance against losses to their property with low deductibles even though increasing the deductible would be in their best economic interest unless they are very risk averse.

- *Category Three*: purchasing the wrong amount of coverage. People buy coverage that turns insurance into a gamble, one that pays off only if some bad events (like cancer or death in a plane crash) occur. Another example is the purchase of inadequate life insurance protection against loss of household earning power, even though the premium loading is moderate.

This chapter shows that there are significant real-world examples of all three types in some settings of risk and insurance. The fact that many individuals deviate from the benchmark model of choice indicates that we need to understand how these buyers make decisions and examine the possible case for public intervention to deal with relatively common apparent errors.

APPENDIX TO CHAPTER SEVEN

Estimation of Loading for Group Cancer Insurance

To estimate an average payout from the Aflac policy for group cancer insurance, we turn to a variety of sources. According to the Centers for Disease Control and Prevention, the average length of stay in a hospital for cancer was approximately seven days (CDC 2006). At a daily rate of $300 this translates into a payout of $2,100 per hospitalization from the Aflac plan. Other cost estimates are taken from a 2004 study in the *Journal of Clinical Oncology* (*JCO*) (Chang et al. 2004). The Aflac plan pays for chemotherapy and radiation at a rate of $300 per day with a monthly maximum of $2,400. The *JCO* study finds the average cost for such treatments is approximately $7,200 per year. This could be an over-estimate of the payout from the policy if the treatments are spread over fewer than three months given the monthly max, but we will use it for our calculations. The Aflac plan will reimburse a maximum of $5,000 for surgery, and the *JCO* study found a monthly cost for surgery of $844, or more than $10,000 per year. We will therefore assume the maximum surgery benefit of $5,000. Finally, this supplemental insurance makes a $5,000 payment conditional on the cancer diagnosis alone (regardless of the cost of treatment).

Although this is not an exact estimate of the annual covered costs under this policy, the exercise is useful for considering the value of such a policy. Adding up these estimates, the average payout from the Aflac policy equals approximately $19,300.[19] At a probability of 0.4 percent (or 1 in 250) of being diagnosed with cancer in a year, the expected annual payout from such a policy is seventy-seven dollars. With an individual premium of $408 per year, this means that only nineteen percent of the premium goes to pay benefits and provides little justification for purchase. The implied loading is very high.

8

Descriptive Models of Insurance Supply

The benchmark model of supply assumes that competitive insurance firms know the loss probabilities and outcomes of the risks they are insuring against and base their premiums on this information. Furthermore, they are able to effortlessly change their premiums to reflect updates in their estimates of the risk. Insurance firms have access to the capital markets (at competitive interest rates) for any needed funds, even after experiencing a large loss. Investors who supply capital to insurers hold diversified portfolios. Losses are independent of one another, so that the law of large numbers minimizes the likelihood of an unexpectedly large total loss and makes it very unlikely an insurer will have to declare insolvency.

In that ideal world, insurance firms are also assumed to have accurate information on the risks of their customers and choose actions that maximize their expected profits. Under this model, firms should be willing to supply virtually any amount of insurance that buyers are likely to find attractive. The premiums they would charge are just high enough to cover their expected claims, including loading costs, which yield a rate of return on capital that investors could have earned elsewhere in the private market. The supply curve of insurance would be virtually horizontal because insurance uses only a tiny fraction of the global capital pool. In other words, the price of coverage should be largely unaffected by variations in the demand for insurance coverage or insurer demand for additional capital.

WHY INSURANCE FIRMS DIFFER FROM THE
BENCHMARK MODEL

It doesn't work that way. The behavior of insurance firms differs from the benchmark supply model for several reasons, which we explore in greater detail in this chapter.

Information imperfections can cause adverse selection or moral hazard problems as discussed in Chapter 5, using automobile insurance and health insurance as examples. In the case of adverse selection, low-risk individuals may have less interest in purchasing insurance because the coverage is priced too high relative to their expected loss. With respect to moral hazard, the price of insurance may increase, because individuals who have insurance often behave with less care than they would otherwise. Although these outcomes are not desirable and may differ from those implied by the ideal competitive equilibrium model, the behavior nevertheless is consistent with the benchmark supply model once it has been modified to take into account this difference in knowledge by buyers and sellers.

Other commonly observed behaviors by insurance firms are, in contrast, *not* consistent with the predictions of the benchmark model of supply. More specifically, insurers often behave as if they are risk averse. Also, their cost of capital rises when they have to obtain more of it, especially following a large loss that depletes their reserves. We will discuss specific examples of such insurer behavior in more detail in the next chapter. Here we characterize insurer behavior and institutional structures that differ from the benchmark model of supply.

Role of Stockholders

One general issue is the relationship between managers of insurance firms and the investors who supply their capital and thus have formal control of the firm. Managers may have more accurate information about circumstances the firm faces than do outside investors. As discussed in Chapter 5, Bruce Greenwald and Joseph Stiglitz posit that managers will behave as though they are risk averse if they are rewarded when profits rise, but fear that they may become unemployed or suffer a loss to their reputation if the firm becomes insolvent (Greenwald and Stiglitz 1990). Now we want to see how this managerial behavior eventually affects the decisions by most insurance firms. If stockholders do not overrule these managers' preferences, the firm will behave as if it were risk averse. In this case, the firm will fail to maximize expected profits because managers set reserves at higher levels than stockholders would prefer.

Such deviations between objectives of owners and managers become more important as the insurer's portfolio deviates from one independent risk to a more highly correlated one. This increases the likelihood that the firm will suffer a large loss in surplus and perhaps become insolvent. To reduce the likelihood of this outcome, insurance firm managers will want to increase the level of capital reserves that they hold. These actions are likely to increase the cost of coverage to consumers as well as drive down average profits. Investors do not have the information to detect and question such behavior.

Conventional wisdom holds that major accidents and disasters are low-probability events. But when you look at a whole state or country, as insurers normally do, such events have a relatively high chance of occurring somewhere in a given time period. It is somewhat sobering, for instance, to learn that the probability is one in six that at least $10 billion of insured property will be destroyed by hurricanes somewhere in Florida next year. This is equivalent to the chance of getting the number three in one toss of a die – hardly a low probability. If we extend the time horizon from one year to ten years while keeping the population of Florida constant, the likelihood of at least one hurricane causing damage exceeding this amount is greater than five in six.[1] With economic development in coastal areas of this state and the apparent increased intensity of hurricanes due to global warming, we are almost certain to experience a disaster of losses exceeding $10 billion in Florida in the next decade (Kunreuther and Michel-Kerjan 2009).

If one extends the event space to include all natural disasters and the sample space to encompass the globe, then we have to modify our definition of a low-probability event. In other words, we are highly likely to experience weather-related catastrophes in the coming years. A large-scale disaster affecting a limited geographic area can turn into a catastrophe for an insurer if its portfolio of risks is heavily concentrated in this region. Diversifying its exposure over more regions can make average claims per exposure more predictable.

In one sense, this diversification could lead to better functioning of insurance markets for another reason: diversified insurers will know that large total losses can occur in practice, and therefore will not be surprised when they do. But it also means that capital needed for reserves will be higher than if such large losses were below the insurer's threshold level of concern. Rating agencies may also play a role by requiring insurers to meet specific standards for higher reserves to maintain or improve their current rating.

Causes of Separation of Ownership and Control

A firm run by managers who pursue their own objectives will behave differently than a firm in which managers reflect what the stockholders want. But why should such a separation of ownership and control emerge? Why would corporate boards representing stockholders choose management teams that overweight the possibility and consequences of ruin in making their insurance pricing decisions? And if managers do not do what is in the investors' best interests, shouldn't that depress the price of stock and leave the firm open to a takeover and management housecleaning?

One answer postulates that the asymmetric information between management and investor-owners gives management the upper hand in providing the firm with day-to-day direction. A second reason is that salaries would have to be higher in the firm that wants management to take chances, so that some of the gain to investors from potentially higher profits is transferred to risk-averse managers as additional payment for their uncertain earnings and uncertain future careers. Of course, if investors have much of their wealth tied up in a particular firm, they may not want the insurer to behave as if it were risk neutral.

We now examine further whether separation of ownership and control coupled with managerial goals (and later, the current role of state insurance regulation) can explain some seemingly anomalous behavior by insurers. Managers in insurance firms have two decisions to make with respect to providing protection against a specific risk: setting the premium and determining how much coverage to offer at that premium. We still assume that firms are operating in a purely competitive environment on the supply side. In a Greenwald-Stiglitz world, however, if they are all owned by stockholders or investors who are kept in the dark, they may all deviate from expected profit maximization due to management concerns with insolvency and other factors. What kinds of behavior by managers are plausible or common, and what is their impact on the supply of insurance?

Risk Aversion and Ambiguity Aversion of Managers

Suppose the management of an insurance firm is risk averse regarding its own compensation, but there are no legal or settlement costs associated with the insolvency of the firm. Although stockholders might lose only a sliver of their portfolios if this firm experiences claims that exceed its reserves, managers might experience a significant cut in their bonuses at the end of the firm's fiscal year.

To reduce the costs the firm will bear, management may want the insurer to charge higher premiums than those that would maximize expected profits if doing so would reduce the firm's likelihood of insolvency. More to the point, managers will reduce the probability of losing their jobs or receiving lower salaries or smaller bonuses at the end of the year. The higher premiums would be one source of the higher level of reserves. Management also might want the firm to turn down some business at premiums that yield positive expected profits if selling these policies significantly raises the chances of insolvency.[2]

The problem is that owners of the firm (stockholders represented by the board of directors) almost surely have less information than management about the risks the firm faces. They thus cannot evaluate managers' actions regarding premiums charged, reserves accumulated, and coverage offered. That is, current owners and the stock market in general cannot distinguish between losses due to bad management of the firm from those outcomes due to bad luck. Hence they punish managers for negative outcomes regardless of the cause. Managers then react by choosing strategies, such as high but costly reserves, that make such outcomes less likely.

In deciding what premiums to charge and how much coverage to offer, insurers also need to take into account the response of potential policyholders. For example, if premiums are increased, some potential buyers will now view insurance as overpriced and therefore cancel their policies and search elsewhere for a better deal or decide to remain uninsured.

If we hypothesize that in a competitive market an insurance manager has chosen a higher level of reserves than buyers desire and translates the increased transaction costs associated with holding more reserves into higher premiums, then the firm's total revenue will fall as a result of the price increase and therefore total expected profits will fall.[3] The extent to which managers will prefer to have more reserves but lower expected profits depends on the degree of risk aversion of those making these decisions.

Insurance managers are also likely to be ambiguity averse: they worry about the uncertainty of the probability of a loss occurring. There is an illustrious history supporting these concerns by insurers. More than ninety years ago, two of the leading economists of the day, John Maynard Keynes and Frank Knight, distinguished between precise measurable probabilities and those with considerable uncertainty and limited knowledge of the likelihood of their occurrence (Keynes 1921; Knight 1921). Both economists pointed out that individuals are likely to be more concerned with events where there is more uncertainty regarding the outcome.

In a famous experiment conducted forty years later, Daniel Ellsberg (1961) showed that individuals preferred to bet on known rather than unknown probabilities. This finding, which demonstrated that these individuals violated one of the axioms of expected utility theory – the independence of irrelevant alternatives – had a powerful impact on research in this area, as many of the proponents of utility theory made choices inconsistent with the model that they were promoting.

In the insurance world, actuaries and underwriters utilize rules of thumb that reflect their concern about those risks where past data do not indicate with precision what the loss probability is. Consider estimating the premium for wind damage to homes in New Orleans from future hurricanes. Actuaries first use their best estimates of the likelihood of hurricanes of different intensities to determine an expected annual loss to the property and contents of a particular residence. When recommending a premium that the underwriter should charge, they increase this figure to reflect the amount of perceived ambiguity in the probability of the hurricanes or the uncertainty in the resulting losses. More specifically, if the premium for a nonambiguous risk is given by z, then an actuary will recommend a premium of $z' = z(1+\alpha)$ where α reflects the degree of ambiguity regarding the risk (Kunreuther 1989).

Underwriters then utilize the actuary's recommended premium as a reference point and focus first on the impact of a major disaster on the probability of insolvency or some prespecified loss of surplus to determine an appropriate premium to charge. Given underwriters' concern with losing their jobs should their firm experience a catastrophic loss, insurers will also choose to limit coverage so that the chances of insolvency are kept at or below a prespecified probability. In 1973, Insurance Commissioner James Stone of Massachusetts suggested that an underwriter who wants to determine the conditions for a specific risk to be insurable will focus on keeping the probability of insolvency below some threshold level (p^*) rather than trying to maximize expected profits (Stone 1973). From discussions with insurance underwriters today, this safety-first model still characterizes their behavior.[4]

Are buyers willing to pay more for coverage when the probabilities of a loss are ambiguous? If they are, they will continue to buy insurance at the higher premium. If they are not, they will reduce purchases when underwriters charge a higher premium due to actuaries' responses to ambiguity. Of course, if the premium recommended by the insurer's actuaries is higher than the one that maximizes expected profit, the firm will not on average collect as much revenue as it could. But there will now be more reserves per policyholder to cover catastrophic losses, so with fewer policyholders the insurer is safer.

The safety-first model proposed by Commissioner Stone explicitly concerns itself with the likelihood of insolvency when determining whether to provide insurance against a particular risk and, if so, how much coverage to offer and what premiums to charge. More specifically, a preassigned annual probability p^* reflects a firm's tolerable threshold insolvency probability. The value of p^* is likely based on rating agency

criteria with respect to reserves that an insurer needs to cover catastrophic losses. Suppose that the insurer sets $p^*=1/250$. This implies that
it will want to set premiums so that the likelihood of the insurer suffering
a catastrophic loss is no greater than 1/250.

The safety-first model also implies that insurers might *not* pay attention to events whose likelihood of causing insolvency of the insurer is
below p^*. As we will show in Chapter 9, this may explain why insurers
were not concerned about terrorist events prior to 9/11 or did not focus
on the probability of severe disasters such as Hurricane Andrew until
after they occurred.

Empirical Data on Insurers' Pricing and Coverage Decisions

Actual insurer behavior often seems to follow a safety-first model rather
than an expected-profit-maximizing model. More specifically, the empirical evidence based on surveys of underwriters supports the hypothesis
that insurers will set higher premiums when faced with ambiguous probabilities and uncertain losses for a well-specified risk.

Underwriters of primary insurance companies and reinsurance firms
were surveyed about the specific prices they would charge to insure a
factory against property damage from a severe earthquake[5] under the
following four different cases:

- *Case One*: well-specified probabilities (p) and known losses (L);
- *Case Two*: ambiguous probabilities (Ap) and known losses (L);
- *Case Three*: well-specified probabilities (p) and uncertain losses (UL);
- *Case Four*: ambiguous probabilities (Ap) and uncertain losses (UL).

For the nonambiguous cases, the probability of the earthquake (p)
was set at either 1 percent or 0.1 percent and the loss should the event
occur (L) was specified at either $1 million or $10 million (Kunreuther,
Hogarth, and Meszaros 1993). Table 8.1 shows the ratio of each of the
other three cases relative to the nonambiguous case (p,L) for the four
different scenarios, which were distributed randomly to underwriters in primary insurance companies. For the highly ambiguous case
(Ap,UL), the premiums were between 1.43 to 1.77 times higher than if

Table 8.1. *Ratios of underwriters' premiums for ambiguous or uncertain earthquake risks relative to well-specified risks*

SCENARIO	CASES				
	1	2	3	4	
	Well specified p Certain L	Ambiguous p Certain L	Well specified p Uncertain L	Ambiguous p Uncertain L	N
$p = .005$ $L = \$1$ million	1	1.28	1.19	1.77	17
$p = .005$ $L = \$10$ million	1	1.31	1.29	1.59	8
$p = .01$ $L = \$1$ million	1	1.19	1.21	1.50	23
$p = .01$ $L = \$10$ million	1	1.38	1.15	1.43	6

Note: Ratios are based on mean premiums across number of respondents for each scenario; N = number of observations.

underwriters priced a nonambiguous risk. The ratios for the other two cases were always above one, but less than the (Ap, UL) case.

It should be noted that these are the premiums that underwriters would *like* their firm to charge. In practice they may not be able to do so because of rate regulation. In addition, if buyers do not focus on credit risk and are highly price sensitive, demand can fall so much that the strategy of raising premiums becomes unattractive to insurers. Finally, the marketing department, usually rewarded on the basis of sales, may be more eager to charge lower prices so as to increase the firm's market share.

Recent research reveals that insurers are sensitive to whether experts agree or disagree with each other with respect to a specific forecast and/ or in their premium recommendations (Cabantous et al. 2011). To illustrate, assume that two advisers, A_1 and A_2, are asked to provide estimates about the probability of a given scenario, for instance a Category 3 hurricane hitting the city of New Orleans in the next fifty years. If both advisers agree that there is, say, a fifty percent chance that the hurricane will occur, there is consensus on a precise probability. In contrast, under the situation labeled "imprecise ambiguity," the two advisers arrive at an interval that is identical. For example, they may both think the likelihood is between twenty-five percent and seventy-five percent. "Conflict ambiguity" occurs when both advisers provide a precise point estimate but the two probabilities differ from each other. For instance, A_1 strongly believes that the hurricane will occur with a probability of twenty-five percent, and A_2 strongly believes it will happen with a probability of seventy-five percent.

A Web-based experiment provided actuaries and underwriters in insurance companies with scenarios, such as the one just discussed, in which they seek advice and request probability forecasts from different groups of experts and then must determine what price to charge for coverage. The data revealed that insurers charge higher premiums when faced with ambiguity than when the probability of a loss is well specified. More specifically, across three hazards (floods, hurricanes, home fires), we find that on average, insurers report they would charge premiums for ambiguous damages between twenty-one percent and thirty percent higher than the premiums they would charge for damages under a well-specified risk situation. Furthermore, they would likely charge more for conflict ambiguity than imprecise ambiguity for flood and hurricane hazards (8.5 percent and 14 percent more for a one-year contract, respectively) but less in the case of fire (nine percent less for a one-year contract).

A complementary strategy that insurers can follow to deal with their safety-first constraint is to restrict explicitly the number of policies they offer. They can do this by raising the premium so that demand for coverage is decreased and/or by not offering insurance to some potential customers.

SUPPLY BEHAVIOR OF MUTUAL AND NONPROFIT INSURERS

Mutual and nonprofit insurers may behave in very different ways than insurance companies owned by stockholders. We now discuss why such firms exist in the first place and if they mitigate some of the anomalies and inefficiencies that might otherwise exist.

As discussed earlier, mutual insurance is a form of a consumer cooperative in that customers technically own the firm. It also comes closest in form to the ideal way of risk pooling among a set of agents subject to similar risks. Although a modern mutual insurer has reserves and collects premiums to maintain those reserves, its fundamental principle is to return dividends to its policyholders during years when losses are small relative to premiums collected. Larger than expected losses are first covered by company reserves. If there is still a deficit, policyholders are assessed an additional premium to recover the shortfall in revenues.

After a mutual has been in business for some time, and it has had more experience setting premiums appropriate to risks, and builds up reserves, it often drops the power to assess members in case of a severe loss. In this situation, members are at risk should the mutual insurer become insolvent or should the state regulatory agency order another insurer to take it over because it is in dire financial straits. If management is sensitive to the desires of the customer-owners, a mutual insurance company can offer benefits to its members that avoid anomalies. Most obviously, buyers need not be worried about being charged much more than expected benefits plus loading, in contrast to stock companies concerned with producing profits for their shareholders. The premium may still be high but, in principle, any realized net income remains the property of the policyholders and could be distributed back to them.

Less obvious, a mutual arrangement is a way of dealing with a set of individuals who all agree they face a similar risk but have quite different beliefs about the magnitude of some of its aspects. For example, homeowners in a storm-prone area may disagree on the likelihood of the next catastrophic storm. Should these individuals form a mutual arrangement, there needs only to be consensus by all members that the probability (whatever it is) and the consequences of specific events are the same for everyone covered by the company. All members agree that each house has no greater chance of being damaged than any other house in the collective. Even though members can disagree about the likelihood of the storm that will affect them, they still will want to buy insurance from their mutual company.

Mutuals also can work when risks differ in some dimensions (value of the property at risk, presence of features that will mitigate damage once a storm occurs) as long as all agree on the *relative* differences in expected loss due to such characteristics, so-called *rate relativities* in insurance parlance. That is, if we all agree that a home closer to the shore is twice as likely to suffer damage when "the big one" hits, owners of homes both nearer and farther from the shore will still gain from being in a mutual insurance arrangement. In this case, the person closer to the shore pays twice the premium than paid by the one farther away.

Perceived estimates of the risk may differ from the best scientific evidence because individuals use different information to form their subjective estimates of probabilities and consequences from an untoward event. In addition, two individuals with different risk perceptions may have joined the same mutual insurer for different reasons. For example, a mutual insurer would be attractive to someone who thinks "it will almost never happen because it hasn't happened for a long time" and to another individual who feels that "it hasn't happened for a long time so we are due," both potentially anomalous ways of determining probabilities. The first group will think that the expected benefits to be paid out will be small, but will still buy coverage because it expects any excess premiums to be returned. The second group will believe that the expected benefits are worth the premium and then some. Based on this logic, both adherents and deniers would join a mutual that provides insurance against the potential consequences of global warming or flooding due to sea level rise.

Nonprofit insurers by contrast are, surprisingly, responsible neither to investors nor to customers. Their initial equity capital is likely to come from philanthropic donors such as foundations. Nonprofit insurers also benefit from legislation that gives them special privileges, including tax advantages. (The tax advantages, however, have been curtailed in recent years as many plans have converted to for-profit status.) There usually is some recognition of a social mission, and often regulation exists that pays attention to the way that mission is carried out. For example, many Blue Cross health insurance plans were nonprofit and chartered by special state enabling acts that provided tax and other advantages with the objective of providing hospitalization insurance at reasonable premiums to middle-class people in a community. They are still subject to scrutiny with respect to rate increases, reserves, policies offered, and populations served.[6]

ROLE OF RATING AGENCIES

To the extent that they facilitate information sharing between buyers and sellers of insurance, rating agencies should foster supply behavior consistent with the benchmark model in a perfectly informed competitive process. But some measures used to evaluate the financial soundness of insurers may also lead to actions that differ from what would emerge in a competitive market without these restrictions. For example, high ratings can lead insurance buyers to trust insurers' promises to pay benefits to a greater extent than is warranted by the facts. Suddenly eroding ratings can lead buyers to overestimate the likelihood of insolvency and hence cancel their coverage. Those supplying capital may require a higher return on their investment because they had perceived the insurer's credit risk to be significantly lower than the new ratings imply.

Rating agencies, such as A.M. Best, Standard & Poor's, Moody's, and Fitch, provide independent evaluations of insurers and reinsurers' financial stability and their ability to meet their obligations to policyholders. A low rating has an impact on premiums charged because it increases the reluctance of capital or debt institutions to provide additional funds except at higher interest rates. A downgraded rating will have a negative effect on the share price of publicly traded insurance firms and may trigger requirements for them to add reserves. This occurred in the fall of 2008 with the American International Group (AIG) as a result of the large losses incurred by the 377-person London-based unit, AIG Financial Products, run with almost complete autonomy from the parent company.

During the past few years, rating agencies have paid increasing attention to the impact that catastrophic risks will have on the financial stability of insurers and reinsurers. To illustrate how ratings are determined, consider the rating agency A.M. Best, which undertakes a quantitative analysis of an insurer's balance sheet strength, operating performance, and business profile. Evaluation of catastrophe exposure plays a significant role in the determination of ratings, as these are events that could threaten the solvency of a company. Projected losses from disasters occurring at specified return periods (a 100-year windstorm/hurricane or a 250-year earthquake) and the associated reinsurance programs to cover them are two important components of the rating questionnaires that insurers are required to complete.

For several years, A.M. Best has been requesting such information for natural disasters. Until recently, the rating agency included probable maximum loss (PML) for only one of these severe events (wind damage from a 100-year hurricane or 250-year earthquake) depending on the nature of the exposure risk of the insurer's portfolio. In 2006, A.M. Best introduced a second event as an additional stress test. The PML used for the second event is the same as the first event in the case of wind damage from hurricanes (a 1-in-100-year event; the occurrence of one hurricane is considered to be independent of the other one). Suppose the main exposure facing the insurer is an earthquake. Capital requirements for the second event are reduced from a 1-in-250-year event to a 1-in-100-year event (A.M. Best 2006).

These new requirements have increased the amount of capital that insurance companies have been forced to allocate to reserves. Insurers are now more reluctant to provide catastrophic coverage unless they are able to purchase additional reinsurance and/or increase premiums sufficiently to reflect any additional capital costs.

Standard and Poor's, another rating agency, has also revised its criteria for measuring catastrophic risk by examining insurers' reserves relative to their net expected annual aggregate property losses for all perils at 1-in-250-year return periods. This criterion was previously applied only to reinsurers. Moody's has shifted the industry likelihood of insurers experiencing severe losses from hurricanes upward to reflect recent storm activity (Fleckenstein 2006).

To what extent do such rating processes and associated rules affect supply behavior? For one thing, the requirement of additional reserves to avoid a rating downgrade will cause insurers to increase the premiums they charge, due to the costs associated with obtaining the added capital and the need to hold this capital in liquid forms that earn a lower return than other investment options open to them. The magnitude of this additional cost in ordinary times is fairly modest, but can become very high in times of individual insurer or industry distress, whether caused by losses on policies or losses on investments of their premium income.

We suspect that these phenomena can lead to a supply curve in which premiums increase by a larger amount as more coverage for potentially catastrophic risks is supplied than if there were no rating agencies.

ROLE OF REGULATORS

In the United States, insurance is regulated at the state level with the principal authority residing with insurance commissioners.[7] Primary insurers are subject to solvency regulation and rate and policy form regulation. *Solvency regulation* addresses the question as to whether the insurer or reinsurer is sufficiently capitalized to fulfill its obligations if a significant event occurs that inflicts major losses on its policyholders.

Rate and policy form regulation refers to the price and terms of the insurance contract. Insurance commissioners often regard solvency as a principal objective even if it means requiring higher premiums or other insurer adjustments such as reducing their catastrophe exposures or holding more capital reserves. On the other hand, insurance regulators face political pressure to keep insurance premiums "affordable" and coverage readily available. In balancing solvency and consumer protection goals, insurance regulators are required by state law to ensure that rates are adequate but not excessive and not unfairly discriminatory. Regulators' assessment of insurers' rates and other practices involves some degree of subjectivity, which can result in rate restrictions that reduce the supply of insurance or cause other market problems and distortions. "Parameter uncertainty" and different opinions on the level of risk of loss can lead to disagreements between insurers and regulators over what constitutes adequate rates and appropriate underwriting practices.

SUMMARY

The ideal world, in which insurance companies maximize their expected profits, is far from the world in which they actually operate. In the real world, insurance companies may have imperfect information relative to potential buyers. This can lead to adverse selection and moral hazard, both of which may result in lower profits than would be expected and may even cause the demise of the firm. Once we recognize the asymmetry of information between insurance buyers and sellers, resulting insurer behavior can theoretically fall within the confines of the benchmark supply model.

Because insurers are overly concerned with ambiguity and risk relative to the benchmark model, they will want to set higher premiums for catastrophic events above their level of concern (p^*) and limit the amount of coverage they provide to those who face potentially large losses. On the other hand, if insurers are unconcerned about events whose likelihood is below p^*, they will not exclude these risks from coverage until after a catastrophic event occurs.

At the root of this anomalous behavior is the separation of ownership from control in many insurance companies. The owners, represented by the board of directors, simply have much less information about the company and its risks than do the managers. The managers know that unacceptable losses or the demise of the firm will mean the loss of their jobs and probably their reputations. Thus they are risk averse with respect to their own income and future earnings and act in their self-interest rather than that of their stockholders. The managers' resulting behavior is compounded by their aversion to ambiguity. If the likelihood and consequences of a future loss are highly uncertain, the managers will follow their instincts for preserving their jobs and assume these risks are higher than the best estimates provided by experts. They will charge a higher premium to reflect this ambiguity. The result is lower expected profits of insurers than that implied by the benchmark model of supply.

Nonprofit insurers, especially mutual insurers, may behave in very different ways than firms owned by stockholders, because the managers and boards of stock companies will be more apprehensive about insolvency or failure. More specifically, mutuals and nonprofits are more concerned with their balance sheets while stock companies focus on their profitability.[8]

Mutual insurance comes closest in form to the ideal way of risk pooling among a set of agents subject to similar risks. If properly managed by individuals sensitive to the desires of the customer-owners, a mutual insurance company can offer some benefits that help to avoid anomalies. Most obviously, buyers need not be worried about being charged much more than expected benefits plus loading because they are part owners of the firm and thus will share in the positive returns (as well as the losses in excess of premiums) and the earnings from investing them. Nonprofit insurers benefit from legislation that gives them special privileges.

Rating agencies and state regulators may impose additional constraints on insurers by requiring more capital reserves than insurers would otherwise hold for dealing with catastrophic events. In addition, insurance commissioners may impose rate restrictions so premiums are "affordable."

9

Anomalies on the Supply Side

This chapter focuses on empirical examples of specific types of anomalies by insurers and those who supply capital to insurers. They may be caused partially by some of the concerns of insurance firm managers discussed in the previous chapter, such as fear of insolvency and the impact that this would have on their future job prospects. They may also be due to the effect rating agencies and regulators may have on the premiums insurers can or want to charge and the reserves they are forced to hold. Other deviations from benchmark supply behavior may be a result of the decision processes and heuristics used by insurance managers.

We first consider specific examples of insurer firm and manager behavior that do not adhere to the benchmark supply model and attempt to identify which, if any, of these behaviors can be classified as anomalies. We then consider anomalous behavior on the part of investors and other capital suppliers to insurance firms that create supply problems for insurers.

DECISION TO OFFER OR NOT OFFER TERRORISM COVERAGE

Insurers, like everyone else, have difficulty dealing with the uncertainty associated with terrorism.[1] The likelihood of an attack is highly ambiguous and the actions taken by terrorists may change depending upon what protective measures are undertaken by those at risk. This latter feature distinguishes terrorism risk from other low-probability, high-consequence risks, such as hurricanes and other natural catastrophes where nature does not try to outwit the adoption of preventive measures and where catastrophe models using scientific and engineering data can help insurers determine premiums.

The limited confidence in the accuracy of likelihood estimates for terrorism has driven insurers to use deterministic approaches rather than the usual probability-based approaches for managing insurance exposures to this risk. In other words, insurers prefer to construct scenarios that characterize specific terrorist actions without taking into account the likelihood the event will occur. Even so, we can calculate the implied probability of a terrorist attack by looking at the premium the insurer charges.

To illustrate, suppose an insurer charged $50,000 to provide up to $1 million of coverage against terrorist damage to a firm's property. If this premium were actuarially fair, then the implied probability of a terrorist attack producing $1 million worth of damage to the property could not exceed one in twenty (i.e., $50,000/$1,000,000). If the probability were less than this figure or the damage was less than $1 million, then the insurer would expect to make a profit in the long run, assuming no administrative costs. If the probability were greater than one in twenty, then the premium would be less than the expected loss.

It is widely believed that the large ambiguity associated with the likelihood and consequences of a terrorist attack persuaded insurers to refuse to continue offering coverage at moderate premiums after the terrorist attacks of September 11, 2001. David Cummins and Christopher Lewis (2002) hypothesized that insurers and reinsurers dramatically increased their estimates of the potential frequency and severity of terrorists events in the United States after 9/11 leading to disruptions in insurance and reinsurance markets. They attribute this response to an increase in the uncertainty and probability updating with respect to the likelihood of another terrorist attack coupled with capital market imperfections that make external capital more costly than internal capital. Prior to 9/11, for example, Chicago's O'Hare Airport carried $750 million of terrorism insurance at an annual premium of $125,000; after the terrorist attacks, insurers offered only $150 million of coverage at an annual premium of $6.9 million (Jaffee and Russell 2003). This new premium, if actuarially fair, implies the likelihood of a terrorist attack in the coming year on

O'Hare Airport to be approximately one in twenty-two ($6.9 million/$150 million), an extremely high probability – and one very inconsistent with what insurers estimated before the 9/11 attacks. Concern about such erratic pricing and supply behavior by insurers was one of the reasons the U.S. Congress passed the Terrorism Risk Insurance Act (TRIA) at the end of 2002, which provided a federal backstop up to $100 billion for private insurance claims related to terrorism.

In a provocative paper, Kent Smetters (2004) argues that if insurance and capital markets were allowed to function unfettered by regulations, then the private sector would be capable of insuring large terrorism losses, even those ten times larger than the $35 billion loss incurred on 9/11. The relevant question here is not the theoretical potential of private markets but how these markets actually behave. After 9/11, a set of constraints and perceptions persuaded many insurers that terrorism was no longer an insurable risk in the United States (Wharton Risk Management and Decision Processes Center 2005). A principal reason that U.S. insurers refused to offer terrorism coverage after 9/11 was that global reinsurers, unconstrained by premium regulation and U.S. taxes, refused to provide protection to insurers against losses from another attack.

In most countries today, problems with pricing and supply by the private sector exist. When insurers offer terrorism protection, it is usually part of a public-private arrangement, as in the German terrorism insurance pool, Extremus, and in the French pool, Gareat. In Germany, the first layer of 2 billion euros is covered by a mix of fifteen primary carriers and reinsurers from the national and international markets. In France, the first 400 million euros in losses is covered by all property risk insurance companies doing business in France. Several layers between 400 million euros and 2 billion euros are covered by 185 small and large insurance and reinsurance companies. In both countries, the national government provides a reinsurance guarantee that insurers pay for.

In contrast, the federal government in the United States provides free reinsurance up front, but plans to recoup part of its claims payment from insurers following a terrorist attack. This policy thus overcomes the liquidity problem that private insurers face after a severe loss (Michel-Kerjan and Pedell 2005, 2006). Insurers do not offer terrorism coverage on their own. If they were to offer such coverage without government assistance they would either have to purchase reinsurance against losses from a terrorist attack or raise external capital to have sufficient reserves to cover a potentially large loss. However, insurers and the investor community at large were reluctant to provide funds to support terrorism insurance following 9/11, and reinsurers refused to offer coverage against terrorist attacks after 9/11. During the fall of 2001 it was not unusual for investors to require an annual rate of return of twenty percent to provide capital for terrorism coverage (Kunreuther 2002). If the normal rate of return were eight percent, this implies that risk-neutral investors were behaving as if they thought there was a one in ten chance they would lose their entire investment.[2] If they turned to the capital market for financial support, insurers would then have to charge a very high premium to cover the costs of replenishing their reserves.

Another reason for the relatively thin market for terrorism coverage following the attacks of 9/11 was a misperception of the risks by buyers and sellers. Prior to 9/11, insurers and property owners were unconcerned with terrorism risk and there was no problem with market supply. The reason insurers did not charge explicitly for terrorism coverage before 9/11 was that they had not experienced significant losses from this risk. After the terrorist attacks of 9/11, insurers wanted to reduce the chances of insolvency to an acceptably low level given that the industry had just suffered the most devastating loss in its history. Meanwhile, buyers who possibly had been unaware as to whether their insurance covered terrorism losses now wanted to be sure that it did and were willing to pay more for that assurance. As far as we can tell, this anomalous perception was an equal-opportunity contagion, affecting small businesses, major real estate holders, giant insurance firms, even larger reinsurance firms, and the supposedly sophisticated global capital market.[3]

CHANGES IN PROPERTY INSURANCE MARKETS

Rate regulation has had more impact on property insurance than on any other line of coverage, particularly in states at risk of potentially catastrophic losses from natural disasters. Rate regulation, when combined with insurer perception of risks, can lead to anomalous behavior by insurers.

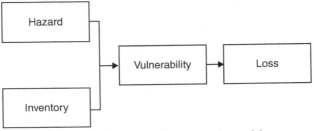

Figure 9.1. Structure of a catastrophe model.

Consider the case of Florida. After Hurricane Andrew (August 1992), nine insurers became insolvent as a result of losses from the disaster. Only then did insurers and reinsurers realize that they needed to manage their natural hazard exposure more precisely and begin to utilize catastrophe models that provided quantitative estimates of the risk. These models helped them to determine the types and locations of property they would like to insure, what coverage to offer, and what premiums to charge to reflect their risk. Some also used catastrophe models to justify the need for rate increases to the state insurance commissioners.

Role of Catastrophe Models

Catastrophe models identify and quantify the likelihood of occurrence of specific natural disasters in a region and estimate the extent of incurred losses. The four basic components of a catastrophe model are: *hazard*, *inventory*, *vulnerability*, and *loss*, as depicted in Figure 9.1.

First, the model characterizes the likelihood of the hazard occurring. In the case of a hurricane, scientific procedures have been developed to simulate storm tracks for each ocean basin of concern. Historical track data are used to generate probability matrices that answer questions such as "If the direction of the hurricane movement at some location is *a*, what is the probability that its next direction will be *a, b, c, d*, etc."[4] Next, the model characterizes the inventory or portfolio of properties at risk as accurately as possible. Geographic coordinates such as latitude and longitude are assigned to a property based on its street address, ZIP code, or another location descriptor. Other factors that characterize the

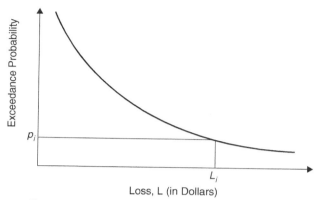

Figure 9.2. Sample exceedance probability (EP) curve.

property are the construction and occupancy types, the building height, and its age.

The hazard and inventory components enable the calculation of the vulnerability or damage susceptibility of the structures at risk. This step in the catastrophe model quantifies the physical impact of the natural hazard on the property at risk. Finally, based on this measure of vulnerability, the loss to the inventory is evaluated.

Using these data, the catastrophe model can generate an exceedance probability (EP) curve that specifies the probability that a certain level of loss will be exceeded over a given time period. To illustrate, suppose an insurer was interested in using the output from a catastrophe model to construct an EP curve for his portfolio of insurance policies covering wind damage from hurricanes in coastal communities in Florida. The insurer would be provided with information on a set of events that could produce a given dollar loss for the portfolio and the corresponding probabilities that these events would occur. Based on these estimates, an EP curve is constructed, such as the one depicted in Figure 9.2. The *x-axis* measures the insurer's loss in dollars and the *y-axis* depicts the probability that losses will exceed a particular level. If the insurer focuses on a specific loss L_i, one can see from the figure that the likelihood that insured losses exceed L_i is given by p_i.

The insurer can use this EP curve to determine the scope of coverage to offer for various properties in the region, given the current risk profile and given some target probability that its losses will not exceed some critical loss level. More specifically, if the insurer wants to remain below a loss level L_i^*, with probability p_i^* it may have to reduce the number of policies in force, raise its premiums to increase its reserves, or decide not to offer this type of coverage at all (if permitted by law to do so). One key feature of EP curves at any point in time is that they reflect the likelihood of future losses as a function of past losses and scientific information on the risk (Grossi and Kunreuther 2005).

Anomalous Insurer Behavior Following Recent Hurricanes

Rather than using catastrophe models to justify premium increases to the state regulator in Florida, insurers pointed to their large losses following Hurricane Andrew as a basis for that request, without considering the likelihood of another disaster of this magnitude occurring. This behavior highlights an availability bias by insurers, similar to their behavior with respect to terrorism insurance following 9/11. Furthermore, insurers were assuming that regulators were subject to a similar bias and would thus agree to the requested rate increases. They were not quite right.

Florida regulators resisted this recommendation and allowed insurers to only gradually raise rates over the decade while restricting their ability to cancel existing homeowners' policies. More specifically, in May 1993 the state imposed a moratorium for six months on the cancellation and nonrenewal of residential property for the upcoming hurricane season for insurers that wanted to continue to do any business in Florida. In November 1993, the legislature enacted a bill that these insurers could not cancel more than ten percent of their homeowners' policies in any county in Florida in one year and could not cancel more than five percent of their property owners' policies statewide for each of the next three years. During the 1996 legislative session, this phase-out provision was extended until June 1, 1999 (Lecomte and Gahagan 1998). Insurers reduced the supply of new homeowners' policies, using guidelines based only on recent loss history, not on analytic models. They concluded that there was substantial rate inadequacy at those regulated premiums (Grace, Klein, and Kleindorfer 2004).

Given the tendency for insurers as well as consumers to focus on recent events in making their decisions, it is unclear to us whether this concern was justified. Had they based their requests for premium increases on the results of valid catastrophe models, and used them to calculate the price, insurers would have had a more solid argument. Instead, they based premiums on actual losses from Hurricane Andrew and, because their views about the premium clashed with regulators' views, the result was a reduction in supply.

Over time, as insurers were allowed to further increase rates, their concerns eased, either because they increased premiums or because they reduced their estimates of hurricane probability as time passed; probably a combination of both. By the beginning of 2004, most insurers probably viewed their Florida rates as being close to adequate except in the highest-risk areas, and there was no substantial pressure to further increase rates until after four major hurricanes battered Florida in 2004. This change again represents anomalous behavior by insurers relative to the benchmark model, because there is no good reason why the mere passage of time should cause insurers to accept premiums they previously regarded as inadequate – unless something happened during that interval to lower the affected loss probability.

After the 2004 and 2005 experience, many insurers began to file their first major wave of rate increases in Florida. The magnitude of the rate increases filed varied among areas within the state based on insurers' estimates of the inadequacy of their existing rate structures. Regulators approved or allowed the initial wave of rate increases to go into effect but denied a second wave of rate filings by Allstate, Nationwide, and USAA in the latter part of 2006. More specifically, the Allstate Group filed a 24.2 percent increase for Allstate Floridian and a 31.6 percent increase for Allstate Floridian Indemnity. The increases were ultimately approved at 8.2 percent for Allstate Floridian and 8.8 percent for Allstate Floridian Indemnity. Nationwide filed for a 71.5 percent rate increase that was overturned. It appealed the rejection to a Florida arbitration panel that ruled in favor of a fifty-four percent increase. USAA filed for a 40 percent increase but received only a 16.3 percent increase. There were no demands placed on how much coverage these insurers had to provide to homeowners, as was the case following Hurricane Andrew.[5]

Early in 2007, Florida enacted legislation that sought to increase regulatory control over rates and roll them back based on new legislation that expanded the reinsurance coverage provided by the Florida Hurricane Catastrophe Fund (FHCF). Insurers were required to reduce their rates to reflect this expansion of coverage, which was priced below private reinsurance market rates. This requirement applies to every licensed insurer even if an insurer did not purchase reinsurance from the FHCF.

Formation of Citizens Property Insurance Corporation

Florida's residual market mechanism for property insurance, the Citizens Property Insurance Corporation, has experienced a significant increase in market share of the Florida residential property market in recent years with legislative changes in 2007 accelerating that growth. Consumers were allowed to purchase a policy from Citizens if a comparable policy would cost twenty-five percent more in the voluntary market; this was reduced to fifteen percent with the passage of new legislation in 2008. Citizens' assessment base was expanded from property lines of insurance to include all lines of business except workers' compensation, medical malpractice, accident and health, the National Flood Insurance Program, and the Federal Crop Insurance Program. The net effect is that fewer insurers are profitable in Florida.

State Farm, the largest private insurer in the state, had made plans to leave the market until the Florida Insurance Commissioner issued a consent order in December 2009 permitting the insurer to not renew up to 125,000 of its 810,000 residential property policies. The consent order also grants State Farm Florida a 14.8 percent rate increase for all homeowners and condominium unit owners' policies.[6] One reason for this consent order is a concern with the potential problems created by the large number of homeowners searching for alternative insurance had State Farm left the Florida market.

In the ideal world of the benchmark supply model, a residual mechanism should be a source of last resort. The transformation of the insurance market in Florida following the severe hurricanes of 2004 and 2005 can be viewed as a failure of the private insurance markets to protect against a well-specified risk. Insurers appear to have overreacted to the large losses they incurred, regulators resisted proposed rate increases, and a state-funded company, Citizens, filled the gap by providing relatively inexpensive insurance (Kunreuther and Michel-Kerjan 2009).

In summary, insurers may have behaved anomalously in Florida by overreacting to high claims from Hurricane Andrew and by reducing supply when they were forbidden to raise premiums. That reaction in turn generated a large market share for the government insurer, Citizens. Whatever anomalous behavior insurers may have exhibited, an additional factor played a role in restricting the supply of insurance. Political pressure from residents in hurricane-prone areas to restrict homeowners' premiums led the state legislature to allow Citizens to charge premiums at highly subsidized rates, thus undercutting the private market.

Formation of the California Earthquake Authority

The marketing of earthquake insurance in California provides another example of how insurers who suffered large losses from a disaster are reluctant to continue offering coverage against this risk.[7] In 1985, the California Legislature passed a law requiring insurers writing homeowners' insurance on one- to four-family units to offer earthquake coverage on these structures. While insurers were free to set whatever rates they wanted, typical premiums were moderate (e.g., $400 per year for a $200,000 house with a $10,000 deductible, which was based on five percent of the value of the property). There was no requirement by the state that the owners had to buy earthquake insurance, only that the insurers had to offer it. Lenders required homeowners' or commercial coverage against the usual perils, but not the purchase of earthquake insurance.

The Loma Prieta earthquake that struck in October 1989 was a magnitude 7.1 that caused $6 billion in property damage. Two smaller earthquakes in the state in 1992 led to significant homeowner demand for earthquake insurance, as detailed by surveys of homeowners in 1989, 1990, and 1993 (Palm 1995). But the *coup de grâce* from the perspective of the insurance industry was the Northridge earthquake of 1994 that caused insured losses of $19.6 billion (in 2007 prices) and led to even greater demand for earthquake insurance. For example, in Cupertino

County, more than two-thirds of the homeowners surveyed purchased earthquake insurance in 1995 (Palm 1995).

In that same year, private insurance companies in California reevaluated their earthquake exposures and decided that they could not risk selling any more earthquake policies on residential property. As with terrorism insurance and coverage against hurricanes, insurers were concerned about the impact of another catastrophic event on their balance sheet, almost without regard to the likelihood of it occurring. Fixating on the worst-case outcome, they decided not to offer coverage at any price. Based on the benchmark model of supply, where insurers are expected to utilize both the likelihood of specific events and the resulting losses to determine premiums, this behavior must be viewed as anomalous.

In view of the law requiring inclusion of earthquake coverage in homeowners' policies, the only legal response to their fear of high losses was for insurers to stop offering new homeowners' policies. The California Insurance Department surveyed insurers and found that up to ninety percent of them had either stopped or had placed restrictions on the selling of new homeowners' policies. After extended discussions between the California Insurance Department and the large insurers in 1996, an advisory group of insurers and actuaries proposed the formation of a state-run earthquake insurance company – the California Earthquake Authority (Roth, 1998).

In many parts of the state, the CEA set the premiums – which had to be approved in advance by the California Insurance Department – at higher levels than insurers had used prior to the Northridge earthquake of 1994. The minimum deductible for policies offered through the Authority was raised from ten percent to fifteen percent of the insured value of the property. This price-coverage combination was not especially attractive to homeowners in the state. A fifteen percent deductible based on the amount of coverage in place is actually quite high relative to damages which typically occur. Most homes in California are wood-frame structures that would likely suffer relatively small damage in a severe earthquake, although there is still a chance that the house could be seriously damaged or totally destroyed. For example, if a house was insured at $200,000, a fifteen percent deductible implies that the damage from the earthquake would have to exceed $30,000 before the homeowner could collect a penny from the insurer.

The rates insurers charged under the CEA's rules, which are based on the estimates of losses from catastrophe models, are approximately three dollars per $1,000 of coverage for wood-frame houses on good soil, and up six dollars or seven dollars per $1,000 for houses in higher-risk locations or near known faults. For a high-value house in a high-risk area, the additional premium can easily run into thousands of dollars per year. If those insurers and investors who have provided the capital for different layers of the CEA actually do incur very small claim payments following severe earthquakes in relation to the premiums they are collecting, then earthquake coverage of this form could be a highly profitable activity. If the catastrophe models are right, they should expect to break even.

The higher rates and the perceived small chance of collecting on a claim (due to the high deductible) apparently prompted many homeowners to drop their coverage as the last damaging earthquake receded in memory. As of the end of 2010, only twelve percent of homeowners in California had earthquake coverage, considerably below the thirty percent of homeowners who had earthquake coverage at the end of 1994, presumably because the homeowners think that expected benefits above the deductible are not large enough to offset the high premium. If a major earthquake were to occur in California next year it is likely that the uninsured losses would be very large.

Two features of earthquake insurance in California lead us to classify it as an anomaly driven primarily by suppliers. First is the reaction by insurers following the Northridge earthquake: they decided that they could no longer offer coverage against this peril rather than reassessing their portfolios and determining whether this risk was insurable. Second, when the CEA began charging rates that appeared too high relative to the risk, there was little interest by private insurers in offering competing coverage to homeowners even though there was no regulation preventing them from doing so. In fact, today, private insurers usually file rates with the California Department of Insurance that are so high in earthquake-prone areas of the state that they clearly do not want anyone in these regions to purchase this coverage. One reason for this behavior is that if insurers sell homeowners' insurance in California they must also offer earthquake insurance, but they only want to cover this risk if they obtain a very high premium in return.

ANOMALOUS INSURER SUPPLY BEHAVIOR WHEN CATASTROPHES OCCUR OR DO NOT OCCUR

As illustrated by both terrorism risk and risk from natural disasters, a common theme is that recent disasters have an inexplicably large impact on rates insurers charge and their interest in offering coverage.

Rate Increases after a Disaster

As just discussed, Florida regulators resisted large rate increases after Hurricane Andrew and only allowed insurers to raise rates gradually over the decade. They concluded that there was no scientific evidence that this disaster was more severe than scientists expected it to be or that its occurrence meant that such disasters were more likely in the immediate future.

This and other supply-side anomalies may be explained by heuristics and biases utilized by insurance companies that do not conform to behavior consistent with firms maximizing expected long-run profits. More specifically, the availability bias occurs when an insurer over-weights a recent event in estimating the probability of loss compared to some benchmark of probability based on scientific modeling. Regulators' views toward a particular risk can also be influenced by an availability bias. They are likely to approve a substantial rate increase after a large loss from a hurricane or other disaster by perceiving the likelihood of a future catastrophe to be higher than scientific estimates. Some emotions – fear of the financial impacts of another severe loss immediately after a disaster, and then increasing nonchalance as time passes without another catastrophe occurring – may very well influence the behavior of managers of insurance firms and cause them to deviate from actions designed to maximize expected profits.

Refusing to Provide Coverage after a Disaster

A distressing and recently all-too-common problem in the supply of insurance is the behavior of insurance markets after an unusually large loss from a natural or man-made disaster. Premiums spike, most insurers refuse to offer large amounts of coverage even at those prices, and some insurers withdraw altogether. Again, the most glaring example of this behavior was the refusal of many insurers to offer explicit protection against terrorism losses after 9/11, supposedly because they could not obtain reinsurance or had to charge extraordinarily high rates (partly due to the cost of capital as part of their loading cost) even though they had not charged one cent extra for coverage against this peril before this event.[8] Similar behavior occurred after the severe Mississippi floods of 1927 when no insurer was willing to offer flood coverage again, eventually leading to the passage of the National Flood Insurance Program in 1968 (Dacy and Kunreuther 1968).

One way to explain premium spikes is to assume that suppliers of capital to insurers raise their prices when large additional reserves are demanded in a short period of time, as illustrated by the more formal models of Anne Gron (1994) or Ralph Winter (1994). What remains most puzzling, however, is the apparent rationing/withdrawal behavior by insurers. If there are those who still want coverage at a price for which insurers are willing to provide it, shouldn't a market, albeit perhaps a smaller one, still exist at moderately elevated premiums?

Much of the discussion of insurer behavior after major disasters, especially by journalists, posits correctly that insurers and reinsurers are affected by timidity and fear. After a disaster, risk analysts often raise their estimates of the probability of a future event and (more important) admit that they are more uncertain with respect to the likelihood of another disaster of this kind occurring in the future. As pointed out in Chapter 8, insurer reaction to ambiguity of probability should result only in higher premiums (if they are allowed to charge these prices), not their exit from the market. However, if insurers have the freedom to price their products and estimate that the resulting demand will be close to zero at very high premiums, they may choose to avoid embarrassment and bad press by withdrawing altogether rather than being accused of price gouging.

The empirical evidence does not support the view that buyers will resist those price increases. Following a disaster, individuals and firms *are* willing to pay premiums much in excess of actuarially based risks if they can find an insurer willing to provide them with coverage. As pointed out in

Chapter 3, an example was the actual purchase six months after 9/11 of a terrorism insurance policy of $9 million at a cost of $900,000 to cover losses from a terrorist attack over the coming year. It is hard to believe that the managers of the company who bought this coverage actually perceived the likelihood of such an event to be anywhere close to one in ten, the implied probability that would make this premium actuarially fair. Given the limited supply of terrorism insurance, a company may have paid such a high price because they were forced to have a terrorism policy as a condition for their mortgage but also because there was pressure from their board of directors to have this protection.

The refusal of most private insurers to offer coverage, even at extremely high premiums, may be economically rational if there is a high fixed cost to market a policy and the resulting demand will not cover these costs as was the case in providing environmental insurance coverage (Freeman and Kunreuther 1997). Alternatively, an insurer's (or reinsurer's) management may anticipate that if it sells insurance in the face of a very uncertain market and there is a recurrence of the disaster, the management will suffer the humiliation and job loss that results from climbing much too far out on a limb.

Limited Impact of Financial Instruments in Securitizing Insurance Risk

New alternative risk transfer instruments were developed in the 1990s to transfer part of an insurer or reinsurer's exposure to catastrophic risk to additional investors in the financial markets. Catastrophe bonds, the payouts of which are tied to the occurrence of disasters, offer insurers and corporate entities the ability to hedge events that could otherwise impair their operations to the point of insolvency. Catastrophe bonds typically cover several consecutive years while offering investors a unique opportunity to enhance their portfolios with an asset that provides a high-yielding return shown to be uncorrelated with the market (Litzenberger, Beaglehole, and Reynolds 1996). Despite the attractiveness of these investments, there have been fewer bonds issued than had been anticipated by investment bankers (about 100 since their creation).[9]

This catastrophe bond market has not taken off as expected despite their much higher spread compared to other debt-issuance instruments. The limited activity in this market is not just a consequence of the lack of investor familiarity with a new asset but also signals some deeper issues that need to be resolved. Ambiguity aversion, myopic loss aversion, and fixed costs of learning can account for the reluctance of institutional investors to enter this market. Worry regarding the impact of a catastrophic loss on the performance of the bonds may be an additional factor to consider (Bantwal and Kunreuther 2000). Here there does appear to be a true divergence of behavior from that postulated by the benchmark model of supply.

Reinsurance Prices Decline if there are No Recent Disasters

Reinsurance markets also appear to fall victim to anomalous behavior, despite the financial sophistication of their owners and actuaries. Reinsurance is priced on the basis of the amount of capital that the reinsurers have available, not on their perceptions of estimated losses. When they have excess capacity because they have not suffered catastrophic losses, reinsurers are interested in lowering the price of their coverage because of competitive pressure. This may have a behavioral explanation, for example, overweighting the most recent observations in estimating probabilities, or a rational one, such as capital constraints in the insurer's balance sheet become less binding as reserves are rebuilt from underwriting profits after years without a loss.

Even when the managers of the reinsurance firm might feel comfortable charging a lower premium, they may need data to convince capital suppliers (investors) that the price is reasonable. However, there may also be deviations from expected-profit-maximizing behavior on the parts of insurers or suppliers of capital if they exhibit the same kind of availability bias and judge the probability or riskiness based on the salience or timing of loss-producing events.

OVERPRICED INSURANCE

Most of the supply-side anomalies previously discussed are related to coverage for rare and catastrophic risks that is either priced higher than expected losses would indicate or not offered at all. Our demand-side analysis uncovered another potential supply-side anomaly, however, in several examples of insurance that were overpriced for much more moderate and predictable losses. These included cancer and rental car insurance, extended warranties, and seemingly very profitable low-deductible policies.

The arguments made earlier about inefficiently large demand for low-deductible insurance is based on the premise that the additional premium to lower the deductible is considerably in excess of the expected additional benefits from doing so. Whatever the merits of the argument that consumers are behaving anomalously, the existence of insurance with such high premiums relative to benefits is also puzzling if true. We now consider both theory and evidence about such a supply-side puzzle.

If there is relatively free entry into the insurance business and the costs of entry are low, the existence and persistence of insurance or insurance-like products with market prices much in excess of the benefits paid out (or the expected value of the benefits per buyer) seems puzzling. If we plausibly assume that insurance buyers are willing to switch to a lower-priced seller for the same type of insurance policy, even though they may have no idea of what the loss probability is, then competition with only moderate search costs should result in premiums being bid down to levels to yield normal profits.[10] In short, we should not find overpriced insurance, either for a risky event (like an accident with a rental car) or across different levels of coverage (like low-deductible versus high-deductible policies). This conceptual conclusion raises two questions:

- Is overpricing (premiums high relative to expected benefits) of insurance policies associated with above-average profits or above-average administrative costs?
- Have insurance markets changed in ways that reduce or eliminate the overpricing?

We have already discussed the first question to some extent. In the United States, insurers' profits in the long run are at or below those in other industries, but they do fluctuate rather widely between years depending on the occurrence of a large natural disaster or other catastrophic event.

For example, using data on the Fortune 500 firms, we find that the return on equity (ROE) in 2009 for stock life insurers was about five percent and for stock property-casualty insurers was six percent to seven percent (depending on whether or not AIG is included in the sample). (Data are available at http://money.cnn.com/magazine/fortune/fortune500/2009/industries/182/index.html.)

While the property-casualty ROE does fluctuate over time, these returns are almost always lower than the average returns for all large firms in the Fortune 500, which are in the range of twelve percent to fifteen percent. To be sure, some people have become rich from their insurance investments. But as a fraction of total revenues or relative to capital at risk, the returns from investing in insurance firms are not large. Presumably, this is because the physical costs of setting up an insurance company are relatively small since it doesn't require a large investment in plant and equipment. In the United States at least, there are no cartels (as there have been historically in Europe) or additional barriers to entry.

The other potential source of high premiums relative to benefits is high administrative cost. Here there is a possibility of a catch-22: if the costs of marketing insurance are high, premiums will have to reflect this expenditure. The higher the premium, the more the firm will have to expend on marketing its product to persuade people to buy it. The relevant question is whether buyers would then notice if a different insurer offered the same insurance at lower premiums. Would buyers discover low premiums by their own efforts or does insurance have to be sold?

The answer to this question depends on consumers' perception of the need for coverage and whether or not they are required to purchase it as a condition for a loan (e.g., homeowners' insurance) or due to a regulation (e.g., automobile insurance). Some insurance policies emphasize price more than others – for example, auto insurance advertises premium savings, while homeowners' insurance rarely does. The best explanation for differences in administrative costs relative to benefits that persist over time links to the economic theory on advertising. That theory makes the commonsense point that selling expenses will be high if consumers mainly respond to sales activity, while prices will be low if they mainly respond to lower prices (Dorfman and Steiner 1954). So is there something about warranties and rental car coverage that suggests that insurers would find them easier and more profitable to sell than other insurance?

If many consumers are not expected utility maximizers, but are looking for an elusive "something else" from insurance – peace of mind, avoidance of regret, an investment that really pays off – they may be prey to selling efforts targeting such desires. If one's decisions to purchase insurance are based on these goals, which are not considered part of the standard expected utility model or descriptive models of choice like prospect theory, then one can understand why a person would want to purchase policies with low deductibles at a high premium relative to expected losses. Furthermore, if one perceives the likelihood of experiencing small losses to be higher than objective data suggest, a person may feel justified in buying this coverage at the going rate. Still, even if people buy overpriced insurance for emotional reasons, there should be an incentive for other firms to enter and bid down that price – unless the high price per se is what provides emotional reassurance.

An alternative explanation postulates that insurers' administrative expenses extend to services in addition to financial protection, such as advice and reassurance from the insurance agent or salesperson. Some of these services can also be translated into savings in time as well as money. For example, in the case of a warranty, one knows who to contact in order to get the product repaired and knows there is an incentive for the company to do it well, thus reducing transaction costs.

With respect to the second question, over time there appear to be self-correcting mechanisms when the overpricing of coverage gets sufficiently high. We have noted that today, most travelers do not buy flight insurance because they correctly perceive that the expected returns are not likely to justify the premium. Most people do not take rental car insurance because their own auto insurance (or their credit card) will provide protection if they total the car. Only consumers' love affair with low-deductible insurance for car and home makes overpricing somewhat durable even in the face of competition.

SUMMARY

Before the terrorist attacks of 9/11, the insurance industry did not explicitly include or exclude terrorism as a specific peril. In the aftermath of the attacks, however, the insurance industry refused to provide insurance against further attacks or priced it at rates that indicated high expectations of further attacks and heavy losses. Meanwhile, frightened buyers clamored for coverage. Terrorism presents insurers (as well as everyone else) with some vexing economic problems. Terrorism is an intentional act, not an occurrence in nature, and terrorists can change their methods to circumvent defensive measures. Furthermore, there is little historical or scientific data on terrorism. Nevertheless, the industry's behavior – charging little or nothing explicitly for coverage before the attacks and refusing to offer coverage afterward – appears to be an anomaly.

In other instances, insurers may have historical and scientific data on which to base decisions, but for whatever reason they have ignored this information. It appears that insurers responded as do many consumers: an immediate event (Hurricane Andrew in 1992 and the Florida hurricanes in 2004) caused them to overreact. Then, as time passes, they once again become complacent. Insurers' lack of concern in properly estimating the likelihood and potential damage from hurricanes to Florida's heavily developed coastline, and the amount and type of property at risk, appears to be an anomaly.

Florida also serves as an example of how regulators can distort insurance markets. As a result of the 2004 hurricane season and the insurance industry's efforts to raise rates, the state of Florida began to offer coverage to homeowners through Citizens Property Insurance Corporation, a state-subsidized entity. Citizens offered premiums below market rates indicated by catastrophe models, and much below what private insurers were allowed to charge in high hazard regions of the state. As a result, Citizens has a substantial share of this market today.

Regulation has also distorted the market for earthquake insurance in California. When regulators mandated that homeowners' insurance policies include earthquake coverage, many insurers wanted to abandon the market. As a result, the California Earthquake Authority, a state-run insurer, was formed in 1996. The authority set many rates higher than they had been and mandated a minimum deductible of fifteen percent. That meant a house valued at $200,000 would have to suffer damages amounting to more than $30,000 before the owner collected a penny. Many homeowners concluded that the coverage was not worth the price and dropped it. The question now is whether there will be renewed demand from homeowners after the next major earthquake strikes.

These examples highlight several features of insurer behavior that can be classified as anomalous. Following a disaster, insurers focus on the large loss and overweight the likelihood of a similar event occurring in the future. They thus will want to raise their premiums significantly or will refuse to offer coverage against the specific risk. At the other end of the spectrum, insurers and reinsurers may underprice their coverage if they have not suffered serious losses for a period of time. The previously cited examples also illustrate how regulators have compounded the problem by restricting the prices that insurers can charge and setting up state-operated firms that charge subsidized premiums.

PART III

THE FUTURE OF INSURANCE

10

Design Principles for Insurance

We have seen that both buyer and seller behavior in a number of insurance markets is sometimes anomalous when judged by the two benchmark models (expected utility and expected profit maximization). Although buyers and sellers have managed to create and use insurance markets to provide sufficient protection against many of the most important threats to wealth, coverage is limited for some types of risks where the losses can be significant, such as earthquake risk.

Some insurance prices in the market are high relative to the expected loss, such as rental car or renters' insurance. At the other extreme, buyers sometimes purchase coverage against events that have low financial consequences, such as the failure of an appliance, where the expected loss is considerably less than the price of insurance. Sometimes they fail to buy coverage against a catastrophic event, even at very favorable premiums. When such anomalous behavior occurs, what, if anything, should be done to correct it? Are there government regulations, subsidies, or other actions that might be appropriate? What role can insurers themselves play in the process?

At the outset, we should note that overpaying for insurance and risk protection normally has less financial and public policy significance than the failure to purchase or offer insurance against risks where the losses to individuals can be catastrophic. Purchasing insurance with somewhat higher premiums, even purchasing excessive coverage, is unlikely to pose a severe financial strain on the typical middle-class family and provides benefits when a loss occurs. On the other hand, households can go bankrupt if they cannot or do not purchase insurance and suffer a catastrophic loss.

What steps are worth considering to address these asymmetric benefits and costs? It may be feasible to alter social or market arrangements to deal with both underpurchase and overpurchase of insurance by demanders. It may also be feasible to alter arrangements so that insurers do not curtail supply or raise prices substantially after large losses occur. Government responses to demand or supply anomalies through subsidy or regulation can help. However, they may also create market outcomes that deviate further from the ideal benchmark because real-world public policy makers sometimes pursue objectives other than maximizing social welfare. Such objectives may include redistribution according to some equity criterion. Policy makers may also distrust market outcomes and processes, yet be unaware or inattentive to the unintended adverse consequences of their own actions. Sometimes the *health of the insurance industry* is a political issue that distorts the welfare of consumers. In short, whether public sector correctives are warranted depends on the circumstances in the insurance market and in the political arena.

This chapter proposes general principles that we believe should govern consistent answers to these questions. Because governments as well as markets might be imperfect, we consider cases in which public sector actions affect insurance markets in ways that cause anomalous behavior. This leads us to examine whether some types of anomalies would be better left alone by imperfect political and market institutions that characterize the real world.

We then specify a set of efficiency and equity criteria for determining who should bear the losses and costs from adverse events. Based on these considerations, we formulate a set of guiding principles for providing information, designing insurance contracts and guiding regulation. The chapter concludes with four proposals for the public sector to establish organizational arrangements and goals for insurance that differ from current ones.

FORMULATING AND EVALUATING RISK MANAGEMENT STRATEGIES

Insurance can play a key role in addressing two broad questions for decision makers in the public and private sectors to consider when designing strategies for risk management:

- Who should bear the risk of losses caused by specific events (e.g., automobile accidents, hospital expenses associated with a health-related event, losses from natural disasters, and costs of a terrorist attack)?
- What should be the level of resources committed to reducing those risks to individuals, businesses, and other private sector organizations and society?

Two criteria are normally utilized in addressing these questions about risk spreading and risk mitigation (or about any economics policy question): *efficiency* and *equity*. By *efficiency* we mean the allocation of economic resources so that the total net benefit (benefits minus costs of all actions) is maximized. Efficiency is defined in part by preferences and valuations of consumers, and thus the size and distribution of benefits and costs may vary from one constituency to another. These preferences also represent a community's idea of *equity*, where equity refers to concerns about fairness in the distribution of goods and resources and its impact on consumption of goods and services.

In theory, efficient policies should be specified by considering the benchmark ideal models of supply and demand, with the goal of trying to replicate those results as closely as possible. The net benefits should then be distributed as society sees fit to satisfy equity considerations, such as assisting low-income residents with cash transfer payments if they cannot otherwise afford premiums that reflect risk.

EFFICIENCY CONSIDERATIONS

How might public policy affect these goals of efficiency and equity? Competitive insurance markets in theory should produce an efficient allocation of risk bearing among individuals subject to different hazards. If transaction costs are not too large, and if consumers have good information on the risk and make choices to maximize their expected utility, such insurance markets should result in everyone who is risk averse sharing losses by purchasing insurance. But when such markets are impeded by widespread demand-side or supply-side anomalies, society may prefer something different: regulation, foregoing market insurance in favor of social insurance, or having government use taxation to collect revenue which is then spent to cover losses.

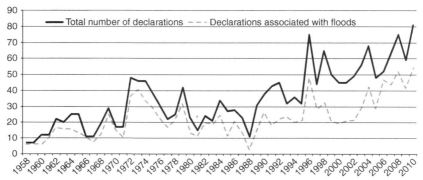

Figure 10.1. Number of U.S. presidential disaster declarations (1958–2010).
Source: Michel-Kerjan, Lemoyne de Forges, and Kunreuther 2011.

A government mandate requiring insurance purchase is another way to guarantee that an insurance market exists. In contrast, a requirement that every policy include certain kinds of insurance benefits but under which individuals can choose whether or not to buy coverage can impede efficient markets by discouraging insurers from offering products that consumers may truly prefer. We will consider public substitutes for voluntary private insurance in more detail in subsequent sections. For now, we simply note that the choice between private provision of insurance on a voluntary basis versus government requirements that consumers must purchase coverage depends largely on decisions by policy makers about whether private insurance is feasible and how the cost of coverage should be distributed.

In effect, this choice appears to be relevant to what happens when government offers subsidized relief to disaster-stricken areas. The fact that politicians can benefit from their generous actions following a disaster raises basic questions as to the capacity of elected representatives at the local, state, and federal levels to induce people to adopt protection measures before the next disaster. The difficulty in enforcing these mitigation measures has been characterized as the politician's dilemma by Erwann Michel-Kerjan, Sabine Lemoyne de Forges, and Howard Kunreuther (2011) and is graphically displayed in Figure 10.1 with the spikes in disaster declarations often coming in election years.

Here is a case in which mandatory purchase of insurance may have a role to play. Rather than pay for disaster losses in one region of the country by taxing the entire citizenry, society could require those at risk to buy insurance to protect themselves financially in advance of the event. In the debate over proposed health reforms in 1993, the Congressional Budget Office insisted on regarding the premiums for mandated insurance as taxes. They reasoned that mandatory insurance functions in the same way as taxes, since both taxes and mandated insurance represent compulsory private payments to achieve social or public goals. The equivalence of a mandate and a tax was reaffirmed in the 2012 Supreme Court decision on the Affordable Care Act.

EQUITY CONSIDERATIONS

Two aspects of equity must be considered. One is the principle of *micro-horizontal equity*, which says that people who benefit from an activity should pay the cost of that activity, and people who do not benefit should not pay. Private markets do this automatically. Similarly, government sometimes chooses to finance its activities with taxes tied to the marginal benefit from those activities. An example would be using federal gasoline taxes to pay for roads, so that people who drive very little do not pay a large share of the cost.

Such a benefit principle of horizontal equity could be employed even when government collects funds as an alternative to relying on a voluntary private market. It is used for unemployment and workers' compensation insurance, where the compulsory taxes are tied to the loss experience of the workforce at individual firms. But proposing to tax older people more than younger ones in order to pay for Medicare catastrophic coverage because they could expect to collect larger benefits from this program was controversial. It led to the repeal of the Reagan-era "Medicare catastrophic" law that would have taxed only the seniors who were going to benefit. In contrast, Medicare financing since this point in time has relied on higher income and payroll taxes for the general population. The only hint of a return to the benefit principle is the recent policy of increased Medicare Part B premiums for higher-income seniors.

A key equity issue in this context may be whether people can alter their behavior in response to taxing a product or activity correlated with a benefit. For example, people can drive less and may do so if they have to pay a high price for gasoline, but they cannot keep from growing older.

So it may be fair to tax activities that people can largely control (like driving), but not things that they cannot do much about (like the occurrence of natural disasters or aging). In reality, there often is an element of necessity in driving to work and an element of choice in where and how you build your house to avoid experiencing a large-scale natural disaster or what steps you take to reduce the impact of aging on health such as not smoking and exercising.

The other principle, *macro-horizontal equity*, looks at the distribution of well-being over all activities but does not concern itself with fairness with respect to specific products. Perfectly competitive markets do not necessarily or even usually produce what many regard as a fair distribution of well-being, especially if the initial distribution of resources is unequal. An equitable distribution of outcomes may thus require special treatment of certain individuals or groups at the expense of others. In welfare economics, the best way to achieve macro equity is to redistribute income or wealth while at the same time allowing resources to be allocated efficiently. In Richard Musgrave's (1959) classic terminology, government has both an "allocation branch," whose task is to oversee an efficient mix of inputs and outputs, and a "distribution branch," whose task is to assure that the distribution of well-being is regarded as fair by whatever social welfare function a society is using.

Sometimes, however, society may have preferences as to how a particular good should be distributed among the affected population. In such cases, one option is for government to provide a prespecified number of vouchers or credits to assist households needing special treatment. For example, it might provide *insurance stamps* for low-income families to use in paying for a portion of the cost of their homeowners' or renters' insurance just as it provides *food stamps* today for families who cannot afford the market prices of groceries.[1]

There can also be political benefits from earmarking funds for use in specific ways rather than giving transfer payments that individuals can spend on goods and services about which there is little social concern. In the case of an insurance voucher, low-income homeowners in hazard-prone areas would be able to afford to purchase coverage against losses from a disaster, thus reducing the provision of government assistance following the next flood or hurricane.

Attempts at redistribution of income following a specific event may have a cost in terms of efficiency by distorting incentives. Provision of public assistance immediately after a natural disaster may be viewed as equitable but can be inefficient from a longer-term perspective if it encourages more people to move into harm's way. If uninsured disaster victims are guaranteed (or anticipate) grants and low-interest loans that enable them to continue to build or rebuild in hazard-prone areas, and if more people therefore build in those areas, then taxpayers or purchasers of community-rated insurance will be subject to increasingly larger expenditures for bailing out victims of future disasters. This kind of government aid may also cause many people to fail to invest in protective measures or fail to purchase insurance.

If insurance is to play a central role in implementing risk management strategies for the public sector, an ideal arrangement would be one in which everyone subject to losses is personally responsible for the financial consequences of disasters and so bears the costs and benefits of any risk-reducing measures or activities. Those low-income persons needing special treatment could then be provided with predetermined subsidies from the public sector for insurance purchase rather than through regulatory-induced insurance premium reductions. The rationale for such an arrangement is that those residing in hazard-prone areas will make a more appropriate effort to avoid losses if they expect to bear the costs of an adverse event than if they do not. This should lead to smaller distortions and less free riding than strategies in which government bails out everyone after a disaster.

GUIDING PRINCIPLES FOR EVALUATING POLICIES

We think that these broad considerations of equity and efficiency could apply to any market. We now identify principles more specific to insurance that are still general enough to cover a range of anomalies. These guiding principles provide a framework for developing and evaluating strategies involving insurance in concert with other policy tools such as well-enforced building codes, reducing risks, and financially assisting those who suffer large losses through insurance claim payments. These principles fall into two categories: (1) *information principles* to foster the availability of risk data necessary to implement good policy; and (2) *policy design principles* given that risk data is available.

Information Principle One: Make Accurate Risk Assessments Available to Everyone

Information on the likelihood and consequences of specific events and the uncertainties surrounding these estimates should ideally be made available to all participants in insurance markets; no party should have any special informational advantage. If buyers and sellers have common knowledge and state-of-the-art information about risks, many anomalies can be avoided.

One key issue is what government or the insurance industry might do when risk perceptions differ among insurers, customers, and lawmakers – even after much effort is made to produce accurate and consistent assessments of the risk. Another issue is whether an entity, either government or private, might be charged with the task of developing accurate information about risks and then convincing buyers and sellers that these estimates are indeed valid. Once the information is verified by credible sources there is little cost to making it available to everyone. It may be appropriate for government to play this role if the public sector is viewed as more trustworthy by the citizenry than private sources.

In reality, however, fiscal constraints can often hamstring what government agencies can do in this regard. Corporations such as catastrophe modeling firms or industrywide data warehouses may be able to bring more resources to bear, although they will be challenged financially to come up with a business model so they can generate sufficient revenues from the sale of information to make this venture profitable. For example, if the broad contours of the results from a risk assessment model become generally known, there will be less reason for insurers to pay to obtain data from a private firm, unless they need precise estimates that require special information from the catastrophe modeling firm.

When premiums can be tailored to risk, this information can be helpful to potential buyers of insurance. The premium provides buyers with the knowledge about their relative safety regarding a particular hazard.

If, in contrast, premiums for a given type of coverage cannot or are not permitted to vary with risk, then providing more accurate information to individual buyers about their risk may foster adverse selection, with the low risks not buying insurance and the high risks purchasing policies.

Information Principle Two: Identify and Address Interdependencies

It will be useful to have a public agency characterize the nature of the interdependencies associated with risks that impose negative effects on others and deal properly with these spillover effects. To date, the private market has not dealt efficiently or equitably with these negative externalities. An example of an interdependency is a fire that starts in a home without a sprinkler system and then spreads to adjacent houses. In practice, an insurer who provides protection is responsible for losses incurred by the policyholder no matter who caused them.[2] In other words, the insurer is unconcerned with the damage to others that may be created by its policyholders, but is very concerned with the damage caused by others to its clients. This allocation of responsibility inhibits incentives to foster protective actions by residents or insurers of other properties and suggests the need for well-enforced building codes to reduce these negative spillover effects.

In contrast, insurance that shields actors from the full consequences of their negligence (such as medical malpractice insurance, which is rarely experience rated) can make interdependencies even more troublesome by encouraging lax or careless behavior. For example, insurance that covers legal damages due to negligent behavior offsets the intended legal incentives to discourage certain actions by individuals or firms. If premiums depended on the likelihood and expected losses from negligent behavior, then this problem could be avoided. Detecting such actions, however, is difficult and administratively costly. In addition, basing premiums on negligent behavior is politically unpopular. In principle, consumers could be offered insurance at lower premiums if in return they were willing to tolerate insurer monitoring of their risky behavior.

Information Principle Three: Detect and Adjust Strategies for Behavioral Biases and Heuristics

Many people utilize simplified rules in making their choices (e.g., "it will not happen to me"), misperceive probability, and are myopic with respect to their evaluation of investment decisions such as whether to adopt risk-reducing measures. These biases and heuristics need to be taken into account when insurers and regulators develop strategies for managing risks. In a sense, this is the main policy objective of this book: public and private policy makers should know the causes of anomalous behavior and take them into account when planning strategies. Policy makers should have the relevant knowledge and appreciation of the behavior that they believe is likely to occur in order to reduce adverse effects.

The design of the National Flood Insurance Program (NFIP) in 1968 highlights this point. At the time, policy analysts assumed that, by providing highly subsidized premiums, government could induce homeowners residing in flood-prone areas to purchase coverage. In reality, few individuals purchased insurance because they substantially underestimated the risk to such an extent that even subsidized coverage was not attractive. Many believed that no future flood would affect them, so it would be a waste of their money to spend anything on insurance, no matter how modest its cost. As a result, Congress passed the Flood Disaster Protection Act of 1972, which required homeowners with federally insured mortgages to purchase flood insurance if their house was located in a community that was part of the NFIP (Kunreuther et al. 1978). As we discussed earlier, one challenge facing the NFIP today is enforcing this requirement, especially when mortgages change hands.

These three information principles should be complemented by guidelines for designing insurance contracts. Two contract design principles are now specified.

Contract Design Principle One: Premiums Should Reflect Risk

Insurance premiums should be based on risk in order to warn individuals about the hazards they face and to encourage them to engage in cost-effective mitigation measures to reduce their vulnerability to catastrophes. Allowing insurers to charge premiums based on risk also encourages them to supply coverage which they might not do if prices are artificially constrained. It also enables insurers to choose the quality of service that they would like to provide to their clients such as speed of response in settling claims following a loss. Regulations that force premiums below the risk-based price that insurers would like to charge will stifle the supply of insurance.

Contract Design Principle Two: Define Equity across Buyers and Sellers and Apply it Consistently

The costs of any subsidy or special treatment provided by a governmental unit to a subset of potential insurance buyers (for equity or political reasons) should be covered by personal income or consumption taxes. In contrast to cross-subsidized premiums, taxes on income or consumption do not distort the purchase of insurance in a significant way. The costs should *not* be recouped by assessments on other potential insurance buyers through increased premiums because the consequent higher premiums may discourage them from purchasing coverage that they otherwise would have bought if premiums had reflected risk.

Subsidies should be made available so that individuals can purchase coverage from any insurance firm, just as those who use food stamps can shop at any grocery store. Proposals to improve equity should specify why some groups of buyers deserve special treatment and indicate who will bear the cost of that treatment. For example, if a state legislature decides to impose a special tax on all property owners in order to provide a predetermined amount of insurance stamps or subsidies for certain groups, then at least the distribution of the resulting tax burden should be specified.

Note that in the case of property insurance, the voucher system should apply only to individuals who currently reside in a hazard-prone area. Those who decide to move to the area in the future should be charged premiums that reflect the risk. Providing newcomers with financial assistance to purchase insurance would encourage them to locate in hazard-prone areas, thus exacerbating the potential for catastrophic losses from future disasters.

There is no compelling equity argument for redistributing wealth from middle-class households with inland property to middle-class households with shoreline property solely because those on the coast face a higher risk. An argument often used to justify subsidies to middle-class households in high-risk areas is that it will stimulate homebuilding in those areas and increase property values. Even though this may be true, the net social benefits, taking into account expected damages from future hurricanes or floods, would be even higher if these houses were located in less hazard-prone areas. There would then be less damage following the next disaster and hence lower public expenditures to aid the recovery process.

INSURANCE REGULATION IN PRACTICE

We have noted a number of instances in which overregulation has led to private insurance markets disappearing or shrinking where they should be vibrant, as occurred with insurance against wind damage from hurricanes in Florida. It may also lead people to overinsure and cause moral hazard problems due to their failure to invest in protective measures when more modest levels of insurance would provide adequate protection and promote more responsible actions by those at risk. In this way, regulation is inconsistent with the role of government to improve overall welfare and efficiency, not diminish it. Having said this, regulation can play a positive role in designing principles for insurance.

The public sector's intrusion into insurance might be partially explained by differences of opinion about the government's role in measuring and providing information on risk. Political decision makers often have lower estimates of risk than those of insurers and think that their estimates are accurate and should be used to set premiums. Their judgments are reinforced by the universal political appeal of promising lower insurance costs to voters. Inappropriate intrusion is most likely caused by political decisions consistent with public choice theory. That is, regulating premiums can provide large benefits to a minority of citizens, often well-organized and wealthy, who have political power. The cost of this cross-subsidy is spread in a way that is difficult to detect and entails relatively low cost per person over the larger majority of households – and that cost may not occur for a long time. This behavior was illustrated in Chapter 9 with respect to Florida's state-run Citizens insurance company that subsidized insurance premiums to property in the coastal regions of the state, many of which were second homes. On the positive side, requiring a health insurer to cover expensive psychiatric treatments for adolescents provides benefits to families with affected children but raises premiums only modestly across the board, perhaps something voters would support if it was an item on a referendum.

Government regulation causes two broad classes of anomalies: those that affect the structure of insurance benefits and those that impact insurance premiums. There may also be anomalies due to public regulation of insurer reserves. Regulators, as we noted, sometimes mandate that any insurance sold in their state include certain kinds of benefits, and they often restrict premiums that insurers can charge. What kinds of policy remedies exist for such institutions? And who is supposed to bring them to the government's attention?

Although the simplest answer is to remove dysfunctional government regulation, there may be people who made prior commitments based on the existing regulatory framework and who would suffer losses if the regulation were to be rescinded. Thus there may need to be a careful transition from a regulated market to a freer market to address these short-run considerations. It is easy for policy analysts like us to suggest that government refocus its regulatory energy toward improving matters. However, we recognize that the case to constrain, redirect, or expand regulation needs to be made to and through the voters. Next, we specify three principles that we believe should guide regulatory policy for insurance.

Regulatory Principle One: Avoid Premium Averaging

In many settings, regulators are reluctant to let insurers charge premiums that reflect risk. For example, if a decision is made to have premiums fully reflect losses from future hurricanes rather than being partially subsidized by those not subject to these disasters, the burden of this change will fall more heavily on owners of property in vulnerable locations. Taking into account the effect of high premiums on property values as well as current consumption, regulators often try to temper or reduce the extent to which premiums vary with risk.

Lowering premiums for some will require raising premiums for others if insurers are to break even with respect to their expected profits. Sometimes such offsetting premium increases are facilitated by regulators, but often, state insurance commissioners restrict these increases and/or set limits to insurer profits. Sometimes states set up residual market mechanisms that provide protection to those who cannot secure insurance in the open market. The state itself guarantees that the public insurer will be able to pay claims by using its taxing power if revenues and reserves fall short in the event of a serious disaster. In effect, state taxpayers bear the liability should claims be high. If the low-probability event does not occur, the state insurer can cover its actual outlays, and the arrangement may even appear to be a better deal for everyone than market insurance.

In this regard, Florida has so far fared very well since the time it introduced Citizens as a public insurer. From 2006 through 2011 no hurricanes caused damage to the state, and premiums in high-hazard areas have been subsidized with respect to this risk. But should there be a serious disaster that depletes Citizens' reserves, the additional claims are likely to be paid from assessments (taxes) on the premiums charged to all homeowners in Florida. The most serious defect of such a system is that it encourages individuals to locate in high-hazard areas, thus putting more property at risk than would occur under a market system. This is the principal reason not to introduce such a system in the first place.

Remedies here have to be political as well as economic. The best strategy may be to determine who the households are (by wealth and location) that the state wants to assist in its role as proxy for all concerned citizens. There then could be a subsidy in the form of an insurance voucher for low- or modest-income residents in high-risk regions. This system should be buttressed by well-enforced building codes and land-use regulations for locating or improving structures. These measures would include financial incentives, such as insurance premium reductions and long-term loans for encouraging investment in cost-effective loss reduction measures. These improvements would be subsidized by general revenue taxation. This approach relates to Policy Design Principles One and Two because premiums paid to insurers need to reflect risk; the subsidy (in the form of a predetermined insurance voucher) addresses the affordability issue.

Regulatory Principle Two: Do Not Mandate Insurance Benefits Not Worth Their Cost

State regulations that specify minimum benefits that must be provided by an insurance policy can cause anomalies. In the context of health insurance, the state may require that particular kinds of care be covered (e.g., outpatient mental health care, podiatrist care, infertility treatments). Usually, the rationale for such rules is that these mandated benefits are important because the services provided to the insured are useful. They may fail to be covered by insurers voluntarily because these types of ailments are associated with unusually high moral hazard. For example, if the presence of comprehensive insurance coverage for outpatient psychotherapy creates increased demand for visits to the psychiatrist, the premium for such coverage may have to be so high to cover costs that it discourages people from buying generous insurance. It would then not be efficient to have very generous coverage of such a service.

Nevertheless, lawmakers might mandate overly generous coverage even though insurance buyers are willing to sacrifice such protection in order to keep their premiums down. Lawmakers who can convince voters that they can make insurers cover such services without premium increases may be successful; the strategy sometimes is one in which the politician gains twice, first by forcing insurers to provide more generous coverage (for previously uncovered services, such as experimental or unproven procedures) and then by criticizing and limiting the resulting premium increase that the insurer would want to charge.

Not all mandates are inefficient, however. Sometimes, the services covered provide societal as well as private benefits. Vaccination that protects others against contagious diseases is one example. Sometimes, coverage of preventive services that will eventually reduce the costs of future care is mandated because the insurer is unwilling to pay for a preventive service that will save future costs for those customers who have moved on to another insurer or to Medicare. There are some data suggesting that such mandates substantially increase premiums in states that enact them, compared to premiums in other states, other things being equal (Kowalski, Congdon, and Showalter 2008). However, the evidence on this point is not consistent because some mandates involve benefits that include such small increases in premiums that they are difficult for the insured to detect.

A significant potential downside to this kind of regulation is that it can force coverage of something inappropriate to insure, either because the service itself is not necessary or because the individual treatment is relatively inexpensive or is almost certain to occur even if insurance is not provided, such as doctor visits during cold and flu season. More generally, requiring insurance on high-likelihood events is anomalous behavior by the regulator.

Regulatory Principle Three: Examine Impacts of Crowding-out Effects on Behavior

By cushioning the consequences of mistaken choices, one may encourage exactly the kind of behavior targeted for change. In the language of political economy, this phenomenon is sometimes known as "crowding out." By providing a public substitute (even an imperfect and low-quality one) for some private activity that would otherwise be appropriate, people may be deterred from the private activity. We have already commented on the classic example in the case of natural disasters: to the extent that the government bails out uninsured homeowners or small businesses, it deters people from spending their own money on the coverage they should have.

Another example of extreme crowd out is the case of long-term care insurance, voluntarily purchased by only about eight percent of the eligible population. In addition to the usual loading and buyer misinformation problems, Jeffrey Brown, Norma Coe, and Amy Finkelstein (2007), following Mark Pauly (1990), show that a major deterrent is the presence of government Medicaid coverage, which will pay for long-term care even for people with initially moderate means when those people spend enough to become impoverished. As noble and altruistic as such a policy is, it deters people from buying private coverage that will pay for (and charge them for) care that Medicaid would eventually cover. There are bound to be some adverse incentive effects of any government spending program, but the virtual elimination of private insurance by an especially low-quality public option in this case almost surely causes more anomalous behavior than it cures.

ROLES FOR THE PUBLIC SECTOR IN AIDING INSURANCE DECISION MAKING

How might these principles on information, design, and regulation be carried out? Insurance firms themselves might implement them as part of overall industry policy. But often their implementation will require public sector action. What kinds of programs might governments be able and willing to enact for encouraging the wise purchase or efficient supply of insurance? There are four broad models of government decision making and intervention that we will consider.

Model One: Strong paternalism

The first model is what we term *strong paternalism*. To illustrate, suppose public policy is designed to meet the criterion that outcomes should mimic what would happen if consumers maximized their expected utility and firms maximized expected profits in competitive markets. If consumers and firms did not follow this criterion, regulations would be utilized to force the desired behavior. More formally, this would be considered *welfare-maximizing paternalism* in which welfare is defined by the expected utility model, and distributional weights across the affected individuals characterize a social welfare function. For example, demand and supply of insurance might be regulated, subsidized, or mandated as a way of achieving this outcome because individuals do not maximize expected utility or firms do not maximize expected profits.

The government that could oversee such programs is the fabled *benevolent dictator* interested in maximizing a weighted sum of consumer and producer welfare. For example, government could be advised to make all decisions using cost-benefit analysis only. Cost-benefit analysis is sometimes used (and justified) by this kind of welfare economics model, but unrestricted application of those kinds of analyses to actual public sector decisions, untrammeled by politics and special pleading, is rare. If government did behave in this manner, then consumers who bought some insurance, eschewed other policies, or engaged in or avoided investing in protective measures would be subject to subsidies, taxes, or regulations that would push their behavior toward what would have been chosen by a population with the same distribution of incomes taking actions that maximized their expected utility.

In a similar manner, government might intervene with private insurers if they did not offer coverage against certain risks. Federal guarantees of payment in case of catastrophic loss (as with terrorism insurance today) could be justified as a response to the failure of the private market to furnish adequate coverage. In this case, the taxpayers' assets would be pledged as reserves rather than relying on voluntarily supplied capital that might not be forthcoming for reasons described in Chapter 8. Alternatively, the government could provide loans to insurers at market rates of interest following a catastrophic loss so they would be willing to offer coverage both before and after the event occurred (Jaffee and Russell 2003).

Strong paternalism does rule out some kinds of behavior that real-world governments might otherwise engage in, such as using insurance premium regulation to redistribute income by requiring premiums to be lower than expected loss or by requiring insurers to pay claims for risks not part of the contract. On the latter point, following Hurricane Katrina, the attorney general of Mississippi sued insurers for failure to pay for water damage suffered by homeowners even though the insurance policy explicitly excluded this risk. The legal system would be used to prevent such lawsuits.[3]

Many proposals for health reform and health insurance regulation follow the strong paternalism model. For example, proposals for targeted subsidies to reduce the cost of health insurance to those at high risk are intended to encourage these individuals to purchase coverage. They are not specifically motivated by a belief that high risks, many of whom are not poor, deserve a transfer to improve their well-being. On the other side, a proposal to ban appliance warranties or insurance offered by rental car companies, on the grounds that this type of insurance provides low expected benefits relative to its cost, could also be justified in the context of a strong paternalism model.

Welfare-maximizing paternalism is not the only kind of strong paternalism. Another version would substitute preferences of policy makers for those of insurance buyers or sellers. In health economics this version is called *extra-welfarism* and is endorsed by some analysts, especially British health economists looking to explain and justify the heavy involvement of government in the British National Health Service. The idea is that some social values should be considered that are above and beyond the well-being (as they see it) of consumers and input suppliers. In the simplest model, these values are assumed to be known by lawmakers and government officials.

In an extreme version of *extra-welfarism*, it is not the welfare of those citizens being helped (as those citizens judge it) that is the basis for policy makers' decisions. Rather it is the policy makers' judgments as to what they perceive as the appropriate actions that citizens should undertake. For example, a subset of consumers who are not very risk averse might be unwilling to buy insurance at market premiums. It is possible that these consumers were maximizing their expected utility by taking their chances to avoid the loading costs associated with the insurance policy, but a paternalistic government with preferences that everyone should purchase insurance might mandate coverage.

Model Two: Soft Paternalism

In *soft paternalism*, the government moves toward changing rules, information, or incentives in ways that do not appreciably affect well-informed consumers who already maximize their expected utility. Rather, it addresses the behavioral biases and imperfect decision rules used by others. These errors are usually measured relative to some objectively observable benchmark (e.g., choosing the retirement plan that offers the best deal), but the fundamental specification of what constitutes an error by consumers is measured as the difference between actual behavior and that implied by the benchmark model of demand – maximizing expected utility.

This model is intended to recognize the mistakes often present in individuals' behavior in the face of risk, but to correct them gently, by designing what Richard Thaler and Cass Sunstein (2008) call a *choice architecture* that increases the chances that people will generally select the best option, even if they are imperfectly informed and using heuristics. It builds on the strong evidence that framing of choices matters in affecting what people choose. But it still relies on the expected utility model to define goals and mistakes in attaining those goals. The welfare economics that results when government (or whoever is the designated choice architect) tries to gently push people in a particular direction is, as we shall see, not wholly clear. But, as we shall also show, there are some anomalies for which the kind of nudges suggested by this approach would seem like good policy.

Model Three: Public Provision of Accurate Information

Public provision of accurate information limits government intervention to cases in which there is buyer or seller misinformation or misperception of risks. It allows buyers and suppliers to act on their preferences, no matter how these differ from expected utility theory or expected profit maximization; it specifies only that they should use accurate information when making choices. In this case, individuals would be considered justified for making insurance policy choices based on such sentiments as a desire for *peace of mind* or *preference for a low deductible*.

One specification of this model would have the government provide consumers with the best available information on the nature of the risk, or even try to inform consumers as to what expected utility or expected profit maximizing implies with respect to choices. Consumers are free to make whatever choices they wish after they obtain good factual information and clear explanations of their supposed mistakes relative to the benchmark models of choice.

To illustrate this point, consider how such a program would be applied in the following situations:

- Middle-class consumers who buy no health insurance at all would be allowed to go without coverage and told they would experience the consequences;

- Highly risk-averse consumers would be permitted to buy over-priced warranties or rental car insurance after they are informed what the true expected benefits are in relation to costs.

On the supply side, one could provide insurers with the best information available about the risk of adverse events (e.g., future hurricanes), but allow them to stay out of the market (despite the apparent opportunity for high profits) if their management or owners are very concerned about the ambiguity of probabilities or think the best estimates are still too low.

Model Four: Extended Public Choice

In the *extended public choice model*, government engages in regulatory or fiscal behavior when it is preferred by certain members of the voting public. For example, a lawmaker may decide not to implement a policy preferred by citizens (even if the policy is consistent with the benchmark model of demand), because he or she is concerned about not being reelected by other citizens who hold fast to views that differ from choices implied by this benchmark model. Some elected officials, including state insurance commissioners, may stay in office based on actions that increase inefficiency in insurance markets but benefit certain important special interest groups, such as high-income residents who have subsidized insurance premiums on their coastline vacation homes.

This model may characterize government behavior more accurately than the conventional welfare maximization model. Homeowners' insurance in Florida, where Citizens, the state insurer, offers subsidized premiums to those residing in hurricane-prone areas, is a good example of this political view. If a storm produces catastrophic losses such that Citizens cannot pay all the claims, then the state will have to find a way to obtain funds to cover this shortfall. Those who do not reside in hazard-prone areas but are likely to be taxed after the storm to provide these funds may not have built this scenario into their thinking and hence did not object to the creation of Citizens.

SUMMARY

This chapter postulates two broad questions central to making good policy decisions about insurance:

- Who should bear the risk of losses caused by specific events?
- Who should bear the costs of reducing the risks when the reductions are large enough that it is appropriate to do so?

Policy answers to those questions should take into account efficiency and equity. Efficient policies should be based on the competitive benchmark model of supply while equity should reflect a society's views of fairness with respect to the distribution of costs and benefits.

We believe that a framework for formulating and evaluating strategies that involves both the public and private sectors can be built using principles aimed at developing and providing accurate information, policy design, and more effective regulation. The information principles deal with accurate risk assessment, the identification of interdependencies that create risks for spillover effects, and identification of the behavioral biases and heuristics that lead to less-than-optimal decisions. The design principles call for premiums that reflect risk and a consistent and efficient application of equity across buyers and sellers. Regulatory principles avoid premium averaging, carefully evaluate the impact of mandated insurance benefits, and take into account crowding-out behavior in which a public substitute drives out a more appropriate private solution. The framework in this chapter will be used later in the book to deal with specific anomalies.

The information, design, and regulatory principles may be applied in one of four models of government policy:

- *Model One: strong paternalism*, in which the government becomes the benevolent dictator decreeing the insurance that people will buy and what insurers will offer;
- *Model Two: soft paternalism*, in which the government changes rules or incentives to correct behavioral biases or heuristics among buyers and sellers of insurance;

- *Model Three: public provision of accurate information,* in which government intervention is limited to providing information to correct misunderstandings and misperceptions about the nature of risk;
- *Model Four: extended public choice,* in which government bows to the public will and provides the regulation that the majority or some special interest groups desire.

Strategies for Dealing with Insurance-Related Anomalies

This chapter develops more concrete examples and strategies that the insurance industry and the public sector can use to deal with the problems raised by anomalies on the demand and supply sides, based on the principles formulated in the previous chapter. The first section focuses on strategies for dealing with the demand side. These strategies involve providing information, reframing choices, changing incentives, and assuring coverage in various ways to improve individual and social welfare. We then turn to anomalies on the supply side by examining ways that risk information could and should affect insurers as they determine what premiums to charge, the types of coverage to provide, and the role that the public sector can play in making insurance more widely available. The chapter concludes with suggestions for future research on ways to more effectively utilize insurance as a cornerstone for creating risk management strategies for individuals, firms, and society.

PUBLIC POLICY TO DEAL WITH DEMAND-SIDE ANOMALIES

The least controversial argument for trying to correct apparent anomalies on the demand side exists when they result from errors that buyers of insurance make due to incomplete or biased information, or when they use overly simplified models of choice.[1] Government's role here is not to change preferences, but to take steps that bring behaviors more in line with the hypothetical choices of a fully informed decision maker with a correct understanding of the relationships between risk and premiums.

The strategy is designed to foster an efficient private market for insurance, not impede it.

Going beyond the provision of information, there are several other ways the government can address demand-side anomalies. As noted in Chapter 10, the *soft paternalism model* frames the "choice architecture" so that consumers are led to make the appropriate choices by the way options are presented. This option need not present new information. The more controversial alternative is *strong paternalism*, which uses regulation or taxes to compel citizens to do what the government believes is in their best interests. But strong paternalism models may not pass the public choice or practical politics test if people do not believe they are not fully informed and/or trust that the government knows better. The pushback against mandating health insurance (and the resulting weak mandate) in the recent health care reform debate is a good example of the political difficulties confronting paternalism in American democracy. Providing information or reframing may ultimately be more politically feasible.

As pointed out in Chapter 5, many consumers decide not to purchase insurance, or decline even to explore the option of purchasing, when they perceive the likelihood of the insured event occurring to be below a threshold level of concern. In some cases this behavior may be rational if the search costs associated with getting information on insurance premiums are sufficiently high (Kunreuther and Pauly 2004). But in other cases, this behavior may lead to nonoptimal decisions. To correct this behavior one can reframe the problem so that consumers will pay attention to the likelihood of a loss and consider purchasing insurance coverage. We now characterize two specific demand-side policy options that may be helpful in this regard.

Demand-Side Policy Solution One: Provide Accurate Information to Correct Biases

Many of the demand anomalies discussed in Chapter 7 arise either because the potential buyer has misinformation or because the insurance options are described in a way that unnecessarily biases typical consumer choice away from behavior consistent with the benchmark model.

The government might play a useful role here by providing accurate information, as illustrated by the following example. Today, the Center for Medicare and Medicaid Services provides information relevant to selecting a Medicare drug insurance plan. Medicare's website supplies an online decision tool that will tell the beneficiary how much out-of-pocket expense to expect under each of the Medicare drug plans, given information the beneficiary inputs about the drugs he or she is now taking.[2] There is no direct interference with voluntary choice regarding beneficiary plans. The taxes to pay for the provision of this information and to finance most of the cost of the insurance fall on the entire citizenry.

Of course, the mere fact that consumer decisions could be improved by publicly provided information is not enough to argue for such information. For one thing, the value of the benefits from improved choices has to be large enough to justify the cost of furnishing the information. For another thing, all the other necessary conditions for efficient markets should ideally be in place if more information is to be guaranteed to improve matters overall. For example, some critics have pointed out that Medicare Compare makes adverse selection in community-rated Part D Medicare insurance easier, and so could have negative side effects (Handel 2010). Still, better information is generally more effective.

Demand-Side Policy Solution Two: Present Probabilities and Consequences Using Concrete Comparisons

People have great difficulty evaluating low-probability risks, but they do a better job when the data are presented in the context of risks that they understand. They might not know what a one in a million risk means as an abstract concept, but they can more accurately interpret the figure when it is compared to the annual risk of an automobile accident (one in twenty), or lightning striking their home on their birthday (less than one in a billion). Empirical research indicates that comparisons of risks are much more effective in helping decision makers better assess the risk than translating the risks from probabilities into a specific measure such as an insurance premium (Kunreuther, Novemsky, and Kahneman 2001).

Presenting information in this form can also help people avoid thinking of insurance as an investment to be discontinued if it does not offer a short-term payback in the form of claims payments. It is not easy to convince policyholders that *the best return on their insurance is no return at all* when they have not gotten a benefit payment lately. Presenting information on the magnitude of the potential loss along with information that convinces people that they can suffer the loss in the future may prevent them from canceling their policies. Such a presentation may, for example, help convince more people to obtain health insurance. To be sure, health insurance is expensive, and some people are not able to take advantage of tax breaks and economies of large-group insurance purchase. Even so, deciding not to purchase insurance looks less attractive if the potential buyer understands that, without insurance, a very high medical expense could lead to bankruptcy, not to mention the inability to undertake treatments because of its high cost to them.

Determining how to deliver this better information is more of a challenge. People may not want to see more information if they have already decided that the risk is of low concern to them. More generally, Americans appear reluctant to let their government decide and endorse probability estimates which may be controversial, as the debate over global warming indicates. Individual political parties advance agendas using alleged probabilities (sometimes even correct probabilities), but people do not trust such partisan information. Who (if anyone) should be given the power to decide the likelihood of the next hurricane in south Florida – insurers and their political allies who think it likely, or regulators and opposing lawmakers who think it unlikely? Simply anointing a risk-modeling firm as the unbiased source seems doubtful. Deciding how to provide, present, and pay for this information poses challenges, but it is a step forward to recognize its importance and determine its form.

Demand-Side Policy Solution Three: Extending the Time Frame

Probability of loss is also easier to understand when a longer time frame is utilized to characterize the likelihood of the event occurring. A probability of four percent per year translates into about a one in three chance of having one or more losses in ten years, or, alternatively, only a two-thirds chance of being accident-free over that period. People are more willing to wear seat belts if they are told they have a one in three chance of an accident when a seat belt will matter over a fifty-year lifetime of driving, rather than a one in one hundred thousand chance of an accident on each trip they take (Slovic, Fischhoff, and Lichtenstein 1978).

Adjusting the time frame can also affect risk perceptions. For example, if a homeowner or manager is considering earthquake protection over the twenty-five-year life of a home or factory, these individuals are far more likely to take the risk seriously if they are told that the chance of at least one earthquake during the entire period is greater than 1 in 5, rather than 1 in 100 in any given year (Weinstein, Kolb, and Goldstein 1996). Studies have shown that even just multiplying the single-year risk so the numerator is larger – presenting it as 10 in 1,000 or 100 in 10,000 instead of 1 in 100 – makes it more likely that people will pay attention to the event (Slovic, Monahan, and MacGregor 2000).

In other words, most people feel small numbers can be easily dismissed, while larger numbers get their attention. Of course, the small annual probability will be linked to a loss that will be large relative to someone's annual income but not so large relative to his or her lifetime income. So effectiveness of the communication depends on whether people are motivated more by loss probabilities or by the consequences of a loss, when ideally they should be motivated by both, a point we mentioned earlier in critiquing journalistic advice on insurance.

One challenge for future research is to determine ways to present information to individuals so that they understand the meaning of low and high probabilities. Insurers might choose to offer policies with longer time frames, such as five, ten, or twenty years (Jaffee, Kunreuther, and Michel-Kerjan 2010). In offering such a contract, they could provide information on the likelihood of a low-probability event occurring during the term of the policy. Individuals are then more likely to take into consideration what the consequences of such an event would be.

Long-term framing should be in the insurance industry's interest as a way to increase sales, but there is a danger that the information could be presented in a way that misleads consumers. For example, some sellers of long-term care insurance to middle-aged adults are fond of pointing out that about forty percent of people will be in need of nursing home or home health care at some point in their lives. What they fail to mention is that most of those episodes are brief convalescences after hospitalization, which are not covered by long-term care policies, and some of them are institutional stays for the mentally and physically disabled who have obtained governmental help from childhood. Furthermore, these insurers normally do not point out that the proportion of people over the age of sixty-five in nursing homes in any given year is less than five percent, implying a low probability of collecting benefits each year in return for one's annual premium.

Demand-Side Policy Solution Four: Have Insurers Bundle Low-Probability Events

The probability that one particular event will damage property may be low, but many other events can cause the same type of monetary loss; property can be damaged by fire, wind, water, or ice. Accordingly, it may be better to avoid *individual peril* insurance (like cancer-only coverage) or *named perils* insurance that covers some specific causes but not all causes of a given loss. Rather, insurers should consider offering consumers an *all perils* policy that covers damage to an asset regardless of cause, as is the case in France, Spain, and New Zealand with respect to property insurance. Then people may be more likely to buy the coverage they will need. Some soft paternalism by government might be helpful in nudging insurers to at least make this option available.

Demand-Side Policy Solution Five: Discourage Purchasing Insurance with Low Deductibles

People often purchase policies with low deductibles that are financially unattractive according to the benchmark model of demand. If a deductible of $1,000 can save significant administrative costs over a deductible of $500 because it avoids having to process many small claims, a higher deductible may be desirable for all but the most risk-averse individuals. By providing information on the relatively small expected benefits of the lower deductible in relation to its extra cost, consumers may understand why this is not a good use of their money. For example, by presenting competing plans in multiple temporal frames, a small deductible that seems to carry a low price in one year looks much worse when the expense is viewed over ten years and contrasted with the expected benefits over the same time frame.

To illustrate this point, consider an event with a loss greater than $1,000 that has a one in twenty annual chance of occurring that remains constant over time. Assume that there is a proportional loading cost that is 100 percent of the expected loss (that is, loading is fifty percent of premiums) so that reducing the deductible from $1,000 to $500 costs the consumer an extra premium of fifty dollars (that is, 2 x 1/20 x [$1000-$500]). If one pays this extra premium over a ten-year period, the total cost to the consumer is $500, but the chances of never collecting the extra $500 during that time interval is sixty percent.[3] By presenting the information in this way, consumers should be much more likely to take the higher deductible than if they were only looking at the differential cost in the next year. Paying an extra $500 when a loss occurs is painful for most people, but may seem more manageable if they know it is very unlikely to occur over the next ten years.

If this line of argument fails, another alternative is to take advantage of individuals' preferences for rebates (another anomaly) by offering them a check if they switch to a higher deductible. The agent could indicate to the policyholder that by converting his or her policy from a $500 deductible to $1,000, the policyholder would be mailed a check for fifty dollars at the end of each policy year if he or she maintains this coverage. This might be viewed as a very attractive option by the consumer, particularly if it is coupled with information explaining why low deductibles are unattractive in the long run.

Another way to encourage individuals to avoid low deductibles is by making the high deductible the default option in the spirit of the soft paternalism prescriptive recommendations by Richard Thaler and Cass Sunstein (2008). The insurance industry might do this voluntarily, or it could be required to do so by regulation. The standard insurance policy would have a high deductible, but there could be a policy with a low deductible available at additional cost to those willing to go to the trouble of requesting it. The individual would then be told how much extra the policy would cost and how much more it would pay out on average;

he or she must stipulate in writing that he or she knows the terms of the supplemental policy as a condition for purchasing it.

If these efforts at soft paternalism do not work, government might, as a last resort, forbid the sale of policies with low deductibles when the premium savings from increasing the deductible are very large relative to the expected increment in benefits. Whether such a clear case for strong paternalism on financial grounds can be found is an open question. Public choice theory suggests that this kind of regulation might be politically difficult if voters have strong preferences for low deductibles. For example, few lawmakers would want to force people to pay a high deductible on their health insurance even if on average it saved much more in premiums than it costs. The media would locate people who suffered many losses after taking the higher-deductible policy so that their premium savings for the past two or three years was more than wiped out. The media would be unlikely to note as part of the story that over time, say ten years, the premium savings from taking a high deductible would cover the policyholders' extra out of pocket costs.

Demand-Side Policy Solution Six: Discourage Insurance Policies that Use Rebates

When viewed in isolation, without any other distortions in insurance choices, insurance policies with rebates are not generally a good deal, precisely because they generate confusion rather than clarity. One should be able to present consumers with comparative data to show why this is the case. Using the example of disability insurance presented in Chapter 6, one could show that a person would be paying $600 more for a less than certain chance of obtaining a rebate of $600 at the end of the policy year because that money would be forthcoming only if there were no claims during the period. Furthermore, a rebate reduces the incentive to make a claim, defeating the purpose of purchasing insurance in the first place.

Alternatively, the government could just forbid such policies, thus avoiding the cost of presenting the information just discussed to insurance buyers. But there is potentially some scope for offering policies with "no-claims discounts" upon renewal, which is a form of experience rating used in America for automobile insurance and in Switzerland for health insurance. Such policies typically promise a premium discount in the next contract period if one has made low or no claims in the current period, similar to the "good driver" discounts in auto insurance. There is a difference between explicit cost sharing and premium adjustments. With cost sharing, if a policyholder who incurs high losses also incurs an out of pocket expense, the premium at the next renewal is unaffected. With experience rating or the Swiss "bonus-malus" arrangement for auto insurance, a person who incurs high losses pays a higher premium next period which may cause him or her to not buy insurance. It is probably no accident that, when premiums are based on experience, insurance is made compulsory so that those at risk cannot drop it, as in third-party auto liability insurance, coverage that is compulsory in Switzerland and the United States.

Demand-Side Policy Solution Seven: Requiring or Mandating Specific Insurance

If alternative framing and information strategies are either ineffective or very costly, welfare might be improved if government regulation requires that everyone obtain policies to cover risks that consumers would have wanted protection against if they were well-informed but that they do not value given their current state of understanding (or misunderstanding). Similarly, one may want to propose banning some insurance that an informed person would never want to purchase. In this regard, our earlier cautions about the political acceptability of strong paternalism should be kept in mind when imposing such requirements.

Regulatory agencies do ban certain goods and service and specify minimum product quality levels when they know that well-informed consumers would favor such policies. For example, no one would want contaminated baby food, no matter how cheap, so the Food and Drug Administration takes steps to prevent such products from being sold. With respect to insurance, one may require individuals to purchase certain types of coverage and ban other coverage where the cost is greater than the expected benefit. Today, banks normally require homeowners' policies as a condition for a mortgage and all states require some form of automobile insurance. There are few laws today banning specific coverage even when the annual premium is high relative to expected benefits, but there are provisions in the health reform legislation forbidding insurers from charging premiums that exceed a certain percentage of average claims. In practice, there is unlikely to be unanimity in people's preferences with respect to banning or requiring specific features of insurance. In this setting, soft paternalism may be a more appropriate strategy to follow.

There is, however, a downside to a government requirement that insurers provide coverage for specific risks in a policy that can be purchased voluntarily: this requirement may cause the premium to rise to such an extent that some people refuse to buy any coverage, presumably a worse outcome than their purchasing insurance when certain risks are excluded. Some believe this is what happens with state-mandated benefits for health insurance. There is thus a fine line that regulators must walk between making insurance comprehensive and making insurance prohibitively expensive for some individuals.

Not All Anomalies May Need Correction

We now turn to the obvious point that anomalous behavior of only moderate consequence will have only a minor financial impact on the affected population and thus may not require public intervention; it can best be left alone, given all the other demands on government. For example, the data on annuities presented in Chapter 7 reveal that upper middle-class people often make mistaken choices in deciding how to provide for their retirement. A combination of misplaced self-confidence and poor framing leads them to prefer investing their wealth in risky portfolios of securities and real estate rather than annuities, so that they fail to protect against their income needs should they live into their late eighties or nineties. An ad e-mailed to faculty at the University of Pennsylvania in June 2011 posed the question: "To Annuitize or Not Annuitize?" with the tagline, "Sometimes doing nothing really is the best option." Purchasing immediate annuities guarantees consumption levels as long as the person lives, yet only about two percent of current retirees have this kind of insurance.

But is this potential defect in retirement planning by families with wealth a compelling candidate for public intervention? Public policy in this case differs from that in many other insurance markets because Social Security sets a safety net to retiree income. The main adverse consequence of high-income individuals failing to convert a large portion of retirement assets into an annuity is that their post-retirement consumption patterns will be uneven or at least not ideal, but there may be little basis for direct social concern over the consequences of these choices.

The laissez-faire policy on annuities in the United States differed from that in the United Kingdom where, until recently, people at all income levels were required by law to annuitize a large share of any retirement resources they had. This rule was substantially weakened in 2006, when people were permitted to invest in deferred annuities, which do not provide explicit protection against long life and are largely investment vehicles. The United Kingdom may be moving in the direction of Singapore, which requires people to save a significant proportion of their working years income (through compulsory contributions to the Central Provident Fund), and which controls the nature of those investments until retirement, but then does not require annuitization – and only ten percent of retirees pick annuities there.

The Obama administration has recently discussed a more aggressive soft paternalism approach for the United States. At present, almost all workers have the option of taking any 401(k) retirement fund as a lump sum upon retirement, to be invested however the person chooses. The suggested policy would require employers to hold back some of their employees' retirement fund to provide for a two-year trial annuity period after retirement. After that period, the worker could opt out of the annuity and utilize what is in the retirement fund in whatever way he or she wants (Gale et al. 2008). In effect, the program gives people a trial run on an annuity in the hope that if they try it they will like it.

Other solutions have been considered. Liran Einav, Amy Finkelstein, and Paul Schrimpf (2010) consider mandates as a solution to adverse selection in the UK annuity market, and generally come to a negative conclusion. James Poterba, Steven Venti, and David Wise (2011) and Shlomo Benartzi, Alessandro Previtero, and Richard Thaler (2011) propose that consumers be provided with better information on how annuities work so they can make well-informed choices about their retirement income options, including delaying their Social Security benefits. Benartzi, Previtero, and Thaler also recommend that the government encourage Americans to take annuities by waiving or modifying current regulations so that employers find it easier to reframe choices and/or set default options to encourage retirees to convert their defined contribution accounts to annuities. For example, they propose delaying the retirement age at which individuals can start claiming Social Security benefits and having automatic enrollment in specific annuity plans as the default option.

These different approaches show how difficult it is to define an explicit role for the public sector in retirement income planning for moderate-income to high-income households. Social insurance that provides a floor to retirement incomes (e.g., Social Security in the United States) is accepted in many countries, but it is unclear whether the benefits from taking additional steps are worth the cost, given the many other items on the government's agenda.

Anomalies Caused by Alternative Simple Decision Rules and Preferences about Risk

Specifying good public policies is much more complex if the anomaly is due to consumer heuristics or choice processes that differ from those that would maximize expected utility. Because individuals have different objectives, or process information in ways that deviate from the benchmark model, it is unclear whether there is a role for governmental intervention. Consider the widow who pays premiums for life insurance rather than purchasing an annuity or the student who buys a warranty on a new MP3 player even though the cost greatly outweighs the expected benefits. It may be that these consumers seek the peace of mind that insurance provides them, even if the risk protection seems very expensive relative to its potential financial benefits.

Since only a small fraction of travelers purchase flight insurance, and few middle-class people do not have health insurance, this anomalous behavior is unlikely to trigger a call for government intervention.[4] Soft paternalism, in which the default options in these cases are *not purchasing flight insurance* and *having health insurance*, might be enough to save many more people with normal preferences from mistakenly choosing a financially undesirable course of action given the time and attention required to select the other option.

A more complex situation is one in which individual choices do not reflect unusual or extreme preferences, but rather more common attitudes toward risk that nevertheless differ from the expected utility model. If many people make choices consistent with prospect theory, for example, they are not really making a choice inconsistent with the facts but rather with a particular kind of utility function. Government actions to direct or channel consumer actions to be closer to those consistent with the expected utility model may *not* be appropriate, if one has determined that consumers do have good information and know what they are doing. In this case, government should leave consumers and insurance markets alone; they are competent adults and it is their choice as to how much protection they want.

The problem is how to draw a line between decision processes that are acceptable and those that are not when the consumer's objective differs from expected utility maximization. Is it acceptable for people to buy insurance that provides benefits only if the disease is cancer, and at a high price relative to expected benefits, because it gives them peace of mind with respect to a dreaded cause of death?

Should policy makers tolerate such preferences? Our judgment is that the answer to this question should generally be "Yes." Adults who have enough information to know what they are doing should be allowed to make choices – but they should also bear the consequences. Tolerance for such preferences should be matched with institutional structures that make sure that the decision makers bear the full consequences of their actions and do not impose costs on others.

The homeowner who drops insurance coverage after years of no claims should not be given public assistance when a hurricane strikes. And the consumer who chooses an expensive form of health insurance to gain peace of mind should not receive financial assistance to cover the extra cost of that insurance. The middle-class healthy person who goes without health insurance cannot claim to be a charity case, but might be required to post a bond to cover medical costs before being allowed to remain uninsured. And the uninsured property owner with underground petroleum storage tanks should have to bear the costs of damages to others should the tanks leak.

Although these assertions are easy to make, it is unclear if they will be carried out in a public policy setting where there are often concentrated special interests. The wind-in-your-hair, anti-motorcycle-helmet lobby has often prevailed and avoided even some type of imposed financial protection (e.g., posting a bond before you get on the bike). The few who would be harmed from their poor choices often lobby government for assistance after suffering losses on the grounds that they were unaware of the dangers they faced or did not know that insurance protection was available. Forcing people to sign "hold (society) harmless agreements" if they do not buy insurance is rarely done, and such agreements, when signed, are not easily enforceable.

PUBLIC POLICY AND SUPPLY-SIDE ANOMALIES

In this section, we suggest several strategies that should be required, or at least encouraged, for insurers and reinsurers in making their decisions as to whether to offer coverage.

Supply-Side Policy Solution One: Utilize Valid Risk Estimates in Determining Premiums

Although expected loss appears to be an obvious foundation for determining how much to charge for protection against a given risk, insurers do not always follow this principle when they have the freedom to set premiums. The prime example in recent years is the pricing of terrorism coverage.

As discussed earlier, prior to 9/11, insurance losses from terrorism were viewed as so improbable that the risk was not explicitly mentioned or priced in any standard policy. Following the 9/11 attacks, most insurers swung to the other extreme: they refused to offer coverage at all rather than attempting to calculate a premium reflecting their best estimate of the risk that also incorporated the ambiguity associated with the likelihood of future terrorist attacks (Kunreuther and Pauly 2005). Before 9/11, terrorism coverage was free, and then its price was exorbitant.

We have argued that this is an anomaly, because expected-profit-maximizing insurance firms could surely have calculated such a premium and offered this coverage at moderate premiums. Those few insurers who did provide terrorism insurance set very high premiums that increased premiums dramatically for property-casualty coverage or workers' compensation insurance. When some insurers did charge high premiums for terrorism coverage after 9/11, there were cries of profiteering from regulators, buyers, and buyers' advocates. Logically, it is not correct to assert massive overcharging when information about a loss probability is incomplete, as was the case with the likelihood of a future terrorist attack, especially when some buyers were willing to purchase insurance at the stated, though high, price. Whether a premium is too high cannot be determined on the basis of different views of insurers and politicians for event probabilities where there is limited knowledge. Studies should be undertaken to estimate the probability and consequences of future events with greater certainty. Creativity here should be positively received by all interested parties. But, even in the absence of such studies, it is not reasonable to assume that the likelihood of further terrorist attacks jumped so substantially as implied by short-term premium increases.

Insurers knew about the possibility of terrorism (from the 1993 World Trade Center attack) but did not appear to explicitly include these events in generating scenarios about future losses from terrorism. But requiring all insurance companies to operate as if they were managed by *Star Trek*'s Mr. Spock is a difficult thing to do. It is not clear what steps one can take to force them to pay more attention to such low-probability events prior to the occurrence of a future disaster, and to deal with them with less emotion after losing billions. As Nassim Taleb (2007) notes, we may never think about the existence of a black swan until we see one. There is nothing wrong with behaving as if black swans were very unlikely to appear before one actually sees one. Most people do not check life vests under their airplane seat but assume they are there if they should need them.

Supply-Side Policy Solution Two: Higher Premiums Should Mirror Increases in Risk

This is precisely the terrorism case just discussed, except that here, the explicit premium for standard commercial coverage was zero before

9/11. Following large-scale losses, insurers and reinsurers belatedly recognized the risk and raised their premiums, even when there was incomplete or inconclusive evidence to suggest that the risk had changed. One reason that they did this was that they had difficulty obtaining reinsurance to cover large losses and raising new capital for this purpose except at extremely high interest rates (Kunreuther and Pauly 2005). Hence they did not have the financial capacity to provide coverage at lower premiums while still maintaining their classification by rating agencies such as A.M. Best, Standard & Poor's, and Moody's that judge the soundness of a company in part by examining its surplus and reserves for catastrophic events.

In addition to this institutional concern, a core issue related to this anomaly is that insurers have a tendency to increase their premiums following a large-scale loss because they exhibit availability biases, just like consumers do. For example, insurers may have exhibited an availability bias after 9/11 by estimating the probability of another terrorist attack to have become extraordinarily high without any substantive evidence to defend this position. With the benefit of hindsight, we can say that there was a bias because no subsequent attack has been perpetrated in the United States. But an attack could have happened. So what kind of public policy might deal with this?

After a low-probability catastrophic event occurs, it is unlikely (though not impossible) that a similar one will occur in the near future if the events are considered to be independent, such as a flood or hurricane with a 100-year return period. With respect to man-made catastrophes such as a chemical accident or terrorist attack, it is more complicated to estimate the odds because the initial event may signal future disasters but it also leads to increased vigilance. If the probability of a future disaster has not changed significantly, but insurers are behaving as if it has, an independent but government-organized insurance entity might therefore stand ready to provide coverage temporarily at only moderately increased premiums by filling in for traditional sellers who have temporarily withdrawn from the market.

If private insurers don't want to provide coverage because of the availability bias, government-sponsored insurance should be able to more than cover its costs in the long run, even without raising premiums

drastically after a disaster. Sometimes, both private insurers and governmental entities (like Citizens in Florida) could be adversely affected
by a sequence of extreme events: one hurricane or one terrorist attack
or even one capital submarket panic will occasionally follow another.
However, the likelihood that a series of extreme events will repeat itself
in the next few years is extremely low, so there should be little reason for
insurers to raise premiums very much to reflect this risk unless the cost
of capital is increased to reflect the concern of investors in committing
funds to insurers.

Supply-Side Policy Solution Three: Public Sector Involvement for Catastrophe Risks

What mix of public and private policies might be appropriate for events
in which losses are highly correlated and whose risks are ambiguous?
The problem here is that no one, whether in the private sector, in government, or in academia knows the "truth," so any situation must be one in
which someone is taking a chance that others think is unwise. Consider
the behavior of insurers and reinsurers following a large loss. At least
for a time, some insurers tend to withdraw from providing this coverage. One reason for this is that reinsurers are no longer eager to provide
insurers with protection against catastrophic losses. This presumably
happens because, after events such as 9/11 or a natural disaster, the supply of capital normally provided to reinsurers and primary insurers from
individual investors, pension funds, and endowments often dries up
because investors share the same availability bias.

Given that government does not have the capital constraints that
insurers and reinsurers face, it could function as a temporary reinsurer
against catastrophic losses should another large-scale disaster occur.
One problem here is the old adage, "nothing is more permanent than the
temporary." Pennsylvania still levies a tax on wine and liquor enacted
to temporarily cover the cost of disaster relief following the Johnstown
Flood of 1936, an excise tax increased several times in the years since the
flood occurred. Similarly, there could be concern that it might prove difficult to remove temporary public insurance, since there probably would

be some buyers who would like it and some public employees who would benefit from it.

Government provision of insurance or reinsurance at premiums close to pre-catastrophe levels, or guarantees of reserves for reinsurance, are not costless. Usually, the expense will be borne by taxpayers in the form of a potential – and potentially large – future tax liability should disaster strike again soon or should the extent of losses be greater than anticipated. At one level, such a policy has a desirable effect, as it spreads the risk of a rare but high-loss event over all taxpayers, a much larger pool of people or wealth than any reinsurer or capital market could likely assemble. As Paul A. Samuelson said, "We, Inc." may efficiently bear risk in many situations (Samuelson 1964). But the risk borne by each taxpayer is likely proportional to that person's tax share and not related to his or her attitude toward risk, so this is not ideal insurance.

Collecting prespecified taxes that vary with the risk facing particular individuals or regions might be a way of equalizing the expected net benefit from the plan. For example, the government could decide to levy an extra tax that would fall more heavily on people who own more property in places where data indicates a higher risk of a terrorist attack. In the end, the decision on the amounts that different citizens should be taxed depends on society's view of who should pay. This decision should be made in advance of a disaster rather than in the chaos of the moment.

Supply-Side Policy Solution Four: Regulation of Reserves – Safety-First Meets Regulation

We argued in the section on insurance supply that insurance firms, especially those concerned with the level of reserves, may choose strategies inconsistent with expected profit maximization. In particular, management may choose a level of reserves that increases the likelihood that the insurer survives an expectedly large total loss beyond that implied by the benchmark profit-maximizing model of supply, but we also noted that in many cases, public regulators require a certain minimum level of reserves to reduce the likelihood of insurer insolvency to a politically acceptable level. Patricia Born (2001) shows, however, that most insurers were holding reserves above the legal minimum. For this reason she does not find any significant negative effect of such regulation on profits in general. The small impact of the regulation she does find is concentrated not surprisingly on insurers with low reserves who are forced to raise them.

The level of reserves determines the probability that an insurer will be able to pay all claims in full, versus the possibility that it will be able to only make partial payment and may become bankrupt.[5] If consumers utilize an expected utility-based model, they may prefer to purchase coverage in which there is some chance of partial protection following a catastrophic loss rather than paying the additional higher premium associated with greater protection. That is, they may want to share some of the risk of a large but very rare total loss when the insurer does not have the financial ability to pay all the claims. The insurer could then remain solvent since policyholders were enabling the firm to retain enough assets to continue as a going concern.[6]

When and why might regulation come in? One possibility is that regulators are unaware of or inattentive to consumers' willingness a priori to pay lower premiums in return for some chance of receiving only partial payment from a low-probability, high-consequence event. To protect the insured against this situation, regulators may choose a level of reserves higher than the socially optimal level. The other possibility is that, in their role as guardians of product quality, regulators set minimum reserve levels. Even if most insurers follow safety-first principles, regulations may be designed to address those firms that pursue other objectives. For example, it is surely possible that some insurers with relatively low reserves might try to sell coverage at high prices that buyers would pay because they were unaware of the danger of insolvency.

Is there an anomaly here? If expected utility-maximizing but misinformed consumers place too low a value on safety by inadvertently choosing risky insurers, then regulation may be needed that deals with market failure rather than anomalous behavior. But suppose regulators choose, for political reasons, to require insurance reserves so that the insurer is too safe and the resulting premiums higher than if insurers and informed consumers were free to operate on their own terms. Regulation will have created an anomaly in that insurers hold more reserves than they would prefer and consumers are forced to pay higher premiums than they would otherwise choose. The result may lead to market failure in that insurers do not offer policies against this risk because demand is too low to cover their fixed costs of designing and marketing the product.

SUMMARY

True anomalies can be found in insurance markets on both the demand and supply sides. On the demand side, a variety of policies are available to deal with anomalies, ranging from attempts to improve the information available to consumers and how choices are framed through default options to situations in which the choice is either mandated or subsidized by government. On the supply side, it is not only the insurance firm or its management that needs to be influenced, but also investors who provide capital to insurance and reinsurance firms. All these decision makers need to avoid fixating on recent large losses and consider the likelihood of future claims payments. Some new capital instruments might help, but ultimately the solution here involves government as a potential alternative source of funds or guarantor of capital following a major disaster.

Innovations in Insurance Markets through Multiyear Contracts

INTRODUCTION

This chapter focuses on a proposal to help insurance markets avoid some of the worst current supply-side and demand-side anomalies. Multiyear policies can satisfy two key objectives of insurance – controlling actual losses and providing financial protection against the consequences of those losses – in ways that annual policies, typical of current insurance contractual arrangements, do not.

Using examples of multiyear insurance currently offered in the areas of life and health care coverage, we explore the challenges involved in developing multiyear insurance for standard property coverage under the current regulatory system. We further propose that the government consider modifying the National Flood Insurance Program so it is structured as a multiyear policy tied to the property rather than the individual.

TWO OBJECTIVES OF INSURANCE

Insurance has a dual role in dealing with risk. First, it should cause individuals, as well as private and public sector organizations, to continue to adopt protective measures when the benefits from such measures exceed their costs, thus reducing future losses from health, safety, and environmental risks. Second, insurance provides financial protection through claims payments following an unexpected loss. Let us consider how each of these objectives is related to multiple time periods.

Objective One: Controlling Future Losses

Actions that are cost-effective in preventing future losses are often not undertaken by those who could benefit from them. The goal should be to encourage individuals at risk to invest in such protective or preventive measures. Insurance can offer incentives to better achieve this objective through premium adjustments that reflect the lower claims when one invests in mitigation or loss-reduction actions.

In insurance markets in which premiums accurately reflect expected future losses, the premium reduction associated with loss reduction measures that reduce the likelihood and magnitude of insurance claims would offer an ideal incentive for encouraging such investments. Individuals who stop smoking have a lower risk of getting lung cancer than those who go through one or two packs of cigarettes per day.[1] Cars that have air bags or automatic seat belts reduce the likelihood of severe injuries or death from an accident; insurance that offers premium reductions equal to what safety devices would save in life insurance claims would provide the right incentives for buying and using those devices.

Residences and commercial establishments that have stronger roofs are likely to experience less damage from hurricanes than poorly designed structures, as highlighted by research by the Insurance Institute for Business & Home Safety's Research Center in Chester County, South Carolina. A full-scale windstorm test demonstration was conducted during which a pair of thirteen-hundred-square-foot, two-story homes was subjected to severe thunderstorm and straight-line wind conditions, including wind gusts of 90 mph to 100 mph. One test house was built to the IBHS FORTIFIED for Safer Living® standard, while the other was built to conventional construction standards. The conventionally constructed home collapsed when wind gusts reached 96 mph, while the FORTIFIED home remained standing with little damage (Figures 12.1a and b).

The insurance-oriented model most appealing today in this regard takes us back to the nineteenth century. At that time, the factory mutuals required industrial companies to invest in protective measures before issuing an insurance policy and regularly inspected the factory after coverage was in force. Without such requirements, the existence of insurance

Figure 12.1a and b. During a windstorm test demonstration, the house constructed to conventional standards (left) collapsed when wind gusts reached 96 mph. The house built to the IBHS FORTIFIED for Safer Living standard (right) remained standing.
Source: The Insurance Institute for Business & Home Safety.

for damages might itself cause underuse of preventive activities, a kind of moral hazard. Poor risks had their policies canceled; premium reductions were given to factories that instituted loss-prevention measures (Bainbridge 1952).

The Boston Manufacturers Mutual Insurance Company worked with industrial lantern manufacturers to encourage the firms to develop safer designs, and then mandated that all its policyholders use lanterns from companies whose products met its specifications if they wanted to be insured. The Spinners Mutual insured only buildings in which sprinkler systems were installed. The Manufacturers Mutual in Providence, Rhode Island, developed specifications for fire hoses and advised mills to buy their hoses only from companies that met these standards (Kunreuther and Roth, Sr. 1998). Hartford Steam Boiler provided insurance only if a boiler met certain standards upon inspection (Er, Kunreuther, and Rosenthal 1998). Sometimes it was administratively cheaper to keep track of what precautions the firm was taking than to make direct estimates of risk and adjust insurance premiums, so insurers appropriately got involved in the actual design, production, and installation of risk-reduction measures.

Objective Two: Providing Financial Protection

As emphasized by the benchmark model of demand, a principal role that insurance plays is to provide coverage against losses that would severely affect the wealth or consumption of an individual or organization. The challenges on both the demand and supply sides in meeting this objective highlighted in earlier chapters are magnified if insurance is bought and sold for risks that grow or persist over a long period of time.

On the demand side, consumers and firms need to be convinced that if they do not suffer a loss, they should celebrate their good fortune in being insured rather than perceive their premiums as wasted. They need to look at future benefits of insurance from a longer perspective than the few years during which they paid premiums but made no claims. Individuals need to understand that insurance offers those at risk the opportunity to avoid a much larger loss in the future at a relatively small cost today. If they do suffer damage and make a claim, they need to be assured that they will not have their insurance policy cancelled or experience large premium increases.

On the supply side, insurers may not be willing to offer coverage against catastrophic events that affect everyone in a given geographic area if they are concerned about suffering a significant loss in their surplus that could lead to severe future financial problems and even insolvency. As pointed out in Chapter 2, when risks are independent, as in the case of automobile accidents, fire damage to property, illnesses, and most diseases, then the insurer can rely on the law of large numbers to protect itself against such an event. On the other hand, for events in which the potential losses are highly correlated, such as claims from severe hurricanes and floods, the insurer may be unwilling to provide protection against a large number of individuals in hazard-prone areas at a moderate premium. It wants to be assured that it can cover the rare but possible catastrophic losses through risk transfer instruments from the private sector (e.g., reinsurance, catastrophe bonds), diversified across a large number of areas, or from the public sector through state catastrophe funds or federal reinsurance.

THE POTENTIALLY COMPLEMENTARY NATURE OF THE TWO OBJECTIVES

If individuals and firms invest in cost-effective loss-reduction measures for risky events, insurers are more likely to expand their provision of coverage because the likelihood of suffering a large loss with their existing portfolio is now lower relative to their assets and more predictable. To illustrate this point, suppose that insurers used premium discounts to encourage property owners in a hazard-prone area to invest in a risk-reduction measure such as bolting house walls to foundations to reduce losses from future earthquakes. Suppose the damage to each home is reduced by $20,000 from a severe earthquake with an annual probability of 1/100 and the insurer has covered 1,000 homes in the area. Then the insurer's total loss will be reduced by $20 million should an earthquake occur and the reduction in its premiums, if they reflect expected losses and a loading cost of fifty percent, will only be $300,000.[2] A prespecified level of reserves prior to the adoption of the mitigation measure will now protect a larger number of policies.

The lower premiums offered by the insurer to those adopting the mitigation may also have demand-side effects. Offering buyers a way to lower their premiums may make buying coverage more attractive and lead some uninsured to purchase a policy. In other words, when insurers provide economic incentives (e.g., premium reductions) to control future losses (Objective One), they can also enhance their ability to provide financial protection (Objective Two) for more property owners at risk.

Furthermore, insurers may be willing to charge lower insurance premiums reflecting not just their lower claims, but also their reduced need for risk transfer instruments to protect themselves against future catastrophic losses. These lower premiums will stimulate even more demand for coverage. However, while performance of loss reduction measures may complement the demand for insurance, the presence of generous coverage without premium adjustments may discourage investments in loss reduction measures.

A ROLE FOR MULTIYEAR INSURANCE

We now turn to the role of insurance policies designed to provide multiyear coverage in reducing risk and providing individuals with protection against future losses in ways consistent with the above two objectives. As pointed out earlier, insurance buyers often tend to focus on the short run and as a result do not invest in loss-reduction measures if the upfront cost is high relative to the short-term benefits. They also cancel their policies if they have not collected on their policy in the short run. Multiyear insurance has the potential of dealing with both these problems in ways that annual policies cannot. It also has the potential of reducing the costs to insurers of marketing policies and avoids search costs for consumers whose annual policies are canceled and are now trying to find another carrier.

Two Alternative Multiyear Policies

We now consider two forms that multiyear insurance policies could take. The simplest but also the most challenging one of the two is to extend the term of insurance for many years and charge a commensurate premium before the period of coverage begins. For example, a person might buy homeowners' or health insurance for the next twenty years at a single lump sum premium. This would lock in both the availability of coverage and the premium. The insurer would offer a premium discount to those who invest in loss-reduction measures. But it would require buyers to come up with a large upfront payment in order to purchase the policy. The originator of this type of insurance contract in the United States is Benjamin Franklin, who started the Philadelphia Contributorship for Insuring of Houses from Fire in 1752. In return for the large fixed premium at the time of insurance purchase, the interest earned on this "insurance investment" covered the annual premiums on the property.

Another less financially demanding alternative is termed *guaranteed renewability at class-average rates*, which has been proposed as a form of health insurance (Cochrane 1995; Pauly, Kunreuther, and Hirth 1994; Pauly et al. 2011). The intuition here is that the person in effect buys two insurance policies in each period, one to cover expected benefits for the next year, and the other to cover any jumps in future premiums associated with a change in risk status in the upcoming year. In return, the insurer promises not to single out any insured for premium increases based on changes in his or her risk or levels of claims, although it still reserves the power to increase premiums for all policyholders. Here, some of the long-term premium is paid in advance, but not all of it.

Individual (but not group) health insurance was sold for many years with guaranteed renewability protection, even before being required by law. The cost of this provision raises health insurance premiums, but they are still usually affordable even for young buyers (Pauly and Herring, 2006).

Insurers do offer some long-term or multiyear contracts for life coverage. Similarly, term-life insurance is usually guaranteed renewable. It is typically sold with premiums locked in for five to ten years; buyers can choose whether they want to pay extra for such guarantees, and they may drop coverage at any time. Policyholders are then certain what their life insurance premiums will be over the next five or ten years, regardless of what happens to their health or the overall mortality rate. Igal Hendel and Alessandro Lizzeri (2003) examine 150 term life insurance contracts, some of which have level premiums for five, ten, or twenty years, while others are one-year renewable policies. They show that, on average, the extra prepayment of premiums to protect consumers against being reclassified into a higher risk category for a fixed period of time is more costly over the total period of coverage than a series of annual term policies that can be renewed but under which premiums may fluctuate from year to year. However, if individuals view the stability of premiums as an important attribute in their utility function, they may prefer the multiyear life insurance policy with level premiums over one-year policies.

Challenges in Developing Multiyear Property Insurance

In his seminal work on uncertainty and welfare economics, Kenneth Arrow defined "the absence of marketability for an action which is identifiable, technologically possible and capable of influencing some individuals' welfare ... as a failure of the existing market to provide a means whereby the services can be both offered and demanded upon the payment of a price" (Arrow 1963, 945). Several factors may have contributed to the lack of marketability of multiyear insurance at stable annual premiums for protecting property owners against losses from fire, theft, and large-scale natural disasters. We discuss elements that affect both the supply and demand sides.

On the supply side, political pressure frequently causes insurance rates to be artificially low for those in high-hazard areas. The result is that the risks most subject to catastrophic losses also become the most unattractive for insurers to cover. Forced to charge low premiums ostensibly to help buyers, some insurers withdraw from the market altogether, harming potential buyers even more. Uncertainty regarding costs of capital and changes in risk over time may also deter insurers from providing multiyear policies. Of course, insurers could add a component in their premiums to account for the costs and risks created by these factors if the regulators would allow them to do so. Today insurance regulators, presumed to be representing consumers' interests, are unlikely to allow these costs to be embedded in the approved premiums.

Even in the absence of rate regulations, insurers might also have difficulty dealing with possible changes in the level of risk over time. For example, global warming could trigger more intense weather-related disasters or local environmental degradation might change the risk landscape in the next several decades. One way to address this concern would be to have renegotiable contracts every few years based on new information validated by the scientific community in much the same way that there are renegotiable mortgages with adjustable rates.

On the demand side, those contemplating a multiyear contract may worry about the financial solvency of their insurer over a long period. Consumers might also fear being overcharged if insurers set premiums that reflect the uncertainty associated with long-term risks or worry that insurers will renege on coverage or services. Thus those who have not suffered a loss for ten years but have a twenty-five-year policy may believe the premiums are unfairly priced. It is therefore essential that the design of a multiyear contract anticipates these concerns and be transparent to the policyholder.

Potential Benefits of Multiyear Property Insurance

Multiyear property insurance could encourage individuals to invest in cost-effective loss-reduction measures. Many homeowners are unwilling to incur the high upfront cost associated with these investments relative to the small premium discount – reflecting the expected reduction in annual insured losses – that they would receive the following year. If a multiyear policy with premiums reflecting risk were coupled with a long-term home-improvement loan and both tied to the mortgage, the reduction in insurance premiums could exceed the annual loan payment.

Regulators would have to permit insurers to charge premiums reflecting risk so that premium reductions could be given to those investing in these measures. Insurers or banks holding mortgages could offer mitigation loans to encourage adaptation measures. The cost of the loan each year should be less than the premium reduction if these mitigation measures are cost-effective. The social welfare benefits of these long-term contracts could be significant: there will be less damage to property, lower costs to insurers for protecting against catastrophic losses, more secure mortgages, and lower costs to the government for disaster assistance.

To compare the expected benefits of annual versus multiyear contracts, Dwight Jaffee, Howard Kunreuther, and Erwann Michel-Kerjan (2010) have developed a simple two-period model in a competitive market setting. The authors show that a two-period policy reduces the marketing costs for insurers compared with one-period policies, while lowering the search costs to consumers, relative to a situation in which their insurer might be able to cancel the policy at the end of the first period. If the policyholder is permitted to cancel the two-period policy at the end of period one on learning that the cost of a policy for period two is low enough to justify paying a cancellation cost, then it is always optimal for the insurer to offer a two-period policy and for consumers to purchase them. The insurer will set the cancellation cost at a level that enables it to break even on policies canceled before the maturity date.

In developing any multiyear policy to be marketed by the private sector, the premiums need to reflect risk. This means insurers must charge high premiums to those who are already high risks when they initiate purchase – those who have houses in earthquake-prone areas or who already have chronic and costly health conditions. The time to buy a multiyear policy is before the risk increase occurs. The incentive to buy such insurances is provided by the alternative of risk-based increases in premiums.

Permitting insurers to charge prices that enable them to earn normal profits provides them with incentives to develop new products. Under the current state-regulated arrangements in which many insurance commissioners have limited insurers' ability to charge risk-based premiums in hazard-prone areas, no insurance company would entertain the possibility of marketing a homeowner's policy greater than one year. Insurers would be concerned about the regulator clamping down on them now or in the future regarding what price they could charge, so that a multiyear contract would not be feasible from a financial point of view.

For the private sector to want to market coverage, there needs to be sufficient demand to cover the fixed and administrative costs of developing and marketing the product. Demand should not be a problem in the case of homeowners' coverage, because banks and financial institutions normally require insurance as a condition for a mortgage. The open question is how to make a multiyear policy attractive to consumers who may have a choice between purchasing this insurance or a standard one-year contract. Regulators will still have a role to play in monitoring insurers to make sure that they have sufficient surplus on hand and are charging a sufficiently high premium to reduce the chance of insolvency to an acceptably low level.

Even if regulators permitted insurers to price property coverage freely, how can it deal with uncertainty about variations in risks and expected benefits over multiple periods? Providers of long-term care insurance and guaranteed renewable health insurance now face a similar problem. Uncertainty about changes in the risk of the causal event, and even more important, uncertainty about changes in the dollar amount of damages, must be taken into account by insurers. Hedges potentially exist against some aspects of future risk – for example, against economy-wide inflation – and, in principle, there could be futures markets to hedge against losses from natural disasters in specific areas or the relative price of health care.

MULTIYEAR FLOOD INSURANCE AS A PROTOTYPE MODEL

Given the tension between regulators and the insurance industry as well as the challenges facing private insurers with respect to offering multiperiod policies, we believe it would be easiest to introduce the broader use of multiyear policies by focusing on flood insurance, which in the United States is provided by a single insurer – the federal government through the National Flood Insurance Program (NFIP).[3]

Why Buy a Multiyear Flood Insurance Policy?

A multiyear flood insurance program would offer homeowners residing in flood-prone areas a fixed premium for a prespecified period of time (e.g., five, ten, or twenty years).[4] If the homeowner sold his or her house before the end of the policy period, then the insurance policy would automatically be transferred to the new property owner at the same rate. From the perspective of the relevant stakeholders – homeowners, the federal government, banks and other financial institutions, and the taxpayer – there are several reasons such long-term flood insurance policies would be a great improvement over the current annual policies.

As noted previously, it would provide financial incentives for property owners to invest in cost-effective mitigation measures by taking a long-term home improvement loan. If flood insurance were required for all homeowners residing in hazard-prone areas, additional financial revenue would be generated over time from a much larger policy base than currently available. That larger base would produce larger total claims, but the spread of risk across multiple geographic areas would help risk pooling and spread insurer fixed costs across a large number of policyholders. Multiyear insurance would also prevent homeowners in high flood risk areas from cancelling policies after several years, thus reducing the magnitude of disaster assistance.

Consider the flood in August 1998 that damaged property in northern Vermont. Of the 1,549 victims of this disaster, the Federal Emergency Management Agency found that eighty-four percent of the homeowners in Special Flood Hazard Areas did not have insurance, even though forty-five percent of these individuals were supposedly required to purchase this coverage (Tobin and Calfee 2005). Some of these uninsured individuals obtained low interest disaster relief loans from the Small Business Administration, which represents a cost to U.S. taxpayers. Even with this form of assistance, these victims were forced to bear the costs of recovery using their own resources.

Pricing Multiyear Flood Insurance

Pricing a multiyear flood insurance policy so that premiums reflect risk means taking into account the possible impacts of global warming, principally intensity of future hurricanes and rising sea levels. There is considerable uncertainty surrounding the estimates of what the risks associated with losses from hurricanes and flooding may be ten, twenty, or thirty years from now. To develop actuarially based flood premiums, there is a need for accurate flood maps and for FEMA to update them regularly to reflect these long-term changes and define a pricing formula that evolves over time as maps are revised (U.S. GAO 2008).

To understand more fully how climate change is likely to affect flood risk in the United States in the coming years and decades, a set of realistic scenarios with respect to losses from inland flooding and storm surge from hurricanes that reflect scientists' best estimates regarding climate change are needed. To be of most use to insurers and federal, state, and local governments, scientific studies should address the following questions and provide appropriate uncertainty bands surrounding the relevant estimates:

- How much will sea levels rise and how will natural environmental protection (such as wetlands) change over the next half century in five-year intervals in specific parts of our coasts? What effect will these changes have on riverine flooding and storm surges from hurricanes?
- How many major hurricanes (Category 3 or greater) are estimated to form in the Atlantic Ocean in the next six months to eighteen months (short term) and in the next ten years to thirty years (long term)? Of those hurricanes, how many are estimated to make landfall? How far inland is damage likely to extend, and how closely can the storm tracks be predicted?
- Do today's topological maps accurately reflect risk of inundation? What steps are needed to improve them and update them over time?

Recent analyses by insurers and modeling firms using the latest estimates by scientists studying climate change enable one to undertake simulations of alternative scenarios of global warming's effect on the price of flood insurance for multiyear policies (Heweijer, Ranger, and Ward 2009). A recent study by Lloyd's of London (2008) in conjunction with the modeling firm Risk Management Solutions indicated that the potential risk from sea level rise could double the average annual losses from storm surge by 2030.

One of the principal findings from these studies is that risk-reducing measures can reduce the losses from future disasters significantly. For example, the Lloyd's study showed that loss-reduction measures could reduce annual losses from storm surge for properties in high-risk coastal communities in the 2030s to below today's levels, with high-risk property losses being reduced by seventy percent through investment in measures to the property and flood defenses such as levees. This suggests that multiyear flood insurance coupled with long-term home improvement loans that give homeowners the incentive to invest in loss reduction measures will make a significant difference in reducing the damage from future floods and hurricanes.

Moving from the Status Quo

The evidence on increasing losses from disasters, notably floods and hurricanes, indicates that the current structure of the National Flood Insurance Program is not adequate to cover truly catastrophic floods. It is thus somewhat limited in achieving its twin objectives of reducing property losses from future disasters and providing protection to those who suffer severe water damage for a simple reason: many of these residents do not invest in risk-reduction measures voluntarily and cancel their flood insurance coverage if they haven't suffered a loss for several years.

Those who purchase insurance policies often have a difficult time understanding what risks are covered, what risks are not, and the basis for being charged a specific rate. The problem is likely to be compounded for a longer-term contract. The opportunity to educate consumers about the basis for the premiums being charged lies in providing more detail on the nature of the risk covered and the amount charged for different levels of protection. It would be very useful for the NFIP to reveal this information much more clearly so that homeowners can make tradeoffs between costs and expected benefits, which they are not easily able to do with information currently provided them.

Richard Thaler and Cass Sunstein (2008) argue for this type of disclosure by proposing a form of government regulation that they term RECAP (Record, Evaluate, and Compare Alternative Prices). In the case of flood insurance, the government would disclose the elements of the insurance program in a form easy for the homeowners to understand. What risks are they covered against and which ones are they not? What types of premium reductions will the policyholder obtain for investing in specific mitigation measures? What might happen to premiums when they are renewed after a prespecified time and how will the change in premiums be determined?

The flood insurance program should combine the strengths of the public and private sectors and take into account how people make decisions so that the key interested parties will consider solutions to be win-win propositions. Real estate developers, the construction industry, and financial institutions play an important role in promoting this concept. Third-party inspectors will be needed to certify that the adaptation measures are in place and building codes are enforced.

The NFIP may also want to partner with communities to encourage homeowners to invest in loss-reduction measures by providing "seals of approval" indicating how safe the structure is with respect to future flooding. This may increase property values for these homes in the area, thus serving as an additional incentive for homeowners to undertake these measures, knowing that it will likely increase the selling price of their residences.

Whether decision makers will view multiyear flood insurance policies as an attractive alternative depends on how the program is designed and presented to key interested parties in relation to the current structure of the NFIP. If the stakeholders have a common understanding of the goals and objectives of an innovative and comprehensive disaster management program, we may be able to trade a status quo that encourages myopic thinking for a long-term strategy for reducing losses in this new era of catastrophes. The renewal of the National Flood Insurance Program in July 2012 authorized studies by the Federal Emergency Management Agency and the National Academy of Sciences to examine ways of incorporating risk-based premiums coupled with a means-tested insurance voucher into the program. If these two principles are adopted by the NFIP, the likelihood of multiyear insurance policies will be enhanced. (See Title II in http://www.govtrack.us/congress/bills/112/hr4348/text)

SUMMARY

Multiyear policies have the potential of improving our ability to satisfy the two principal objectives of insurance – reducing future losses and providing financial protection – more effectively than annual policies. Individuals residing in hazard-prone areas would be encouraged to invest in cost-effective loss-reduction measures. Presently they are unwilling to incur the high upfront costs of these measures in return for the small premium savings on a typical one-year policy. If insurers are able to charge premiums that reflect risks for a five-year or ten-year period, then the reduction in premiums is likely to be larger than the costs of a home improvement loan for undertaking the mitigation measures.

The overall benefits of a multiyear insurance program include coverage to homeowners for damage to property, lower costs to insurers for protecting against catastrophic losses, and lower costs to the government for disaster assistance. And a policyholder could be protected against a large change in premiums in the future because of unexpected changes in that person's risk level.

The National Flood Insurance Program offers an opportunity to experiment with multiyear policies as the federal government assumes the risk today and is concerned with the lack of investment in loss-reduction measures. If premiums reflect risk and insurance vouchers are given to those requiring special treatment, then multiyear flood insurance should encourage homeowners to invest in cost-effective loss-reduction measures since the resulting premium reductions will be greater than the annual cost of mitigation loans to cover the upfront expenses associated with the mitigation measure.

There are still a set of open questions that need to be addressed regarding the pricing of coverage. For example, premiums for hurricane coverage rely on the impact of global warming on sea level rise and storm surge from hurricanes. Premiums for health coverage depend on the model of lifetime evolution of chronic conditions. In these and other cases, compared to unexpected and wide premiums fluctuations, even a less than perfect model is likely to be beneficial to insurers and consumers.

13

Publicly Provided Social Insurance

Up to this point we have been primarily concerned with private insurance markets in which buyers and/or sellers behave in different ways than postulated by conventional economic norms of individual and firm choices under risk. But there are some kinds of insurance for large segments of the population that are financed and sometimes produced by the public rather than the private sector: flood insurance discussed in the previous chapter, insurance for retirement income (Social Security), insurance against job loss (unemployment insurance), and insurance for medical care costs (Medicare and Medicaid, to be expanded under health care reform).

Although potential anomalous buyer behavior provides some of the rationale for the development of these types of publicly financed insurance (as was the case with flood insurance when the private sector stopped offering coverage after the Mississippi floods of 1927), an equally if not more important rationale for such coverage is based on equity or distributional considerations. More specifically, some people have incomes in retirement or after job loss that others in society judge to be too low; some people would not obtain what others regard as adequate amounts of medical care. These are deemed unacceptable situations that the public sector steps in to correct.

In this chapter, we consider how these *social welfare* rationales interact with the potential for anomalous behavior. We first consider the rationale for government subsidy to social insurance by showing that private markets may produce socially undesirable outcomes even when there are no anomalies, even when informed buyers maximize expected utility and insurance firms determine the optimal price and amount of coverage that maximizes their expected profit. We then consider how the potential for anomalous behavior by buyers or private sellers interacts with this more traditional rationale. When people behave anomalously, how does that affect the rationale for or the design of social insurance? When considerations of welfare, equity, and anomalous behavior are taken into account, how can these programs satisfy the goals of allocating resources efficiently while at the same time meeting equity or distributional considerations? Concretely, do social insurances provide the appropriate incentives for risk protection and risk mitigation?

We also ask the subsidiary questions of whether such insurances are better supplied by private firms or the public sector. We give the most extensive treatment to health insurance because of the prominence of Medicare and health insurance reform recently. The question as to what role the public sector should play in providing protection for individuals' health, labor income, and retirement needs is too important to ignore in any discussion of insurance and insurance markets.

GOALS AND BEHAVIOR UNDER SOCIAL INSURANCE

Social insurance is designed to address the public's concerns with goals such as protection from high (possibly bankrupting) medical expenses, access to needed medical care, and inadequate income after retirement or job loss. These concerns arise in large part as a form of altruism that uses taxes from the entire population to subsidize insurance protection. Historically, social insurance subsidies in the United States have been targeted at special groups, such as older people, the unemployed, young children and their mothers, and the disabled. All taxpayers provide financial support for certain insurances but not for other items of consumption like clothing or entertainment (Pauly 1970).

The special character of this redistribution and reallocation of resources can be illustrated with an example. Suppose lower-income consumers make their health insurance decisions based on maximizing their expected utility. It is surely possible that many people in this group who do buy insurance would choose such very low coverage that fellow citizens, especially those with higher incomes and altruistic concerns, would feel it to be inadequate.

It is also likely that some people in lower-income groups would rationally choose to purchase no coverage, perhaps because health insurance
is not attractive at current prices compared to other uses of their limited
income. They may say – and it would be true – that they cannot afford
coverage, in the sense that it would bite too deeply into their ability to
buy other things. Eschewing something you cannot afford in this sense is
rational. The low-income individuals may also reason that if they needed
medical care and were uninsured, they could go to the emergency room
for free (Herring 2005). For these reasons it makes sense for some
low-income people to avoid health insurance and for less risk-averse
people to avoid expensive health insurance.

This behavior, while seemingly rational for these individuals, may not
be socially optimal if others have concern for this group's health status
or financial protection. Hence, there may be a demand for a social insurance program that helps people get sufficiently generous coverage – to
be financed, if necessary, through public expenditures. This altruistic
demand was a large part of the basis for the passage of Medicare (directed
primarily at low-income elderly) and Medicaid (directed primarily at
low-income children and their parents), and was also an important consideration in the recent health care reform legislation, which subsidizes
and mandates health insurance purchase.

The conflict between rationality and altruism is only part of the story,
however. There surely are also some people who underestimate their
expected benefits from health insurance relative to the premiums they
would have to pay and so choose to be uninsured, even though their
incomes are not very low. More specifically, reasonably well-off young
people sometimes misjudge their vulnerability and believe that they will
not incur high medical expenses.

Table 13.1 shows the distribution of uninsured people by family
income relative to the poverty line in 2008 (before the recession hit).
It shows that the proportion uninsured falls as income rises, just as one
would expect. But it is perhaps surprising that, even in households with
incomes above 300 percent of the poverty line (combining the 300-400
percent and greater than 400 percent rows in the table), there were 11.6
million uninsured people, representing twenty-six percent of the total
uninsured. These are households with incomes close to or above the

Table 13.1. *Insurance Status of Individuals under 65 by Relationship of Household Income to Federal Poverty Level (FPL): Numbers in Millions and Percent of Income Category*

% of Federal Poverty Level	Number in Millions (n) and % of Income Category	Uninsured	Government	Private	Total
<100%	n	11.4	17.0	5.7	34.1
	%	33.4%	49.8%	16.8%	100.0%
100–125%	n	3.6	4.5	3.1	11.2
	%	32.2%	40.5%	27.3%	100.0%
125–150%	n	3.7	3.8	4.0	11.5
	%	32.6%	33.1%	34.3%	100.0%
150–175%	n	2.8	2.9	4.7	10.5
	%	26.8%	28.1%	45.0%	100.0%
175–200%	n	3.0	2.4	5.5	10.9
	%	27.3%	21.9%	50.8%	100.0%
200–300%	n	8.8	7.0	27.9	43.7
	%	20.1%	16.0%	63.9%	100.0%
300–400%	n	4.6	3.8	28.3	36.7
	%	12.5%	10.4%	77.1%	100.0%
>400%	n	7.0	7.1	89.5	103.6
	%	6.8%	6.8%	86.4%	100.0%
Total	n	45.0	48.5	168.7	262.2

Source: Pauly 2010, p. 11. (Original data from the U.S. Census Bureau, Current Population Survey, March 2008 Supplement.)

Note: Weighted (n in millions); individuals reporting both government and private insurance are included in government insurance.

median household income in the United States, so they cannot be characterized as poor or even low income.

There is also evidence that many people perceive the premiums to be higher than they actually are (Yegian et al. 2000). They may prefer not to incur the search costs to determine the costs and provisions of health insurance given their belief that the probability that they will realize a net benefit from purchasing health insurance is below their threshold level of concern (Kunreuther and Pauly 2004; Pauly, Herring, and Song 2006). In short, some people may have been subject to demand-side anomalies that led them to remain uninsured. Reform of social insurance detects and corrects such anomalous behavior along with providing welfare benefits and satisfying altruistic taxpayer desires. And it seems that anomalous behavior leading to not purchasing insurance is more likely if a person's income is low than if it is high.

One can justify providing health insurance as social insurance without focusing strongly on anomalous behavior or misperceptions of the value of purchasing catastrophic coverage by some individuals. For the most part, the low-probability, high-cost character of other types of insurance that generate anomalies is not present with respect to health insurance. The policies that the great majority of the population buys include catastrophic coverage and coverage for routine illnesses. Furthermore, people do not drop their coverage because they make few claims during a given time period. In fact, more than eighty-five percent of people make at least some small claim on their health insurance in any year so in this sense they are likely to perceive health insurance to be a good investment as well as a vehicle for financial protection. But the ability of such programs to detect and correct anomalous behavior as well as behavior that distresses others is part of the argument for social insurance.

The risks covered by social insurance are viewed differently than other kinds of risks. For other kinds of insurance such as auto collision and fire insurance, we expect a non-negligible minority to rationally decline coverage on the grounds that its price is high relative to their demand for risk protection. Furthermore, many car owners and homeowners who do buy this insurance are required to do so as a condition for an auto loan or a mortgage. But we do not view the absence of insurance coverage against financial losses to these assets as a serious social problem.

These differences in theory are matched by what we actually do even now. If a single uninsured home burns down or an uninsured person's car is totaled, then the general public is not usually willing to come to the rescue with complete financial support. However, if an uninsured person requires medical attention, he or she can always go to a hospital emergency room and must be accepted for treatment there. (It is true, however, that hospitals will try to collect for the use of the emergency room from uninsured people who have money.) Society judges not having health insurance as being more harmful than not having one's car or house protected against loss.

Some people are privately willing to accept the risk of large health expenditures and/or low use of beneficial medical care by being uninsured rather than sacrificing other items of immediate consumption. We feel compelled to help them should personal disaster strike, but we do not want to be put in that situation. And so under health care reform we will both subsidize lower-income people to have insurance and mandate everyone to do so in order to avoid costly and poorly designed *ex post* assistance.

The history of Medicare further illustrates these points. When Medicare was passed in 1965, being age 65 or older was virtually synonymous with being poor and uninsured; most elderly had much lower incomes even with Social Security payments than the rest of the population, and little private insurance. The problem for this population was almost entirely one of affordability of insurance due to the high costs of private health insurance associated with their high use of care. Publicly provided Medicare insurance was viewed as the solution to the problems of social welfare and anomalous behavior, but it certainly helped that the great bulk of government subsidies then flowed to people who needed them.[1] Current health care reform has been more contentious precisely because the correlation between uninsurance and need is less strong in the under-sixty-five population, with many of the uninsured having incomes higher than the poverty line (though still below average).

Medicare and Social Security were social arrangements designed to improve the welfare of the target population, with the cost covered by taxpayers. Correcting anomalous behavior was not a major rationale for either plan, although it was recognized that some people who could afford insurance did not obtain it. To be sure, establishing a "trust fund" for Social Security and Medicare Part A (the part that covers hospitalization) made it appear that eventual beneficiaries were paying for their pensions and old-age health insurance during their working lives. The bulk of financing for the rest of Medicare comes from general tax revenues, with no long-term trust fund. In reality, the long-term financing for these programs was inadequate and this gesture toward designing self-supporting programs is hard to justify today.

CONTRASTING HEALTH AND PROPERTY INSURANCE

Social insurance is also long-term insurance, while many other insurances are not. To illustrate this point we compare health and property insurance. Health insurance differs from property insurance in several ways. An unusually large property insurance claim for an individual in one time period ordinarily does not change future expected losses to a large extent. Sizable property insurance losses are low-probability events not correlated for an individual over time. In contrast, although a very serious illness is also a relatively rare event, a chronic illness such as heart disease, cancer, or diabetes will often imply a risk of future large claims over a period of time. But even with health insurance, there is a diminishing effect with respect to payments over time. After four years following a claim in the top quintile, only about forty percent of people are still making above-average claims (Eichner, McClellan, and Wise 1998).

In contrast to the property-casualty case in which large premium increases after a loss are labeled as anomalous supply-side market behavior, raising a person's premium after a large loss is not anomalous in health insurance. Observing that someone's house was damaged by a hurricane last year does not imply that it is more likely to be damaged this year, but observing that someone's body was damaged by diabetes last year does imply that more harm may be done this year than if the person did not have the condition.

Hurricanes, floods, and earthquakes cause damage correlated across the insured population in a given area. In contrast, most illnesses are uncorrelated across individuals[2] but are correlated for any individual over time, leading to justifiably higher premiums if a person contracts an illness or has a preexisting condition. So public regulation in health insurance deals with those who are or who become high risks.

OTHER SOCIAL INSURANCES IN MORE DETAIL

Some of the arguments we have made in the health insurance example also apply to Social Security and unemployment insurance. Social Security was passed in part because of the belief that, without government intervention, many people would not save enough or buy enough annuity protection to assure adequate income in retirement. The question of whether people who fail to do so are behaving rationally (according to their preferences) or irrationally because they are not aware of the future or discount it too heavily was bypassed when Social Security was made law, precisely because the social concern of impoverished elderly demanded society's attention whatever the reason for individual under-provision of protection. If anything, the acceptability of paternalism for old age protection was stronger than that for health insurance.

But Social Security involves more than mandated insurance. It also has a sizeable redistribution component, because average benefits for low-wage workers are much higher relative to the earmarked taxes paid for Social Security than for high-wage workers. However, there is still a positive relationship between the benefits one receives upon retirement and the wages (and earmarked taxes) during one's working lifetime. In contrast, even in Medicare Part A, funded by earmarked taxes paid into a trust fund, there is no relationship between benefits generosity and what one paid in, as long as payments were made for the minimum time period needed to establish eligibility. For the other parts of Medicare, as noted previously, general tax financing, which is even more redistributive, is used. Thus we can say that the redistribution and welfare motive for social insurance seems much stronger for health insurance than for pension and annuity insurance.

Unemployment insurance further fills out the spectrum of social insurances because the taxes to pay for unemployment insurance are tied very directly to the risk of unemployment at a given firm. Still, we presumably have made unemployment insurance mandatory (though limited in coverage) for the same mix of reasons discussed earlier.

RISK REDUCTION AND PREVENTION IN SOCIAL INSURANCE

We noted earlier that it is efficient and equitable for markets to offer lower premiums to those who take action to reduce future losses. Alternatively, loss mitigation may be encouraged by having insurance cover some preventive behaviors. How do social insurances deal with risk mitigation? As before, we begin with and emphasize health insurance.

With respect to health insurance, private insurers often provide premium discounts to those who undertake preventive measures or behavioral changes. Most health insurers that sell directly to individuals give discounts to nonsmokers, and some offer reductions for undertaking specific wellness programs or meeting particular health (weight) targets. The strength of such specific programs is, however, quite limited because it is hard for insurers to determine if a person is actually engaging in these risk-reduction measures.

Premium discounts are not allowed in public health insurance as there is concern that basing premiums on risk is inequitable. Hence, explicit beneficiary premiums are the same for a given level of coverage regardless of variation in expected benefits across individuals, even for privately managed Medicare Advantage insurance plans.[3] Explicit Medicare premiums (for Part B or Part D), for example, are uniform across all beneficiaries regardless of age and health status, and private Medigap premiums must likewise be "community rated." Recently passed health reform proposals envision premiums for individual insurance for the under-sixty-five population that are allowed to vary only to a limited extent with beneficiary age but not at all with health status.

Although there are some good reasons for such policies, such as protection against premium increases when risk increases, there is a downside, as we noted earlier in our discussion of principles for insurance: such pricing arrangements distort incentives for insureds to engage in activities that might mitigate losses, like preventive care and lifestyle changes to improve health.

For example, under health reform, the premiums for the under-sixty-five population are to be community rated, and firms are limited in their ability to offer lower premiums to people who behave in ways that result in good health status.[4] Only certain designated wellness programs are permitted, and there are bounds on how much they can affect premiums (regardless of their effectiveness for health and spending). This is due to concern that charging lower premiums for people in good health needs to be offset by higher premiums for those in poor health – exactly what risk-based premium rating would entail.

Determining the Cost-Effectiveness of Prevention

Is this limitation on the ability of insurers to offer incentives for preventive care and preventive behaviors a serious problem? To address this question we need to determine the cost-effectiveness of additional prevention. Is there a large reservoir of currently underused preventive care that could actually save money or at least improve health a great deal for only a little more money? Some forms of preventive care are effective in improving future health status and the quality of life, but most do not lower future medical costs.

One example of a measure that does yield net financial benefits is an inexpensive measles shot given to a child, which actually saves money on average by avoiding a sufficient number of future severe cases of measles and their even more costly consequences in the form of viral meningitis and possibly death. Cancer screening, on the other hand, does not catch or prevent a sufficient number of cases to actually save enough money on future medical costs to offset the cost of the procedure. If, however, one incorporates the indirect costs to other family members when a loved one has cancer as well as peace of mind to the individual who is screened from a negative outcome from this procedure, such tests may be justified.[5]

But if a costly preventive treatment mitigates risk and saves some lives, how should these benefits be incorporated in the design of publicly provided insurance? Consider screening for colorectal cancer through a colonoscopy. In clinical practice, prevention of colon cancer uses various combinations of laboratory testing, colonoscopy, and the less invasive sigmoidoscopy. To focus on colonoscopy alone, we use estimates from a study by Amnon Sonnenberg and Fabiola Delco (2002), who considered the consequences of providing a single screening colonoscopy at age sixty-five (a benefit now covered by Medicare) to a population of one hundred thousand people alive at the age of fifty. Without screening, 5,904 cases of colorectal cancer would have occurred over the lifetime of this population. The single screening at age sixty-five detects and prevents or treats cancers earlier and reduces the number of cancers by twenty-three percent, to 4,552. That, in turn, adds 2,604 additional life years due to avoiding premature deaths from this cancer. To accomplish this benefit, those surviving to age sixty-five all get a colonoscopy that costs $475, at a total cost of $41 million.[6]

Avoiding cases of colon cancer does reduce other medical spending on colorectal cancer for this population from $137 million to $104 million, thus saving $33 million. The net impact – 2,604 additional life years added at a net cost of $8 million – means that each additional life year had a positive cost of only $3,000. Because life years are generally thought to be worth at least $50,000, it appears that this screening program is cost-effective because the expected benefits exceed the cost of the procedure. Of course, this implies that to design publicly provided insurance, we must agree to place a monetary value on life, a delicate ethical and political issue. In this case, one only has to agree that the value of an additional life year has to exceed $3,000 to justify giving individuals a colonoscopy at the age of sixty-five.

Sonnenberg and Delco look at a more costly alternative program, closer to current medical practice, of providing a colonoscopy every ten years beginning at age fifty. That program costs more than the once-in-a-lifetime screen, but also saves two to three times more lives. The additional cost of the more frequent program over the one-time screen saves more lives at a cost of $11,000 per life year, still a bargain.

The point of this example is that even a highly effective preventive measure like a colonoscopy does not reduce total medical costs, but does provide additional years of life while avoiding the pain and suffering associated with having colon cancer. In theory, well-informed middle-class consumers should be willing to pay the $475 themselves out of pocket. There is no obvious reason it must be covered by public insurance for them. Indeed, if the cost of treatment (should cancer occur) is covered by insurance, that diminishes the consumer's incentive to seek the preventive treatment.

The rationale for more generous coverage of colonoscopies might be consumer ignorance – people underestimate the value of the test[7] – or an equity judgment that the social value of health for lower-income people, who might not pay for the test themselves, still justifies coverage. More to the point, the existence of a cost offset would imply that some of the cost of prevention should be covered by insurance; people should face and pay the $8 million net cost, not the $41 million gross cost. This implies they would pay only about twenty percent of the cost of the colonoscopy – by coincidence, exactly the coinsurance in Medicare! But all of these considerations are imprecise and subjective, so it is no wonder that Medicare coverage is often controversial.

What has social insurance actually done? Medicare did not start covering screening at this ten-year interval until mid-2006.[8] Even so, only about half of Medicare beneficiaries avail themselves of this benefit according to the July/August 2006 edition of *Health Affairs*. Some of this choice may be rational; the procedure is uncomfortable, the beneficiary must pay twenty percent of the cost and does not benefit from the cost reduction to Medicare by getting a reduction in premiums. But probably such behavior also is anomalous and reflects imperfect information and inattention to future health benefits among people who think that colon cancer "will never happen to me" or prefer not to know if they have this condition.

Obesity also causes a set of chronic conditions such as diabetes and heart disease that are associated with high medical costs and low quality of life (but, surprising, not shortened life expectancy).[9] There was an increase from thirteen percent to thirty-two percent from the early 1960s to 2004 in the proportion of the population aged twenty to seventy-four labeled obese in the United States. The proportion has since leveled off but remains high. Because obesity adversely affects health and medical costs, though with a lag, this increase in obesity is likely to contribute to the current growth in American health care spending.

Obesity is both behavioral and genetic. Changing obesity producing behavior is now a major public health effort. But, in contrast to colon cancer, there are as yet relatively few medical interventions that cause people to lose weight without side effects. Instead, research has turned to nonmedical programs for changing diets and encouraging exercise, but so far has failed to find incentives that lead to substantial and permanent weight loss (Volpp et al. 2008). There is some evidence that school-based programs that improve lunches and encourage exercise during recess are effective, but such changes are beyond the reach of any insurance, public or private – and there are few similar programs for less regimented adults.

How Lifestyle Changes Affect Health Insurance

How should lifestyle changes be treated in publicly provided health insurance? We first deal with perceptions, some of them anomalous. Then we consider the challenges in designing effective programs, which comes in part from these perceptions. Finally we sketch out what we view to be the best options to pursue in the future.

Consumers are concerned about preventing future adverse health events for themselves. In addition, because of the altruistic externalities mentioned earlier, they are concerned that their fellow citizens have access to effective preventive care, potentially to a greater extent than individuals would choose on their own. But actual individual behavior with regard to preventive activities sometimes reflects imperfect information and anomalous motives, especially limited concern for the long-term benefits of these preventive measures.

The great bulk of medical preventive activities have both financial and nonfinancial costs. In the colonoscopy example, financial costs apply to the inputs for the screening tests and the follow-up, should potentially cancerous polyps be removed during the procedure. The nonfinancial costs apply both to screening and prevention: colonoscopies and sigmoidoscopies are uncomfortable. Prevention of colon cancer may be enhanced by changing one's diet away from red meats and processed foods and toward whole grains, fruits, and vegetables, but insurance does not pay for a healthier diet.

In the case of obesity it is easy to determine when someone is overweight, but the changes in behavior (diet and exercise) needed to prevent obesity are not easily covered by insurance, at least not until an effective weight loss pill is developed. So even when the monetary resource costs of screening or treatment are fully offset by insurance claims payments, a rather large proportion of the population fails to comply with recommendations about screening and prevention because the nonmedical costs of the time and discomfort for testing and changing diet are too high.

Finally, there is a genetic component in prevention of medical risks; people intrinsically differ both in the odds of getting one of these conditions and the extent to which preventive activities are effective. Someone with an unfavorable genetic endowment is, for example, more likely to be obese and have a more difficult time preventing or offsetting weight gain even while sticking to a doctor-approved diet.

There is an alternative to insurer payment for mitigation: adjust premiums to offer incentives by increasing premiums for those who are overweight. But there are still potential problems here for health insurance. In the case of property insurance, it is reasonable to assume that the effectiveness of mitigation is easily determined for structures facing specific risks. Two similarly built homes located near each other will have the same chance of a water heater causing damage from an earthquake and the identical cost of tying down the heater to reduce the chances of future damage. So these two homes can be offered the same adjustment in premium – a higher premium if the tank is not secured – to motivate this protective investment. For colon cancer or obesity, in contrast, the effectiveness of identical preventive measures is likely to vary across people. Two people may get the same periodic screening, spend the same time exercising, and eat the same diet, and yet, due to differing genetic predispositions, can end up with different chances of being obese or of getting colon cancer.

This means that tying health insurance premiums to specific measures of risk (like weight or exercise capacity) may not work so well. The risk and the change in risk depend on more than what people do; it may depend in part on what they were born with. So it may be regarded as unfair to charge higher premiums for health insurance based on higher realized risk levels (as indicated by body mass index, for example, or a history of precancerous polyps). But linking premiums to risk does (as the first policy design principle in Chapter 10 indicates) provide incentives for prevention. So there may need to be a tradeoff in health insurance between efficient short-run incentives for prevention and concerns for equity and longer-term risk pooling.

Alternatively, one could tie insurance premiums or benefits to process measures. Some examples would be a reduction in insurance premiums if one undertakes nutritional counseling or joins a gym. The problem here is that the most effective changes in behavior, like time and sweat spent in exercising or controlling food portion size, are hard to measure directly and may not be well correlated with the processes that can be easily observed. So there is a tradeoff between effective but potentially unfair incentives (such as a premium based on body weight) and fair but potentially ineffective programs (such as premiums based on joining [though not necessarily sweating at] a gym).

The implication is that the management of prevention in health insurance may need to reflect a complex balance of incentives, offsets to misperceptions, and concern for others. The political process will necessarily have to consider these tradeoffs, even though it may not always do so in an ideal way. Our proposed solution involves incentives for behavioral change framed in ways that have both initial and long-lasting effects. In addition, any payments for incentives should be linked to savings on claims costs, so that the insurer (or employer paying for insurance) saves as much or more on claims than the amount needed to cover the incentives.

Assuring the provision of incentives for efficient preventive care often requires an arrangement that spans more than the annual time period traditional for insurance. While this year's flu shot is properly motivated by avoiding sickness this year and the associated medical costs, many other preventive measures yield much of their health benefits and associated reduced treatment costs some years into the future. Cancer screenings, medicines for high blood pressure, and better management of care for diabetics all fall into this category.

The predominant employment-based health insurance may cause these future benefits to be undervalued both by insurers and employers, especially if workers move from company to company at a relatively high rate. One insurance plan may pay for the prevention measure, but another insurance plan, and new employer, may reap the benefits. In view of this leakage, the initial decision on prevention may not be as aggressive as it should have been.

Social insurance potentially avoids this problem, and Medicare has been adding coverage for preventive care – although it is still behind many private plans. Individual insurance with guaranteed renewability also deals with the multiperiod issue, since the insurer is obligated to cover future chronic illnesses will want to prevent or mitigate those conditions. Group insurance would also work well if people were in one employment group plan for their entire working life, but this is not typical and is becoming even less common as labor force mobility increases.

Short-term efforts to deal with these problems have involved mandates for preventive care coverage in group insurance (but mandates that can be avoided if the employer self-insures). Health care reform will likely bring more such requirements. A more promising course of action would be to move to a long-term model for group insurance – in the sense that the person would be entitled to buy the same insurance even after leaving a job. Other solutions may also be possible for this problem, which must be addressed.

MITIGATION MEASURES FOR OTHER SOCIAL INSURANCES

The major role played by mitigation in social (and private) health insurance is echoed to some extent in unemployment insurance. We want employers to take steps to avoid layoffs, such as planning in advance for adjustment to demand downturns. The risk-rated nature of unemployment insurance premiums provides a strong incentive to engage in such behavior, and no individual firm can much affect overall macroeconomic instability, so there is no obvious room for improvement here.

For Social Security, presumably we do not want to reduce the risk of living long and claiming high benefits. We do not want to mitigate risk in this sense. But we do want to reduce the risk of low total income in old age by structuring Social Security so that it does not crowd out private pensions, annuities, and savings.

Policy changes that make it easier to supplement Social Security with private savings would seem to have merit – but the effectively high tax rates for those with high incomes on Social Security represent a tradeoff between equity and efficient mitigation of the risk of penury in old age for those in the lower-income bracket.

PUBLICLY PRODUCED SOCIAL INSURANCE

Is there a relationship between the public production of insurance (versus private market production) and anomalous behavior? The primary rationale for social insurance based on anomalous behavior is low demand, and it would seem that this problem could be adequately dealt with by tax-financed subsidies or vouchers for private insurance for lower-income people, and mandates for higher-income ones, that would induce or require them to obtain qualified socially adequate insurance.

There has been considerable controversy that the trust fund structure of Social Security inefficiently discourages private savings (directly or through annuities), although both the theory and the evidence on this point are somewhat ambiguous. We think there are three reasons why publicly produced insurance might be chosen as a vehicle for social insurance. One relates to the demand side, and the other two surprisingly are connected to supply-side anomalies.

The demand-side issue is whether all of the characteristics of insurance about which consumers may err actually occur if privately produced insurance is used. Regulations and rules about what constitutes insurance eligible for subsidies can go a long way, but there may be residual concern that private firms may skimp on or distort needed characteristics. Of course, in the real world, publicly produced insurance may not always provide desired features, especially those concerned with personalizing coverage to the needs and desires of individual consumers (thus the health care reform jokes about the public option having all of the compassion and efficiency of the Department of Motor Vehicles). But there are legitimate differences of opinion here. The argument is the classic one in public economics that argues for public production as a means of quality assurance. That argument postulates that public production can best assure that insurance will have the characteristics consumers need but do not realize they need; private firms, in contrast, will take advantage of them by skimping on needed but hard to detect features and emphasizing features deceptively attractive to buyers.

The controversy over public production also raises a supply-side question: Will private firms reliably supply insurance to satisfy consumer wants and needs? The controversy over the public option in health reform was partly driven by different opinions about whether private health insurance was trustworthy and able to contain medical spending. Some people do trust government managers more than private ones. And a large public insurer armed with political clout might be better able to force down prices paid to hospitals and doctors than private insurers.

There is no doubt that public plans can exercise more buyer market power and more political pressure than can private programs, but it may come at a cost of lower-quality service to patients. In addition, the large size of Medicare or Social Security means that either can achieve greater economies of scale than smaller private insurers and pension plans, and this will reduce administrative costs.

These issues of private insurance quality have been much more controversial for under-sixty-five health insurance than for other social insurance. Social Security was always viewed as a basic foundational benefit for retirement with people permitted and even encouraged to purchase supplementary private annuities or retirement plans. In fact, 401(k) plans are tax subsidized for that reason. Private (though regulated) Medigap insurance has always accompanied the traditional Medicare plan, and private Medicare Advantage plans are available as substitutes for the public plan.

The main remaining controversy over Social Security relates to the tradeoff between potentially higher but more uncertain returns on investment in a private retirement plan relative to what the trust fund based on a public plan could offer. Private plans might invest in risky assets, but the public plan, invested in government bonds and backed in full by the government and its power to tax as a last resort, would be less risky and might even provide better yields in adverse economic times. The argument for the public plan rests on the proposition that the government can offer guaranteed benefits on more advantageous terms than the private sector – the same argument provided by the Florida legislature in establishing the state-owned Citizens Property Insurance Company that provides property coverage to homeowners in hurricane-prone areas. In summary, correcting anomalous demand-side or supply-side behavior is part of the basis for favoring public provision of insurances, but questions can be raised about government's ability to package, manage, and reduce losses in the face of economy-wide risks that are not easily pooled.

MULTIYEAR HEALTH INSURANCE AND RISK RATING

There are two kinds of private health insurance that do not have multiyear issues caused by fluctuating premiums due to risk changes: long-term care (nursing home) insurance and guaranteed renewability of individual insurance policies.

Long-Term Care (LTC) Insurance

We have already noted the relatively low take-up rate of private long-term care insurance. This insurance provides protection against changes in risk and shortsightedness by adopting a payment system similar to whole-life insurance with guaranteed renewability. Specifically, a person starts paying premiums that are high relative to expected benefits during the first few years of a policy in order to be eligible for low (or zero) premiums later. The person who starts paying for LTC insurance in his or her fifties builds up value in the policy, which is used to keep later period premiums low while guaranteeing that those premiums will not increase just because the person does become frail and begins to use long-term care. Without this latter feature it is unlikely anyone would buy LTC insurance.

The implication is that the problems addressed by multiperiod insurance design, such as reclassification risk, are not part of the reason for low levels of private long-term care insurance; it effectively contains a guaranteed renewability feature. Instead, it has other, more serious, problems that account for its scarcity, as already noted, caused by Medicaid crowd out and a low value of money benefits (in excess of what Medicaid would provide) to a frail and incapacitated person.

Individual Health Insurance

As we noted earlier, private individual health insurance also contains guaranteed renewability as a policy provision, which protects the person against unexpected jumps in future premiums because of the onset of a high-cost condition. Of course, premiums will fluctuate as total health-care costs fluctuate.

A serious imperfection in private insurance arises because people must switch to individual coverage if they take a job without group coverage and move out of the group insurance market. Therefore, changes in risk that occur as part of such job transitions (probably motivated by other reasons) are a threat to continuation of coverage. Turnover of group insurance also means that preventive measures that lower future costs are not captured because group insurers expect the person to belong to a different insurance plan in the future. If governmental regulation forbids risk rating, then it may have to mandate or subsidize preventive care that provides long-term benefits. In effect, one governmental action requires another to offset its harmful side effects.

More to the point, the person covered by group insurance in a small firm lacks any protection against high premiums or loss of coverage if the person becomes a high risk; indeed, research by Mark Pauly and Robert

Lieberthal (2008) shows that high risks in small firms are much more likely to lose their coverage from one year to the next compared to those individually insured. Employment-based group insurance does have substantial administrative cost advantages over individual insurance, but is much less effective in providing long-term protection because you can lose group insurance if you become unemployed or change jobs.

AFFORDABILITY IN HEALTH INSURANCE

Multiyear insurance largely addresses the issue of affordability of coverage for individuals who have above average risks, but it does not deal with the problem of affordability to those at average or even low risk who have relatively low incomes. Even for people at average risk, the likelihood they will choose to obtain private coverage falls as income falls.

Is this behavior anomalous? The most obvious answer is "no," because people at the lower income levels rationally decide that they cannot afford expensive health insurance. But that view is too simplistic. For one thing, as noted earlier, there are many uninsured with incomes as high as 400 percent of poverty, suggesting that this is not just an issue of affordability at low income. Less obvious, for low-income but not poor households, the alternative to buying health insurance is the threat of having high medical bills that will be difficult if not impossible to pay.

According to the theory of insurance, people who pay out of pocket for a loss they incur should prefer insurance to protect themselves against this event unless the price of insurance is so high that they prefer to remain uninsured and take their chances that they will not suffer a loss. In the case of health care, it is the increased costs of medical care that has created the affordability problem since it is the cost of medical care that causes insurance premiums to rise. In effect, the growing cost of insurance premiums induces people to drop coverage and take the chance of relying on emergency room care and charity should they become ill.

Whether it is the high cost of medical care or the concomitant high cost of insurance that defines the problem, the rationale for social insurance must be that others in the community want to help these lower-income people. But as already noted, lower-income households do attach some monetary value to health care and health insurance, and many of them do, in fact, pay for both: most households (fifty-one percent) with incomes in the 175 percent to 200 percent of poverty bracket obtain private insurance. Those who do not purchase insurance pay substantial amounts out of pocket for health care costs.

An open question is: How much should one charge for health insurance coverage to find the balance between affordability and premiums that pay for the benefits people will be claiming? Usually this question is answered with a subjective judgment based on social views on how much a household at a given income level should have left over for other consumption goods after paying for health insurance. For example, one rule might be that insurance plus out of pocket payment should not eat up more than some percentage of a household's income.

A problem with this approach is that there is no objective standard for determining what this percentage should be. For example, a study done for the Commonwealth Fund used a cut-off of ten percent of income for the share of explicit premiums plus out of pocket payment for a family with moderate income. Today, many households are willing to spend more than ten percent of their income on health insurance alone, so in that sense their behavior suggests they can afford coverage.

An alternative definition of affordability therefore links it to the proportion of households at any income level willing to buy coverage. There needs to be a social decision on what constitutes evidence of affordability in some population. If more than fifty percent obtain coverage, does that prove insurance is affordable, or should it be seventy percent or even ninety percent? Once this criterion is chosen, we can then calculate how many people without insurance are in subpopulations where the proportion buying indicates insurance to be affordable.

If one household pays a premium less than the actuarial cost of coverage, then other households will have to pay to make up the difference. The analysis is not complete until those who must cover the cost of the subsidy through taxes are identified and the feasibility of collecting the taxes from them is determined.

Analysis of the adequacy of the levels of consumption of other things that can be purchased after paying for health insurance suggests that perhaps as much as half of the uninsured can afford coverage (Bundorf and Pauly 2006).[10] Clearly, the higher the income cutoff for a given subsidy the more households will have to spend on other things and the more households who will be willing to buy insurance – but by the same token, the higher will be the tax burden on their fellow citizens.

Current federal legislation sets these subsidies at levels that extend up to 400 percent of the poverty line ($89,400 for a family of four); households beyond that level receive no subsidy but must pay a penalty if they fail to buy insurance. In most cases the penalty would be less than the insurance premium they would have paid. Legislation passed in Massachusetts in 2006 set a lower (300 percent of the poverty line, or $67,050 for a family of four) income cut-off for eligibility for subsidy, but then judged the subsidies as too low relative to the cost of health insurance to allow people to afford the coverage; hence the legislation was modified before the program was implemented to waive the mandate that they buy coverage.[11] The most we can say at present is that this is an exceedingly unsettled question. It will continue to be debated for a long time.

SUMMARY

Correcting anomalous demand-side and supply-side behavior of consumers and firms is part but not the major part of the motivation for compulsory and tax-financed social insurance. Instead, the major motivation is welfare policy, broadly defined to include social concern for the distribution of income, adequate protection against low income in retirement and unemployment, and adequate use of medical care.

The substantial redistributional components of Social Security and, especially, Medicare show that the goal is not to collect premiums and pay back benefits in proportion to premiums, but rather to collect more from the wealthy and the healthy in order to pay more to the poor and the sickly. The generosity of insurance coverage is probably carried beyond what many perfectly informed, expected utility-maximizing lower-income households could or would choose on their own if they had to pay the full cost themselves. However, both kinds of insurance provide coverage for people who inadequately plan for the future or who feel that poor health (or long retirement) is something that will never happen to them and would have been unprotected if they were making decisions on their own. In other words, Medicare corrects anomalies while at the same time meeting social welfare goals.

Compulsory tax finance is also part of a primary corrective for supply-side anomalies. Public production of social insurance, primarily through government management of Social Security and traditional Medicare, may be motivated in part by the belief that government-run insurance can provide better returns and better risk protection than any private counterpart.

Some of the potential advantage to public plans may be due to large and dominant size (without the same form of monopoly exploitation that would come from similar private plans), but also from governments' ability to tax as a last resort in order to pay promised benefits if reserves and accumulated premiums are inadequate. There is a real and relevant downside: protection for insureds comes at potential cost of risk to taxpayers to make up any shortfall between revenues and the cost of promises, but there may be some advantages of risk pooling. Any potential superiority also depends on political management being superior to private market management in making choices that maximize aggregate welfare, rather than satisfying the goals of government officials – a subject on which there is a wide difference of opinion.

Risk mitigation should be given high priority in designing social insurance. For example, consumer behaviors that reduce future health risk – whether medical care-seeking behaviors or lifestyle behaviors – can matter significantly. But the ability of many variations in insurance coverage and insurance premium policy to strike the right balance between risk reduction and financial protection is limited, and the ability of the potential system to find and choose the best policy is even more questionable. Incentives to lose weight or exercise more can be built into health insurance premiums, but at the risk of politically sensitive risk discrimination. Private savings and amenity purchase should ideally be coordinated with Social Security, but this is easier said than done.

It is probably fair to say that if our only goal were anomaly prevention, public policy toward Social Security and health insurance would be much simpler and less controversial than it currently is. But that transparent situation is not what we face, at least as long as lifetime income is distributed unequally, so we will have to have tolerance for complexity and controversy.

14

Conclusions – A Framework for Prescriptive Recommendations

We have two principal interests in examining how buyers and sellers of insurance make decisions: (1) to characterize and predict their behavior; and (2) to evaluate the impact of their behavior on individual and social welfare. We have reached the following three conclusions based on our empirical analyses:

- *Conclusion One*: The behavior of buyers and sellers of insurance in a number of situations is inconsistent with the benchmark models of choice derived from classical economic theory.
- *Conclusion Two*: There are certain kinds of markets and situations in which anomalous behavior predominates.
- *Conclusion Three*: The public sector can take steps to improve individual and social welfare when insurance markets display such behavior.

In this chapter, we review the anomalous behavior and offer some thoughts as to how political and market frameworks might be structured to facilitate improvements.

CHARACTERIZING ANOMALOUS BEHAVIOR

The richest vein of anomalous behavior occurs when buyers and sellers of insurance confront correlated low-probability, high-consequence events, such as a catastrophic loss from a natural disaster. Before a disaster, buyers often choose to remain uninsured because they ignore events below their threshold level of concern. Many purchase coverage following a disaster because of the salience of the event, and then cancel their policy several years later if they have not suffered a loss because they view their insurance policy as a poor investment.

Insurers exhibit even more erratic behavior than buyers – they often exit the market, sometimes temporarily, after a large loss occurs even though they recognize that future expected losses have hardly changed. Those that reenter the market charge very high premiums difficult to justify on actuarial grounds. As the loss recedes in time and memory, insurers often go to the other extreme by ignoring these potentially catastrophic events because they perceive them as unlikely to happen in the near future. It appears that insurance firms are also responding to spikes in their cost of capital following a loss. The high returns demanded by investors who provide capital to insurers suggests that those investors are also behaving erratically and anomalously in the immediate aftermath of a disaster.

There are other pockets of anomalous buyer behavior, most of them involving situations that fall into two categories: (1) some individuals find it difficult to determine what type of insurance to buy; and (2) unprotected consumers do not seem concerned that they might suffer severe financial losses. The first category may explain why many shoppers buy product warranties after being given a sales pitch for this type of added protection. In fact, sometimes people's confusion and worry lead them to buy insurance at a price considerably in excess of their expected loss and in situations where they could afford to be without coverage if they were maximizing their expected utility.

The second category relates to clear and obvious threats, such as a fire, flood, or earthquake damaging a home; a car collision; or the premature death of a breadwinner in the family. Some people purchase insurance to protect themselves against such events, as they should, even when they are not mandated to do so. Others view these events as below their threshold level of concern and remain unprotected. In some instances, market institutions or public policies have emerged that lead individuals to purchase at least some insurance. The linking of homeowners' insurance to mortgages and automobile collision coverage to auto loans creates a large demand for coverage. Offering health insurance to employees in the form of group coverage with a tax subsidy provides a significant financial incentive to buy a policy.

Our biggest challenge in writing this book was making prescriptive recommendations to address instances when buyers and sellers of insurance behave in ways that deviate from the benchmark models of choice. If buyers utilize decision rules at odds with expected utility theory, what (if anything) should governments and the insurance industry do to change their behavior? Is there a rationale for overriding the choices people make when their actions clash with what classical economic theory says is sensible? If investors are extremely concerned about future losses so make capital available only at very high prices, what role, if any, should regulators, rating agencies, and the public sector play in providing protection or inexpensive access to capital in these situations? Consider the following two questions in this regard:

- Should public policy implicitly endorse choices by individuals that reflect myopic behavior, probability neglect, strongly held incorrect beliefs, or desire for reassurance (peace of mind)?
- Is it appropriate for public policy to override choices that mentally competent adults make?

Our reluctance to interfere is tempered by the thought that, if we eventually have to rescue individuals who have made mistaken choices (such as *not* buying health insurance or flood insurance), shouldn't we support actions that incentivize or require people to do as the benchmark theory of demand and supply recommends?

In Chapters 10 and 11, we outlined ways in which collective action or industry policy might improve welfare. We proposed remedies, some old and some new. But stopping there leaves us distinctly uncomfortable because we would like a rigorous overall normative framework, not just an appeal to common sense, as a way of motivating policy. For example, we criticized cancer insurance that pays a person a predetermined sum when he or she is hospitalized with cancer but does not make payments for other diseases. But many consumers and law makers in some countries (such as Japan and Korea), support cancer insurance largely for cultural reasons having to do with fear or stigma of cancer, but also to fill gaps in their social insurance programs. They would be strongly opposed to discouraging or outlawing such coverage; in fact, they would like more people to purchase this insurance.

A FRAMEWORK FOR MAKING PRESCRIPTIVE RECOMMENDATIONS

We now outline a framework for normative analysis and social choice that might be endorsed by the key interested parties: political decision makers, those employed in the insurance industry, and concerned citizens. We hope that these ideas provide an upbeat ending to the present inquiry and encourage others to carry this line of analysis further.

We have some concerns as well. For one, there is no obvious reason that real-world lawmakers whose primary goal is to get elected and stay in office should be seriously concerned about our recommendations for improving economic welfare when it comes to managing risk if they perceive that an adverse event will be highly unlikely to occur in the next year or two. Elected officials may see no point in supporting measures that satisfy cost-benefit tests or maximize social welfare if they cannot point to short-term benefits resulting from them.

A deeper problem is that some people characterize insurance as a rip-off if it offers net financial benefits only to the few who suffer losses, even though this is precisely the role that insurance is designed to play. If consumers prefer immediate gratification over planning for their future safety and security, leading to nonoptimal behavior in the long run, legislators are likely to be tempted to espouse exactly these same wrong preferences so as to be reelected. To illustrate this point, consider the discussion of Medicare drug coverage during the 2000 presidential election primary debates. Senator Bill Bradley advocated a catastrophic coverage plan. Vice President Al Gore criticized this idea on the grounds that "most people won't collect any money" from such coverage, and went on to defeat Bradley in the primaries.

Turning to the supply of insurance, if regulators think that a future hurricane is much less likely than the predictions derived from catastrophe models used by insurers, these same regulators (for example, in Florida) may then require premiums to be lower than the actuarially fair rate without taking into account the cost of capital required to support the insurers' operations. Alternatively, the regulators may establish a government-run insurer that offers coverage at low premiums so that the taxpayers will be forced to bear the burden should the state be hit by a severe disaster.

One possible alternative is to imagine that there is a higher and more thoughtful level of collective action that structures and constrains day-to-day political decisions, what Nobel-prize-winning economist James M. Buchanan calls a "quasi-constitutional" choice framework (Buchanan 1998; Buchanan and Tullock 1962). He applies this idea to the tax structure and to special-interest legislation, but it could apply as well to insurance and its regulation.

Buchanan notes, for example, that federal tax laws have to apply equally across the country; tax penalties for violating environmental protection laws cannot be lower in West Virginia than in New York, even if representatives from the former state say that industries in their jurisdictions cannot afford to pay the penalties.

In reality, it is legal for federal expenditures to differ widely across states, and they do. The concept of uniform laws and uniform taxation contrasts with the tradition of pork-barrel spending; the former are subject to quasi-constitutional rules, while the latter comes from day-to-day politics. Buchanan also advocates the use of decision processes for making collective choices, like super majorities (e.g., two-thirds of the citizenry or legislature supporting a proposal) that make it harder for special interests to receive special treatment.

Building on this concept of uniform treatment, and recognizing that there is a tendency for legislators to make myopic decisions given their short-run political considerations, we believe that society should have a fair process to decide on the rules of the game when it comes to insurance behavior and regulation. These rules must be determined in a setting in which participants do not know whether they will be winners or losers with respect to specific risks: people may consent to guidelines that are fairer and more likely to lead to better choices on average than if all public choices were made in response to the crisis of the moment.

In an insurance context, those at risk are players in a game in which nature and genetics play a key role. Hence, agreeing on and sticking to rules or principles in advance of particular decisions has even more relevance and appeal precisely because there is considerable uncertainty as to what will occur in the future and who will be adversely affected.

Public policy with respect to insurance should be built on principles, not on expediency, as would be the case if the government provided financial assistance to uninsured victims of a disaster even when it stated in advance that such aid would *not* be forthcoming. A structure based on well-designed principles should lead to better outcomes for individuals at risk and an improvement in social welfare. These principles would require that the insurance industry *not* take advantage of short-term profit opportunities by changing premiums dramatically, abandoning some of its customers and/or leaving the market entirely. The principles would also require that politicians and regulators not demonize the insurance industry or apply pressure for setting premiums too low for the private sector to sustain.

So what kinds of quasi-constitutional rules for public policy toward insurance might be feasible? As a starting point we proposed the following two policy design principles in Chapter 10.

- *Principle One*: Premiums should reflect risk so that consumers have information on the severity of different hazards (health, environmental, and safety) that they face and are encouraged to undertake preventive or protective measures. Socially desired subsidies to high-risk individuals should not come from high premiums paid by low-risk individuals. In other words, premiums should not be averaged, as in the community rating system that is part of the recently passed health reform legislation.
- *Principle Two*: Deal with equity and affordability by providing special treatment to certain groups or individuals through insurance vouchers (similar to food stamps), not through subsidized premiums.

OVERCOMING PROBLEMS IN REGULATION

To implement these principles, we require behavior by regulators that prevents political pressures from dictating policy. In this regard, three main errors in regulation are attributable to political causes and need to be addressed:

- *Error One*: *Public policy that presumes competitive insurers are price gouging.* The hallmark of such policy is regulation that either reduces premiums without reducing benefits or increases benefits without permitting insurers to increase premiums. Subsequent premium regulation may lead to greater fluctuations in insurance availability than would be generated by unregulated insurer behavior.

An example of this controversy occurred during the health care reform debate. A for-profit insurer in California raised premiums, in some cases by as much as thirty-nine percent, for some of its individual insurance policies. Given the uneven pricing in this very small and boutique-type individual market, such actions are not uncommon, and many consumers then switch insurers. But its occurrence during the debate over health care overhaul made the price increase a media event and the insurer then decided to rescind it (Pear 2010). Such haphazard pricing behavior by insurers is clearly undesirable. A permanent solution involves more than just episodic political pressure.

- *Error Two*: *Compelling insurers to deviate from risk-based premiums.* This occurs when regulators require insurers to charge low premiums to residents owning homes in high-risk areas or to those who have health conditions that require costly medical care.
- *Error Three*: *Requiring overly generous insurance through mandated benefits as part of a person's coverage.* For example, many states require that health insurance pays for chiropractic care, acupuncture, or in vitro fertilization, and mandate that the personal injury protection part of auto insurance cover funeral and burial expenses. Some consumers may not want this protection, either because they do not think it worthwhile to use these services or because they want to keep their premiums down by paying out of pocket if they do decide to use them.

With respect to Error One, charges of insurance premium gouging arise when the price of coverage takes a big jump or accounting profits are unusually high. Sometimes, though not always, the higher price reflects a temporarily higher cost of capital. In the latter case, legislators want to stop price increases even if they are based on cost increases. They imagine that there is something called a "fair" profit level to which they should tether prices. More generally, the public often pressures elected officials to limit premiums on the basis of recent favorable but temporarily low loss experience.

When some insurers reveal that they have made higher than average profits during the past year, the public is likely to accuse these firms of price gouging. On the other hand, those insurers who suffered unexpectedly large losses during this period are likely to make the case for premium increases in the next period. Neither of these concerns may be appropriate if the event being insured against has expected losses and a standard deviation that is relatively stable over time. Even in competitive markets, some firms and industries can temporarily make high or low profits. Of course, high prices or lack of insurer competition should be a cause of concern.

ROLE OF MULTIYEAR INSURANCE

Multiyear insurance has the potential to deal with a wide range of anomalies and to address the problem of political pressure as long as regulators agree to let premiums reflect risk. When the risk to be insured is perceived as stable over the next few years, and capital can be obtained inexpensively should an insurer suffer a very large loss, then insurers have an economic incentive to offer multiyear contracts with stable premiums over the length of the contract. There will also be less temptation for political game-playing based on short-term insurer profits.

The assurance of continued coverage means that the consumer need not incur the costs of searching for a new policy (as would be the case should his or her policy be canceled). Multiyear insurance also encourages investments in prevention measures if the consumer knows that he or she will get premium reductions during each year of the contract. In contrast, under annual policies, there is uncertainty as to the stream of benefits that will accrue over time given that the insurer has made a commitment only for the following year. A multiyear policy also creates stability and peace of mind for consumers because they know they are protected over a period of years rather than for just the next twelve months.

A multiyear policy can also be attractive to insurers. There would likely be lower administrative and marketing costs associated with such policies than with a sequence of annual contracts. These reduced expenses relate to gaining new consumers, maintaining existing ones, or regaining those who have left the company. On the negative side, a multiyear policy may create higher capital costs if there is considerable uncertainty with respect to the loss distribution over time or an insurer suffers a very large loss in one period and has promised not to adjust the premium in future periods. But some of this additional expense and bother can be offset or reversed by the lower administrative and marketing costs and the greater flexibility in pricing that insurers will have by introducing multiyear policies.

Regulators may allow the premiums on multiyear policies to be set high enough to compensate insurers for taking on the additional expected capital expense. This assumes that investors ask a high price for insurers to have access to their capital, which may not be the case. Regulators may also be more enthusiastic toward multiyear policies if insurers agree to continue to offer one-year policies as well. Insurers may also deal with the uncertainty of future loss distributions by offering multiyear contracts with adjustable premiums. Put more generally, multiyear insurance will expand the range of policies insurers can offer and thereby enhance regulatory flexibility with respect to risk-based premiums.

PREVENTING FLUCTUATIONS IN PRICING

As we have noted, fluctuations in premiums, even if cost-justified, are troubling. Some kind of arrangement that limits the propensity of legislators to focus on short-term outcomes and yet leads to smoothing of premium changes would be to everyone's advantage. Rules should be built into the insurance policy about what kinds of information (for example, severe extenuating circumstances such as sea level rise that increases the likelihood of flood damage in riverine and coastal areas) would justify significant premium increases. In this context, multiyear insurance with stable premiums would prevent such premium fluctuations.

On the regulatory side, those who control pricing and market structure need to stipulate in advance the degree of industry competition that they will support. If their antitrust arm is doing a good job in fostering competition, reducing barriers to entry, and achieving price transparency, then regulators should not have to react reflexively to challenges of monopoly price gouging or unusually high profits in any given year. Rather, they would have to show that the insurance industry was behaving in noncompetitive ways before taking steps to limit premiums they could charge and would have to explain why their antitrust policy failed.

In the typical insurance market, it would be rare for firms to have significant monopoly power given the ease of entry and exit. If insurers did have the ability to charge higher prices than would be justified based on their costs, this would imply that regulators had been lax in their antitrust oversight and enforcement such as barring or breaking up large firms, controlling collusive behavior, and compelling transparent pricing. To avoid these situations, regulators should be required to act more aggressively in these domains.

APPLYING GUIDING PRINCIPLES

As a starting point for moving in this direction, states that regulate prices today should adopt policy design *Principle One: Premiums should reflect risk* when undertaking any rate-setting procedures or rate review. Any rationale for deviating from this principle should be spelled out in advance and possibly referred to the legislature or formulated as a referendum for review or approval.

Insurance contracts should be clearly written and transparent so that those considering purchasing coverage can understand the contract that they are signing. The basis for setting premiums should be spelled out in the contract with possible requirements by the regulators that insurers disclose their loading factors that reflect their administrative, marketing, and other expenses, as well as their costs of capital for covering potentially catastrophic losses. Rating agencies could be involved in this process by determining whether the insurer was operating on a sound financial footing.

In keeping with policy design *Principle Two: Dealing with equity and affordability issues*, low-income individuals should receive assistance through insurance vouchers rather than subsidized premiums. There needs to be a clear understanding of who will pay for this subsidy and who will administer the program. For example, the state or federal government could administer the subsidy using a specified criterion (such as annual income) and obtain the necessary funds through taxes or other means.

Regulators that attempt to force insurers to offer additional benefits should be required to provide a financial analysis outlining evidence that the additional benefits are worth the cost. For example, suppose some low-income individuals prefer low-cost insurance with a relatively high deductible, believing that they could control their use of health care. A regulation forbidding such an option – as in the current health care overhaul legislation – would have to be justified, perhaps on the grounds that those households will likely default on paying the deductible. The point is that evidence would need to be provided to support this assertion.

ALTERNATIVE ARRANGEMENTS

Legislators and regulators need to be rewarded for bravery. Getting things right, especially when it comes to unpopular public policy on insurance, often brings political risk. Although the majority of states have governor-appointed insurance commissioners, even these regulators need to be shielded from the fact and the appearance of being unduly influenced by the insurance industry.

We support arrangements that reduce biased incentives and provide stability in the insurance market. Among these proposals are multiyear insurance policies and new institutional arrangements for providing capital following a severe loss. We discuss these here.

Providing Stability to the Insurance Market

Cancellation of insurance contracts or highly fluctuating insurance premiums can pose problems to consumers and businesses who desire stability. Yet there is considerable evidence that insurers and those who supply capital to insurers often react to rare high-loss, highly correlated events, leading to premium increases and diminished quantity of coverage. The Florida hurricane, the California earthquake, or the New York terrorist attack can lead to spikes in premiums and temporary shortages, which can best be characterized as an anomalous overreaction to a recent salient event. More specifically, insurers and reinsurers focus on the losses generated by the disaster rather than on the likelihood that a future loss of this magnitude will occur. Discussions with insurers and reinsurers suggest that the main cause of their raising premiums and curtailing coverage is the high cost of replenishing their surplus following a severe loss caused by anomalous behavior by suppliers of capital.

Insurers who suffer a large loss not covered by reinsurance need to find capital to replace their depleted surplus. Following a large-scale catastrophe, it is often difficult for them to obtain protection against future catastrophic losses through reinsurance purchase or catastrophe bonds except at very high costs.

Reinsurers face the same capacity problem as insurers – getting capital to replenish their surplus. Investors are reluctant to provide funds to insurers and reinsurers because they are unclear how profitable these investments will be in the future, even though there is no logical reason the occurrence of the loss should substantially change their expectations of future profitability.[1] This combination of a large loss and a reluctance to invest in an insurer whose surplus is significantly depleted provides considerable instability in the market. This behavior is often characterized as the insurance cycle: hard markets (after a disaster) and soft markets (if there have been no large-scale catastrophes for several years).

Given this behavior by insurers, reinsurers, and the capital markets, what steps can be taken to provide more stability to the system? In our view this problem can be solved with multiyear insurance policies coupled with two complementary strategies: greater diversification of risk and new institutional arrangements that provide inexpensive capital to those who suffer large losses.

Greater Diversification of Risk

In Chapter 2, we discussed the importance of the law of large numbers to enable insurers to provide protection against specific risks. If an insurer's portfolio contains a large number of policies where the potential losses are independent of each other, then the likelihood of the insurer experiencing a catastrophic loss is very small. In contrast, if the portfolio contains a large number of policies whose losses are correlated, then insurers should consider diversifying their risk. The principal reason that insurers are comfortable offering long-term life insurance policies is that they know that it is highly unlikely that a large number of their policyholders will die in any given year.

With respect to property risks, insurers and reinsurers should diversify their portfolio so they are not subject to very large losses should a natural disaster, terrorist attack, or other catastrophe occur. For regionally based insurers, this may not be so easy to do, although reinsurance is an alternative mechanism for achieving diversification. Global insurers still need to limit the number of policies they issue in specific areas so that they know that the likelihood of a large total loss is low.

New Institutional Arrangements for Providing Capital following a Severe Loss

To protect insurers against catastrophic losses over time, there is a need for new alternative risk transfer instruments. Suppose an insurer was considering offering a five-year property insurance policy to its policyholders. It would very likely want to protect itself against potential catastrophic losses by purchasing a five-year reinsurance contract or a five-year catastrophe bond. There are a set of questions that need to be explored in this regard for multiyear insurance policies to be feasible: What conditions would be necessary for reinsurers to offer such a policy? What rate of return would induce investors to provide capital for a five-year catastrophe bond?

Novel institutional arrangements are also possible. For example, insurance pools covering a wide area, such as Gulf Coast states and those in the Northeast, could provide protection to insurers who participate in such an arrangement. The state or federal government could provide loans to insurers who suffer one or more large losses during a five-year period if financing is not available from the private sector. This solution would require a credible index to trigger the availability of inexpensive capital to those who suffer a large loss. Or insurers could charge an additional premium to their normal price that would be used to create a fund to replenish surplus following a catastrophic loss. Such a fund would in effect be a mutual reinsurer.

THE MOST MISUNDERSTOOD INDUSTRY REVISITED

The insurance industry is misunderstood. Buyers of its products have a hard time comprehending what they are getting, partly because insurance policies are often not clearly written and are not transparent, and partly because risk is a complicated concept to explain in simple language.

Sellers of insurance believe they are unfairly blamed as the proverbial bringers of bad tidings. They enter the scene after a disaster occurs and are often accused of not settling claims promptly or denying payments because the losses that occurred were caused by events excluded from the policy coverage (e.g., flood damage is not covered in a homeowners' policy). Insurers compound the misunderstanding by pulling out of the market or raising premiums significantly after experiencing large losses.

One of the remedies for a misunderstood industry is increasing our understanding of what it can and cannot provide – a principal goal of this book. We hope that readers will now avoid reflex reactions when the firms from which they purchase coverage do things that infuriate them. We also hope that insurers take steps to avoid focusing on short-run gains.

Notes

Chapter 2. An Introduction to Insurance in Practice and Theory

1. This point has been made by Marco Arena (2008).
2. Medicare is partly paid for by payroll and general revenue taxes and partly by explicit premiums paid by seniors.
3. The term is also used widely in the academic literature on insurance and economics. See Neil Doherty and Harris Schlesinger (1990, 246) for a representative example.
4. We discuss what happens if the insurer is a mutual insurer in Chapter 5.
5. Investors will expect to get back the ten percent return they would otherwise have earned 99.9 percent of the time, and the extra 0.1 percent will just compensate them for the loss of principal and interest that will happen once in a thousand times.
6. As noted, compared to a situation where it has less capital and is unable to pay full benefits part of the time, if the insurer has more capital it will pay higher expected benefits. The actuarially fair premium will include the expected cost of those additional benefits.
7. As noted by Chris Starmer (2000, 335), "Concavity (of the utility function in money, or diminishing marginal utility) implies risk averse behavior; an agent with a concave utility function will always prefer a certain amount x to any risky prospect with expected value equal to x." James Dyer and Rakesh Sarin (1982) formally show how one can separate diminishing marginal utility from risk aversion in a utility function.

Chapter 3. Anomalies and Rumors of Anomalies

1. A more extended discussion of unwise purchases of insurance can be found in Tobias (1982).
2. Whole life insurance has a somewhat similar feature, but it pays out the policy (death) benefit only in the rare event the individual lives to an advanced age, e.g., 100.
3. See Starmer (2000) for a summary of some of these studies.
4. If the other person has caused the accident and is insured, then Joe will not be responsible for any damage assuming he can collect from the other driver's

insurance company or successfully sue the person causing the accident unless that driver is uninsured or underinsured and without assets.

5. With the exception of employment-based group health insurance and some group life insurance, the bulk of consumer insurance is bought by individuals.

6. This example was provided by representatives of Towers Perrin at a Wharton Risk Center meeting in February 2002.

7. The managed care backlash exacerbated the problem by pressuring insurers to avoid limits on care they had been planning to use as a way of reducing the cost of health insurance.

Chapter 4. Behavior Consistent with Benchmark Models

1. Should coverage be mandated, the actual demand reflects what the consumer is required to purchase, not necessarily what the consumer wants to buy. In some cases, as with homeowners' insurance required as a condition for a mortgage, we may observe high rates of purchase even if many consumers would have engaged in anomalous behavior had they been allowed to do so.

2. In some cases, insurance will make payments only if the vehicle is repaired. In other cases, the insurer sends the insured a check for the estimated cost of repairs; the insured can then decide whether or not to go ahead with the body work.

3. Loss adjustment expenses include insurer payments for things the consumer would otherwise have had to do, like negotiating the cost of repairs, verifying the need for repairs, and writing a check.

4. Insurers have data only on people who did purchase, but not on those who did not.

5. Those whose cars were financed were forced to have collision coverage, but may not have voluntarily purchased it had they been given that option.

6. Maximum contents coverage for a homeowners' policy is normally fifty percent of the coverage on the structure.

7. Such a price would still be consistent with a benchmark model of choice that incorporated fixed cost into the analysis.

Chapter 5. Real-World Complications

1. Insurers themselves might not be all that certain of the risk either.

2. The classic paper discussing this situation is George Akerlof (1970).

3. http://www.cartoonstock.com/directory/i/insurance_fraud.asp.

4. Scott Harrington and Greg Niehaus (1999), pp. 132–3. There may be additional costs associated with the tax treatment of returns from reserves compared to the tax treatment of alternative investments (p. 82).

Chapter 6. Why People Do or Do Not Demand Insurance

1. The source for this figure is Johnson et al. 1993, 43 (Figure 1).

2. The idea that preferences are constructed, rather than revealed, emerged from many lines of research in the late 1980s and early 1990s (e.g., Chapman and

Johnson 1995; Tversky, Sattath, and Slovic 1988; Tversky, Slovic, and Kahneman 1990) and was well characterized by Slovic (1995).

3. For empirical data supporting this behavior see Michel-Kerjan, Lemoyne de Forges, and Kunreuther (2011).

Chapter 7. Demand Anomalies

1. See http://www.sba.gov/services/disasterassistance/ for more details on the SBA disaster loan program (accessed November 5, 2010).

2. Why the insurer was able to charge that much of an excess over claims in a competitive insurance market was not explained.

3. The authors discount the idea that moral hazard might be greater for auto than homeowners' insurance by saying that the deductibles are typically small relative to the total value of the asset – but of course most auto collision claims are small and so a deductible there might impact use for "fender-benders" and the like to a greater extent than for homeowners' coverage where the losses are likely to be larger.

4. The insurer offered policies with deductibles of $500, $1,000, $2,000, and $5,000.

5. A large number of accidents may cause a premium increase.

6. For more details on airline insurance, see http://www.travelinsurancecenter.com/.

7. The accident rate is much higher for privately operated planes for which flight insurance is not available.

8. Today, flight insurance is sold (or at least quoted) on the Web, which indicates there is some demand in advance of the airport.

9. Some rental car companies now charge uninsured customers who had an accident the daily rental fee for the number of days the car is out of service ("loss of use") in addition to the cost of repairs. Unless the car is out of service for months such additional charges still cannot make up for the very high premium loading factor.

10. Employees on business trips are generally told not to buy insurance on rental cars because the company can get the commercial auto insurer to cover all nonowned and hired-car exposures much more cheaply. We are grateful to Jim MacDonald for pointing this out to us.

11. Interesting, a person is much more likely to die from heart disease than cancer, but there are few heart disease specific insurance policies.

12. According to aflac.com, "Aflac insures more than 50 million people worldwide" http://www.aflac.com/aboutaflac/corporateoverview/default.aspx (accessed October 13, 2011).

13. We thank Jeff Brown and Michael Liersch for helpful comments and discussions on this section.

14. In reality, some advisers often ignore the possibility of a much longer than average life and simply report the income that would be received if the person had about the average life expectancy (Jeff Brown, personal communication, May 2010).

15. States also often require that annuity companies contribute to a guarantee fund to protect the promised income.

16. In the case of Enron, all employees whose entire investment was in company stock had nothing when the firm went bankrupt. We thank Michael Liersch for pointing this out to us.

17. If the person is loss averse and is therefore most concerned with parting with a large amount of wealth (after death) if he or she buys an annuity and dies soon after, he or she may not want to purchase an annuity. In other words, loss aversion will outweigh risk aversion.

18. A knowledgeable investor can combine an annuity with an invested portfolio to achieve the balance between risk and the return he or she desires.

19. Hospital care ($2,100) + chemotherapy ($7,200) + surgery ($5,000) + upfront cash ($5,000) = $19,300; this estimate assumes only one hospital stay of seven days. Additional hospital stays would increase the payout. Another estimate has suggested that a $290 Aflac policy has an expected payout of $16,000 which lends some support to our estimate (Bennett, Weinberg, and Lieberman 1998).

Chapter 8. Descriptive Models of Insurance Supply

1. The exact probability of at least one hurricane occurring during the next decade is (1 – Probability of no hurricanes in Florida during the next ten years) = $1 - (5/6)^{10} = .84$. This is a good example of the working of the law of large numbers. We don't know where a hurricane will strike in Florida over the next ten years causing at least $10 billion in damage, but we are fairly certain that at least one such event will occur in the state during this period.

2. These arguments also may explain the demand for reinsurance by property/liability companies (Mayers and Smith 1990). Neil Doherty and Seha Tiniç (1982) have argued that demand for reinsurance is generated by insurers anticipating policyholders' aversion to insolvency.

3. The reason that expected profits will fall is that firms in a competitive market are setting prices on the elastic portion of their demand curves. This implies that if prices are increased, total revenue will fall. If costs are assumed to remain the same, then expected profits will be lower.

4. James Stone also introduces a constraint regarding the stability of the insurer's operation. However, insurers have traditionally not focused on this constraint in dealing with catastrophic risks.

5. The actuaries and underwriters were also asked to price a policy for leakage of an underground storage tank and for a neutral risk where there was no context specified when either or both the probability and losses were well-specified or ambiguous. Their pricing behavior was similar to that described for the earthquake risk.

6. Over time, many such plans have been converted to for-profit firms.

7. See Grace, M. F., R. W. Klein, and Z. Liu (2005); Klein, R. W. (2007); Klein, R. W. (1995).

8. We thank Jim MacDonald for pointing this out to us.

Chapter 9. Anomalies on the Supply Side

1. A more detailed treatment of this decision can be found in Wharton Risk Management Center (2005).
2. If an investor was risk neutral and the risk-free rate of return on capital was eight percent, then it would require a twenty percent return on its capital if it believed that it had only a ninety percent chance of recouping its investment (i.e., 0.9 [1.20] = 1.08). If the likelihood of a terrorist attack were less than one in ten, then the investor would be better off investing in terrorism insurance than earning an eight percent risk-free return. As the risk-free return decreases from eight percent, then investing in terrorism coverage becomes even more attractive to the investor.
3. In the absence of other large-scale attacks like 9/11 and with the government still being largely involved through a backstop today in some of the largest insurance markets (United States, Europe), prices of terrorism insurance have decreased significantly since 2002. By the end of 2008 in the United States, about two-thirds of large U.S. firms had purchased terrorism insurance at an average cost of 12.5 percent of what they paid for property insurance (Michel-Kerjan, Raschky, and Kunreuther 2009).
4. For more details on the use of catastrophe models in the risk assessment process, see chapter 3 in Grossi and Kunreuther (2005).
5. For more details on the interaction between regulators and insurers see Grace and Klein (2007) and chapter 3 in Kunreuther and Michel-Kerjan (2009).
6. More details on the agreement between State Farm and the state of Florida can be found at http://www.floir.com/PressReleases/viewmediarelease.aspx?ID=3375 (accessed September 10, 2010).
7. We appreciate the helpful comments by Richard Roth, Jr. on this section of the paper in an e-mail with the authors on September 2, 2010.
8. Insurers may have added a general "fudge factor" to premiums to take account of all of the perils they had not thought of explicitly.
9. For more details on the catastrophe bond market see Michel-Kerjan and Morlaye (2008).
10. A few phone calls can generate premium quotes for car insurance, extended warranties, or life insurance. There is other coverage, such as health insurance, where searching for quotes is more difficult and time-consuming.

Chapter 10. Design Principles for Insurance

1. Compared to cash transfers, earmarked vouchers ensure that every household given them buys at least as much of the specific good (insurance or nourishing food) as the voucher will cover. Households that previously bought large amounts of the good, however, will just substitute the voucher for their private payments.
2. An insurer who provides protection to a policyholder is responsible for losses incurred by the policyholder no matter who caused them. One reason for this

contractual arrangement between insurer and insured is the difficulty in assigning causality for a particular event. With respect to fire damage a classic case is *H. R. Moch Co., Inc. v. Rensselaer Water Co. 247N.Y.160, 159 N.E. 896*, which ruled that "A wrongdoer who by negligence sets fire to a building is liable in damages to the owner where the fire has its origin, but not to other owners who are injured when it spreads." We are indebted to Victor Goldberg who provided us with this case.

3. The state of Mississippi lost this case. For more details see Kunreuther and Michel-Kerjan (2009).

Chapter 11. Strategies for Dealing with Insurance-Related Anomalies

1. Portions of this section are based on material in Krantz and Kunreuther (2007).
2. The tool is called the "Medicare Plan Finder" at www.medicare.gov/find-a-plan/questions/home.aspx.
3. The probability of not collecting the extra premium is $(19/20)^{10} = .60$.
4. The impetus for national health insurance in the United States is generally held to be the large number of low-income people who are uninsured, not the small number of well-off risk takers without coverage, although there are millions of these individuals as well.
5. Depending on the nature of laws and contracts, partial failure to pay need not necessarily result in bankruptcy of the firm.
6. What actually happens when an insurer is unable to pay all claims, or is forecast to be unable to pay all claims, is complex. Regulators usually intervene and various combinations of buyout, merger, receivership, and liquidation are all possible.

Chapter 12. Innovations in Insurance Markets through Multiyear Contracts

1. A current smoker defending his habit could note that the higher premiums for health insurance would be paid for fewer additional years because of the higher mortality of smokers, but achieving such potential savings on lifetime health premiums by shortening one's lifetime would not appeal to most people.
2. The reduction in expected loss for each home is $(1/100 \ [\$20,000]) = \$200$, so the total reduction in premiums for all 1000 homes with a loading cost of fifty percent is $(1000) (\$200) (1.50) = \$300,000$.
3. The National Flood Insurance Program was created in 1968 because insurers viewed flood risk as uninsurable and refused to cover it. As of April 2012 the NFIP sold more than 5.5 million policies (compared to 2.5 million in 1992) and covered more than \$1.2 trillion in assets (compared to only \$237 billion in 1992;

nominal) (Michel-Kerjan and Kousky 2010; http://www.fema.gov/business/nfip/statistics/pcstat.shtm accessed July 2012.).

4. This subsection is based on Kunreuther and Michel-Kerjan (2010). For more details on the performance of the National Flood Insurance Program since its inception see Michel-Kerjan (2010).

Chapter 13. Publicly Provided Social Insurance

1. The circumstances surrounding the passage of Social Security had a similar history. Private pensions and annuities provided limited financial support and incomes during working lifetimes during the Great Depression were often insufficient to provide savings for retirement.
2. Even pandemics such as influenza usually affect only a very small share of total health claims.
3. Total beneficiary premiums for Medicare cover only about ten percent of total benefits costs, however.
4. Health care reform will allow somewhat more variation in the future.
5. Even after taking these additional benefits into account as well as lowered cost from improved health, some preventive activities appear to be overused, such as prostate cancer screening.
6. The reason that it costs only $41 million is that only 86,316 of the population of one hundred thousand at age fifty survived to age sixty-five.
7. See Pauly and Blavin (2008) for a discussion of optimal coinsurance when consumer demand differs from a correct reflection of marginal benefit. Roughly speaking, if consumers underestimate the marginal benefit from colonoscopies and so are still not pursuing them up to the point where marginal benefit equals marginal cost when faced with a user price reduced by the cost offset, it will be desirable to reduce cost sharing even more until they get close to what would be optimal. Possible risk protection impacts of insurance also should be taken into account, but there is not much risk associated with the cost of a scheduled routine colonoscopy.
8. The conventional Medicare plan will not cover routine colonoscopies at more frequent intervals for people at normal risk. It will pay for those at elevated risk (family member had colon cancer or personal history of colon cancer or precancerous polyps) every two years. Some of the private Medicare Advantage plans may pay for coverage at more frequent intervals.
9. http://www.jhsph.edu/publichealthnews/press_releases/2007/wang_adult_obesity.html.
10. More than half of the uninsured were found to have household incomes high enough that, even after paying insurance premiums, they would still have enough left over to attain a level of consumption above that for households below the poverty line.

11. Following the implementation of the legislation the uninsured percentage in Massachusetts did fall, but primarily among the population made eligible for Medicaid coverage.

Chapter 14. Conclusions – A Framework for Prescriptive Recommendations

1. If that expectation does change because the loss correctly signals some alteration in the loss-generating process, a premium increase would be appropriate.

Glossary

Actuarially fair premium	A premium for a given insurance policy equal to the expected claims under that policy. It does not take into account administrative and capital costs.
Administrative costs	Costs of doing business for an insurer beyond the cost of paying claims that includes marketing costs and staff.
Adverse selection	The tendency of those exposed to a higher risk to seek more insurance coverage than those at a lower risk when premiums do not fully reflect risk. Insurers react either by charging higher premiums to everyone or not offering insurance at all.
All-perils coverage	A comprehensive policy that covers losses from all causes, except those specifically excluded.
Ambiguity aversion	A phenomenon in which insurers will require a markup on the premium to account for uncertainty in the estimates of the probability of a loss.
Anomaly/anomalous	Behavior inconsistent with that predicted by the benchmark models of demand and supply.
Availability bias	The tendency to overweight the impact of recent events in decision making. This bias can be responsible for consumers purchasing coverage after a disaster occurs and for insurers raising premiums after a major catastrophe.
Behavioral economics	Allows for the role of emotions, misperceptions, and other elements outside of expected utility and profit maximization for analyzing individual and organizational decision making.

Capital	Shareholder's equity and retained earnings (for stock insurance companies); initial capital plus retained earnings (for mutual companies).
Catastrophe bonds	A corporate bond that requires the purchasers to forgive or defer some or all payments of interest or principal if the catastrophe loss surpasses a specified amount or trigger.
Catastrophe model	A computer-based model that estimates losses from natural or man-made hazards, s uch as earthquakes, floods, hurricanes, and acts of terrorism.
Choice architecture	The framing of information and options in such a way as to encourage decision makers to make a choice closer to the benchmark model.
Claims	Payment for losses covered by insurance.
Consumer welfare	Individual benefits derived from consumption of goods and services. Often described as the difference between an individual's willingness to pay and the amount actually paid for a good.
Correlated losses	The simultaneous occurrence of many losses from a single catastrophe or disaster.
Coinsurance	Proportional sharing of the losses by an insured party.
Deductible	Dollar amount or percentage of an insured loss that the policyholder must incur before the insurer pays any claims.
Disappearing deductible	An insurance policy where the deductible disappears when the loss reaches a specified amount.
Exceedance probability (EP) curve	A graphical representation of the probability that a certain level of risk will be surpassed during a future time period. The most common form of an EP curve is the annual probability that an economic loss will be surpassed.
Expected loss	The sum of the probabilities of each insured event multiplied by the estimated dollar amount of the loss from each of these events.
Experience rating	Premiums that reflect individual claims history. Automobile insurance coverage is usually experience rated.

Extra-welfarism	Substitutes the preferences of policymakers for those of individuals in efforts to maximize social welfare. Assumes that there are social values above and beyond individuals' valuation of their own well-being that are worth considering.
Fixed costs	Costs that do not vary with output such as rent of a building.
Framing	Different ways of presenting information that can impact on choices between alternatives.
Free entry and exit	An assumption required for the existence of perfect competition in which there are no barriers for firms to enter or exit the market.
Goals and plans theory	A descriptive theory of choice in which financial, emotional, and social goals impact on decision making.
Guaranteed renewability	A provision which allows individuals who pay premiums when they renew their insurance policy to continue coverage and not be singled out for premium increases based on their risk or claims experience.
Heuristics	Rules of thumb used in making decisions.
Independent events	The occurrence of one event is unrelated to the occurrence of other events.
Individual peril coverage	More specific than named-perils coverage. This type of coverage will only protect against losses from one cause. Cancer insurance would be an example.
Information asymmetry	A situation in which two parties have different levels of information. When buyers of insurance know more about their loss probability than insurers, this can lead to adverse selection.
Insolvency	The inability of an insurer or reinsurer to pay all or a portion of its claims obligations because liabilities exceed assets.
Insurance vouchers	A grant, similar in concept to food stamps, to increase equity without distorting market premiums. These vouchers are restricted to payment of insurance premiums.
Interdependencies	Actions or events that can impose negative impacts on others. An example would be a fire that starts in one home, but may spread to adjacent houses.

Law of large numbers	As the risk pool increases and losses are independent, the actual loss approaches the expected loss.
Loading cost factor	The portion of the premium that is not used to pay claims, calculated as a percentage of the premium.
Multi-year insurance	Insurance policies sold for consecutive years as opposed to a traditional annual insurance policy.
Loss aversion	A behavioral phenomenon by which individuals exhibit a stronger preference for avoiding losses than for experiencing gains.
Loss distribution	An enumeration of potential losses and the probability that each will occur.
Loss ratio	The proportion of the premium used to pay claims.
Macro-horizontal equity	The extent to which people have similar levels of welfare.
Market penetration level	The ratio of actual buyers to eligible buyers in an insurance market.
Mental accounting	A behavioral phenomenon by which individuals allocate their income into separate buckets to be used for specific purposes.
Micro-horizontal equity	The principle that people who benefit from an activity should pay the cost of that activity, and people who do not benefit should not pay.
Mitigation measures	Actions an individual or firm can take to reduce the probability or amount of potential losses. This may include driving a safer car or installing storm shutters on a coastal property.
Multi-year insurance	Insurance policies sold for consecutive years as opposed to a traditional annual insurance policy.
Mutual insurance	Form of insurance in which the policyholders are also the owners of the insurance firm.
Named perils coverage	Coverage that applies only to loss arising out of causes listed as covered.
Premium	The price of insurance protection for a specified period of time defined in the insurance contract (normally one year).
Probabilistic insurance	An insurance policy involving a probability that the insured will not be reimbursed for a loss.

Probable maximum loss	The largest economic loss likely to occur for a set of policies when a catastrophic event occurs.
Pseudo-deductible	A threshold above the actual deductible on an insurance policy that governs the decision on whether to file a claim and if so for how much..
Rating agencies	Organizations that provide independent evaluations of insurers and reinsurers' financial stability and their ability to meet their obligations to policyholders.
Reinsurance	Purchase of insurance by an insurer for the purpose of spreading risk and reducing claims to the insurer from catastrophic losses.
Reservation premium	The premium above which an individual will refuse to purchase coverage.
Residual market mechanism	A coverage source of last resort for firms and individuals rejected by voluntary market insurers.
Risk-averse	The attitudes of people whose concern with a risk is such that they are willing to pay more for coverage than the expected claim.
Risk premium	The amount in excess of the expected claims that a risk-averse individual is willing to pay for insurance.
Safety-first model	A model of insurer pricing that reflects the insurer's threshold probability that losses for a specific event will not exceed a pre-specified value.
Social welfare	Overall well-being of society as defined by the preferences of individuals in that society and specific weights on the welfare of different individuals.
Subjective probability	An individual's perception of the likelihood of occurrence of a particular event.
Survivability constraint	The premium an insurer must charge and the number of policies it can offer to keep its probability of insolvency below a threshold level.
Transactions costs	Costs incurred in making economic exchanges or contracts.
Underwriting	The process of selecting risks to insure and determining the amounts of coverage and the terms under which the company will accept the risk.

Bibliography

A. M. Best. 2006. *Methodology: Catastrophe Analysis in A.M. Best Rating*. Oldwick, NJ: A.M. Best.

Abaluck. J., and J. Gruber. 2011. Choice inconsistencies among the elderly: Evidence from plan choice in the Medicare part D program. *American Economic Review* 101: 1180–210.

Abelson, R. 1996. When the best policy may be no policy at all. *New York Times*. November 3.

Aflac Incorporated. 2008. *It's no mystery how Aflac makes a difference: Annual Report for 2008*. http://thomson.mobular.net/thomson/7/2877/3818/ (accessed November 18, 2010).

Akerlof, G. 1970. The market for lemons: Qualitative uncertainty and the market mechanism. *Quarterly Journal of Economics* 84: 488–500.

American Council of Life Insurers. 2008. *ACLI Life Insurers Fact Book 2008*. http://www.acli.com/ACLI/Tools/Industry+Facts/Life+Insurers+Fact+Book/GR08-108.htm (accessed November 5, 2010).

Ameriks, J., A. Caplan, S. Laufer, and S. Van Nieuwerburgh. 2011. The joy of giving or assisted living? Using strategic surveys to separate public care aversion from bequest motives. *Journal of Finance* 66: 519–61.

Arena, M. 2008. Does insurance market activity promote economic growth? A cross country study for industrialized and developing countries. *Journal of Risk and Insurance* 75: 921–46.

Arrow, K. J. 1963. Uncertainty and the welfare economics of medical care. *American Economic Review* 53: 941–73.

Bainbridge, J. 1952. *Biography of an Idea: The Story of Mutual Fire and Casualty Insurance*. Garden City, NY: Doubleday & Co.

Bantwal, V. and H. Kunreuther. 2000. A Cat Bond Premium Puzzle? *Journal of Psychology and Financial Markets*, 1(1): 76–91.

Barrett, W. P. 2010. Annuities aren't all the same. *Forbes Magazine*. March 29.

Barseghyan, L., J. Prince, and J. Teitelbaum. 2011. Are risk preferences stable across contexts? Evidence from insurance data. *American Economic Review* 101: 591–631.

Bell, D. E. 1985. Disappointment in decision making under uncertainty. *Operations Research* 33: 1–27.

——. 1982. Regret in decision making under uncertainty. *Operations Research* 30: 961–81.

Benartzi, S., A. Previtero, and R. Thaler. 2011. Why don't people annuitize late life consumption? A framing explanation of the under-annuitization puzzle. *American Economic Review* 98: 304–9.

——. Forthcoming. Annuitization puzzles. *Journal of Economic Perspectives.*

Benartzi, S., and R. Thaler. 1995. Myopic loss aversion and the equity premium puzzle. *Quarterly Journal of Economics* 110: 73–92.

Bennett, C. L., P. D. Weinberg, and J. J. Lieberman. 1998. Cancer insurance policies in Japan and the United States. *Western Journal of Medicine* 168: 17.

Borch, K. 1962. Equilibrium in a reinsurance market. *Econometrica* 30: 424–44.

Born, P. 2001. Insurer profitability in different regulatory and legal environments. *Journal of Regulatory Economics* 19: 211–37.

Bradford, S. L. 2005. Which life insurance is best? *SmartMoney.com*, February 9, 2005. http://www.smartmoney.com/personal-finance/insurance/which-life-insurance-is-best-16975/ (accessed June 25, 2010).

Braun, M., P. S. Fader, E. T. Bradlow, and H. Kunreuther. 2006. Modeling the "pseudodeductible" in homeowners' insurance. *Management Science* 52: 1258–72.

Braun, M., and A. Muermann. 2004. The impact of regret on the demand for insurance. *Journal of Risk and Insurance* 71: 737–67.

Brown, J. R. 2001. Private pensions, mortality risk, and the decision to annuitize. *Journal of Public Economics* 82: 29–62.

Brown, J., N. B. Coe, and A. Finkelstein. 2007. Medicaid crowd-out of private long-term care insurance demand: Evidence from the health and retirement survey. *Tax Policy and the Economy* 21: 1–34.

Brown, J., and A. Finkelstein. 2008. The interaction of public and private insurance: Medicaid and the long term care insurance market. *American Economic Review* 98: 1083–102.

——. 2007. Why is the market for long term care insurance so small? *Journal of Public Economics* 91: 1967–91.

Brown, J. R., and A. Goolsbee. 2002. Does the internet make markets more competitive? Evidence from the life insurance industry. *Journal of Political Economy* 110: 481–507.

Brown, J. R., J. R. Kling, S. Mullainathan, and M. Wrobel. 2008. Why don't people insure late life consumption? A framing explanation of the under-annuitization puzzle. NBER Working Paper No. 13748. Cambridge, MA: National Bureau of Economic Research.

Buchanan, J. 1998. *Explorations in Constitutional Economics*. College Station, TX: Texas A&M University Press.

Buchanan, J., and G. Tullock. 1962. *Calculus of Consent*. Ann Arbor: University of Michigan Press.

Bundorf, M. K., and M. V. Pauly. 2006. Is health insurance affordable for the uninsured? *Journal of Health Economics* 25: 650–73.

Bundorf, M. K., B. J. Herring, and M. V. Pauly. 2010. Health risk, income, and employment-based health insurance. *Forum for Health Economics and Policy* 13(2): Article 13 http://www.bepress.com/fhep/13/2/13 (accessed October 28, 2011).

Bureau of Economic Analysis. 2010. *Industry Economic Accounts.* http://www.bea.gov/industry/index.htm (accessed July 28, 2010).

Cabantous, L., D. Hilton, H. Kunreuther, and E. Michel-Kerjan. 2011. Is imprecise knowledge better than conflicting expertise? Evidence from insurers' decisions in the United States. *Journal of Risk and Uncertainty* 42: 211–32.

Camerer, C., and T.-H. Ho. 1994. Violations of the betweenness axiom and nonlinearity of probability. *Journal of Risk and Uncertainty* 8: 167–96.

Camerer, C. F., and H. Kunreuther. 1989. Decision processes for low probability events: Policy implications. *Journal of Policy Analysis and Management* 8: 565–92.

Capital Insurance Agency, Inc. 2008. *Personal Cancer Indemnity/Hospital Intensive Care Protection Insurance (Prepared for State of Florida Employees).* Columbus, GA: American Family Life Assurance Company of Columbus (AFLAC). http://www.myflorida.com/mybenefits/pdf/AFLAC.pdf (accessed November 18, 2010).

Cawley, J., and T. Philipson. 1999. An empirical examination of information barriers to trade in insurance. *American Economic Review* 89: 827–46.

Center for Medicare and Medicaid Services. 2008. National Health Expenditure Projections: 2009–2019, Forecast Summary and Selected Tables. Table 3. https://www.cms.gov/NationalHealthExpendData/03_NationalHealthAccountsProjected.asp#TopOfPage (accessed July 28, 2010).

Centers for Disease Control and Prevention (CDC). 2006. FastStats – Cancer. http://www.cdc.gov/nchs/fastats/cancer.htm (accessed July 10, 2010).

Chang, S., S. R. Long, L. Kutikova, L. Bowman, D. Finley, W. H. Crown, and C. L. Bennett. 2004. Estimating the cost of cancer: Results on the basis of claims data analysis for cancer patients diagnosed with seven types of cancer during 1999 to 2000. *Journal of Clinical Oncology* 22: 3524–30.

Chapman, G. B., and E. J. Johnson. 1995. Preference reversals in monetary and life expectancy evaluations. *Organizational Behavior and Human Decision Processes* 62: 300–17.

Chen, T., A. Kalra, and B. Sun. 2009. Why do consumers buy extended service contracts? *Journal of Consumer Research* 36: 611–23.

Chiappori, P. A., and B. Salanie. 2000. Testing for asymmetric information in insurance markets. *Journal of Political Economy* 108: 56–78.

Cochrane, J. H. 1995. Time-consistent health insurance. *Journal of Political Economy* 103: 445–73.

Cohen, A. 2005. Asymmetric information and learning: Evidence from the automobile insurance market. *Review of Economics and Statistics* 87: 197–207.

Consumer Reports. 2005. Extended warranties: Say yes, sometimes. *Consumer Reports.org* 70: 51.

Cummins, J. D. and C. M. Lewis. 2003. Catastrophic Events, Parameter Uncertainty and the Breakdown of Implicit Long-Term Contracting: The Case of Terrorism Insurance. *Journal of Risk and Uncertainty* 26(2): 153–178.

Cummins, J. D., D. M. McGill, H. E. Winklevoss, and R. Zelten. 1974. *Consumer Attitudes toward Auto and Homeowners Insurance*. Philadelphia: Department of Insurance, Wharton School, University of Pennsylvania.

Cutler, D. M., A. Finkelstein, and K. McGarry. 2008. Preference heterogeneity and insurance markets: Explaining a puzzle of insurance. *American Economic Review* 98: 157–62.

Cutler, D. M., and R. Zeckhauser. 2004. Extending the theory to meet the practice of insurance. *Brookings-Wharton Papers on Financial Services: 2004*. Eds. R. Herring and R. E. Litan. Washington, DC: Brookings Institution Press, 1–53.

Dacy, D., and H. Kunreuther. 1968. *The Economics of Natural Disasters*. New York: Free Press.

Doherty, N. A., and H. Schlesinger. 1983. Optimal insurance in incomplete markets. *Journal of Political Economy* 91: 1045–54.

  1990. Rational insurance purchasing: Consideration of contract non-performance. *Quarterly Journal of Economics* 105: 243–53.

Doherty, N. A., and S. M. Tinic. 1982. A note on reinsurance under conditions of capital market equilibrium. *Journal of Finance* 36: 949–53.

Dorfman, R., and P. O. Steiner. 1954. Optimal advertising and optimal quality. *American Economic Review* 44: 826–36.

Dyer, J., and R. Sarin. 1982. Relative risk aversion. *Management Science* 28: 875–86.

Eichner, M. J., M. B. McClellen, and D. A. Wise. 1998. Insurance or self-insurance? Variation, persistence, and individual health accounts. In *Inquiries in the Economics of Aging*. Ed. D. A. Wise. Chicago: University of Chicago Press, 19–45.

Einav, L., A. Finkelstein, I. Pascu, and M. R. Cullen. 2010. *How general are risk preferences? Choices under uncertainty in different domains*. NBER Working Paper No. 15686. Cambridge, MA: National Bureau of Economic Research.

Einav, L., A. Finkelstein, and P. Schrimpf. 2010. Optimal mandates and the welfare cost of asymmetric information: Evidence from the U.K. annuity market. *Econometrica* 78: 1031–92.

Eisner, R., and R. H. Strotz. 1961. Flight insurance and the theory of choice. *Journal of Political Economy* 69: 355–68.

Ellsberg, D. 1961. Risk, ambiguity, and the savage axioms. *The Quarterly Journal of Economics* 75: 643–69.

Er, J. P., H. Kunreuther, and I. Rosenthal. 1998. Utilizing third-party inspections for preventing major chemical accidents. *Risk Analysis* 18: 145–54.

Fang, H., M. P. Keane, and D. Silverman. 2008. Sources of advantageous selection: Evidence from the Medigap insurance market. *Journal of Political Economy* 116: 303–50.

Federal Old-Age and Survivors Insurance and Federal Disability Insurance (OASDI) Trust Funds. 2009. *Annual Report of the Board of Trustees*. Washington, DC: U.S. Government Printing Office.

Finkelstein, A., and K. McGarry. 2006. Multiple dimensions of private information: Evidence from the long-term care insurance market. *American Economic Review* 96: 938–58.

Finkelstein, A., and J. Poterba. 2004. Adverse selection in insurance markets: Policyholder evidence from the U.K. annuity market. *Journal of Political Economy* 112: 183–208.

Finucane, M. L., A. Alhakami, P. Slovic, and S. M. Johnson. 2000. The affect heuristic in judgments of risks and benefits. *Journal of Behavioral Decision Making* 13:1–17.

Fischhoff, B., R. M. Gonzalez, D. A. Small, and J. S. Lerner. 2003. Judged terror risk and proximity to the World Trade Center. *Journal of Risk and Uncertainty* 26: 137–51.

Fleckenstein, M. 2006. Rating agency recalibrations. In *The Review: Cedant's Guide to Renewals 2006*. Ed. G. Dobie. London: Informa UK Ltd.

Frase, M. J. 2009. Minimalist health coverage: The market for mini-medical plans is growing. Is such limited coverage really better than nothing? *HR Magazine*, June2009.http://findarticles.com/p/articles/mi_m3495/is_6_54/ai_n32068534/ (accessed July 2, 2010).

Freeman, P. K., and H. Kunreuther. 1997. *Managing Environmental Risk through Insurance*. Boston: Kluwer Academic Pub.

Gale, W. G., J. M. Iwry, D. C. John, and L. Walker. 2008. Increasing annuitization in 401(k) plans with automatic trial income. The Hamilton Project, Discussion Paper 2008–02. Washington, DC: The Brookings Institution.

Gilboa, I., and D. Schmeidler. 1995. Case based decision theory. *Quarterly Journal of Economics* 110: 605–39.

Grace, M. F., and R.W. Klein. 2007. Facing mother nature. *Regulation* 30: 28–34.

Grace, M. F., R. W. Klein, and P. R. Kleindorfer. 2004. Homeowners insurance with bundled catastrophe coverage. *Journal of Risk and Insurance* 71: 351–79.

Grace, M. F., R.W. Klein, and Z. Liu. 2005. Increased hurricane risk and insurance market responses. *Journal of Insurance Regulation* 24: 2–32.

Greenwald, B. C., and J. E. Stiglitz. 1990. Asymmetric information and the new theory of the firm: Financial constraints and risk behavior. *American Economic Review* 80: 160–5.

Gron, A. 1994. Capacity constraints and cycles in property-casualty insurance markets. *Rand Journal of Economics* 25: 110–27.

Grossi, P., and H. Kunreuther. 2005. *Catastrophe Modeling: A New Approach to Managing Risk*. Boston: Springer Science and Business Media, Inc.

Handel, B. 2010. Adverse selection and switching costs in health insurance markets: When nudging hurts. January 26. Unpublished paper, Northwestern University, Chicago, IL.

Harrington, S. E., and G. Niehaus. 1999. Basis risk with PCS catastrophe insurance derivative contracts. *Journal of Risk and Insurance*, 66: 49–82.

He, D. 2009. Three essays on long-term care and life insurance. Dissertation, Washington University, St. Louis, MO.

Hendel, I., and A. Lizzeri. 2003. The role of commitment in dynamic contracts: Evidence from life insurance. *Quarterly Journal of Economics* 118: 299–327.

Herring, B. 2005. The effect of the availability of charity care to the uninsured on the demand for private health insurance. *Journal of Health Economics* 24: 225–52.

Hertwig, R., G. Barron, E. U. Weber, and I. Erev. 2004. Decisions from experience and the effect of rare events in risky choice. *Psychological Science* 15: 534.

Heweijer, C., N. Ranger, and R. E. T. Ward. 2009. Adaptation to climate change: Threats and opportunities for the insurance industry. *Geneva Papers on Risk and Insurance* 34: 360–80.

Hogarth, R. M., and H. Kunreuther. 1995. Decision making under ignorance: Arguing with yourself. *Journal of Risk and Uncertainty* 10: 15–36.

Hsee, C. K., and H. C. Kunreuther. 2000. The affection effect in insurance decisions. *Journal of Risk and Uncertainty* 20: 141–59.

Huber, O., R. Wider, and O. W. Huber. 1997. Active information search and complete information presentation in naturalistic risky decision tasks. *Acta Psychologica* 95: 15–29.

Huysentruyt, M., and D. Read. 2010. How do people value extended warranties? *Journal of Risk and Uncertainty* 40: 197–218.

Inkmann, J., P. Lopes, and A. Michaelides. 2011. How deep is the annuity market participation puzzle? *Review of Financial Studies* 24: 279–319.

Insurance Information Institute. 2009a. Auto Insurance. http://www.iii.org/media/facts/statsbyissue/auto/ (accessed July 5, 2010).

    2009b. Do I need separate rental car insurance? http://www.iii.org/individuals/auto/a/rentalcar/?printerfriendly=yes (accessed April 1, 2009).

    2008. Homeowners Insurance. http://www.iii.org/media/facts/statsbyissue/homeowners/ (accessed December 9, 2008).

    2010. Online Insurance Fact Book. http://www2.iii.org/factbook/ (accessed June 25, 2010).

Insurance Information Network of California (IINC). 2008. Rental Car Insurance Simplified. http://www.iinc.org/articles/2/1/Rental-Car-Insurance-Simplified/Page1.html (accessed April 1, 2009).

Insurance Research Council. 2006. "Average Premiums for Homeowners and Renters Insurance, United States, 2000–2008." Data table. Insurance Information Institute: Homeowners Insurance. http://www.iii.org/media/facts/statsbyissue/homeowners/ (accessed November 19, 2010).

Insure.com. 2010. *The basics of accidental death and dismemberment insurance.* http://www.insure.com/articles/lifeinsurance/accidental-death.html (accessed February 20, 2010).

Jaffee, D., H. Kunreuther, and E. Michel-Kerjan. 2008. Long term insurance (LTI) for addressing catastrophic market failure. NBER Working Paper No. 14210. Cambridge, MA: National Bureau of Economic Research.

    2010. Long term insurance (LTI) for addressing catastrophe risk. *Journal of Insurance Regulation* 29:167–87.

Jaffee, D., and T. Russell. 2003. Markets under stress: The case of extreme event insurance. In *Economics for an Imperfect World: Essays in Honor of Joseph E. Stiglitz.* Eds. R. Arnott, B. Greenwald, R. Kanbur, and B. Nalebuff. Cambridge, MA: MIT Press.

Jenkins, H. W. 2004. Insurance Update: More alert, less at risk. *Wall Street Journal.* August 11.

Johnson, E. J., J. Hershey, J. Meszaros, and H. Kunreuther. 1993. Framing, probability distortions and insurance decisions. *Journal of Risk and Uncertainty* 7: 35–51.

Kahneman, D. 2011. *Thinking, Fast and Slow*. New York: Farrar, Straus and Giroux

Kahneman, D., and A. Tversky. 1973. On the psychology of prediction. *Psychological Review* 80: 237–51.

1979. Prospect theory: An analysis of decision under risk. *Econometrica* 47: 263–91.

Keynes, J. M. 1921. *A Treatise on Probability*. New York: Macmillan and Co.

Klein, R. W. 2007. Catastrophe risk and the regulation of property insurance: A comparative analysis of five states. Working Paper, Georgia State University, Atlanta, GA.

1995. Insurance regulation in transition. *Journal of Risk and Insurance* 62: 263–404.

Knight, F. H. 1921. *Risk, Uncertainty and Profit*. Boston and New York: Houghton Mifflin.

Kolata, G. 1994. When is a coincidence too bad to be true? *New York Times*. September 11.

Kotlikoff, L. J., and J. Gokhale. 2002. The adequacy of life insurance. *Research Dialogue* 72. New York: TIAA-CREF Institute.

Kowalski, A., W. J. Congdon, and M. H. Showalter. 2008. State health insurance regulations and the price of high deductible policies. *Forum for Health Economics and Policy* 11: 1–24.

Krantz, D. H., and H. C. Kunreuther. 2007. Goals and plans in decision making. *Judgment and Decision Making* 2: 137–68.

Kunreuther, H. 1989. The role of actuaries and underwriters in insuring ambiguous risks. *Risk Analysis* 9: 319–28.

2002. The role of insurance in managing extreme events: Implications for terrorism coverage. *Business Economics* 37: 6–16.

2009. The weakest link: Managing risk through interdependent strategies. In *Network Challenge: Strategy, Profit and Risk in an Interlinked World*. Eds. P. R. Kleindorfer and Y. Wind. Upper Saddle River, NJ: Wharton School Publishing.

Kunreuther, H., R. Ginsberg, L. Miller, P. Sagi, P. Slovic, B. Borkan, and N. Katz. 1978. *Disaster Insurance Protection: Public Policy Lessons*. New York: John Wiley & Sons.

Kunreuther, H., R. Hogarth, and J. Meszaros. 1993. Insurer ambiguity and market failure. *Journal of Risk and Uncertainty* 7: 71–87.

Kunreuther, H., and E. Michel-Kerjan. 2010. From market to government failure in insuring U.S. natural catastrophes: How can long-term contracts help? *In Private Markets and Public Insurance Programs*. Ed. J. Brown. Washington, DC: American Enterprise Institute Press.

2009. *At War with the Weather*. Cambridge, MA: MIT Press.

Kunreuther, H., N. Novemsky, and D. Kahneman. 2001. Making low probabilities useful. *Journal of Risk and Insurance* 23:103–20.

Kunreuther, H., and M. V. Pauly. 2004. Neglecting disaster: Why don't people insure against large losses? *Journal of Risk and Uncertainty* 28: 5–21.

2005. Terrorism losses and all-perils insurance. *Journal of Insurance Regulation* 23: 3–20.

2006. Insurance decision-making and market behavior. *Foundations and Trends®* *in Microeconomics* 1: 63–127. Hanover, MA: Now Publishers

Kunreuther, H., and R. Roth, Sr., eds. 1998. *Paying the Price: The Status and Role of* *Insurance Against Natural Disasters in the United States.* Washington, DC: The Joseph Henry Press.

Kunreuther, H., W. Sanderson, and R. Vetschera. 1985. A behavioral model of the adoption of protective activities. *Journal of Economic Behavior & Organization* 6: 1–15.

Lecomte, E., and K. Gahagan. 1998. Hurricane insurance protection in Florida. In *Paying the Price: The Status and Role of Insurance Against Natural Disasters in* *the United States.* Eds. H. Kunreuther and R. J. Roth, Sr. Washington, DC: The Joseph Henry Press, 97–124.

Lieber, R. 2010. The unloved annuity gets a hug from Obama. *New York Times.* January 29.

Liebman, J. B., and R. Zeckhauser. 2008. Simple humans, complex insurance, subtle subsidies. NBER Working Paper No. 14330. Cambridge, MA: National Bureau of Economic Research.

Litzenberger, R. H., D. R. Beaglehole, and C. E. Reynolds. 1996. Assessing catastrophe reinsurance-linked securities as a new asset class. *Journal of Portfolio* *Management* Special Issue: 76–86.

Lobb, A. 2002. Ouch! Don't forget the disability insurance. *CNN Money*, May 6, 2002. http://money.cnn.com/2002/03/25/pf/insurance/q_disability/index.htm (accessed December 9, 2008).

Loewenstein, G. F., E. U. Weber, C. K. Hsee, and N. Welch. 2001. Risk as feelings. *Psychological Bulletin* 127: 267–86.

Loomes, G., and R. Sugden. 1982. Regret theory: An alternative theory of rational choice under uncertainty. *Economic Journal* 92: 805–24.

Lloyd's of London. 2008. *Coastal Communities and Climate Change: Maintaining* *Future Insurability* (Part of the 360 Risk Project). London: Lloyd's.

Luhby, T. 2004. Money Matters column. *Newsday.* November 28.

Mayers, D., and C. W. Smith, Jr. 1990. On the corporate demand for insurance: Evidence from the reinsurance market. *Journal of Business* 63: 19–40.

Michel-Kerjan, E. 2010. Catastrophe economics: The National Flood Insurance Program: Past, present, and future. *Journal of Economic Perspectives* 24: 165–86.

Michel-Kerjan, E., and C. Kousky. 2010. Come rain or shine: Evidence on flood insurance purchases in Florida. *Journal of Risk and Insurance* 77: 369–97.

Michel-Kerjan, E., S. Lemoyne de Forges, and H. Kunreuther. 2011. Policy tenure under the U.S. National Flood Insurance Program (NFIP). *Risk Analysis.* Article first published online: September 15, 2011. DOI: 10.1111/j.1539-6924.2011.01671.x (accessed October 28, 2011).

Michel-Kerjan, E. and B. Pedell. 2006. How does the corporate world cope with mega-terrorism? Puzzling evidence from terrorism insurance markets. *Journal* *of Applied Corporate Finance* 18: 61–75.

2005. Terrorism risk coverage in the post-9/11 era: A comparison of new public-private partnerships in France, Germany, and the U.S. *Geneva Papers on Risk and Insurance* 30: 144–70.

Michel-Kerjan, E. O., P. A. Raschky, and H. C. Kunreuther. 2009. Corporate demand for insurance: An empirical analysis of the U.S. market for catastrophe and non-catastrophe risks. Working Paper, Wharton Risk Management Center, University of Pennsylvania, Philadelphia, PA.

Miller, M. J., and K. N. Southwood. 2004. *Homeowners Insurance Coverages: An Actuarial Study of the Frequency and Cost of Claims for the State of Michigan.* Carlock, IL: Epic Consulting, LLC.

Mitchell, O. S., J. M. Poterba, M. J. Warshawsky, and J. R. Brown. 1999. New evidence on the money's worth of individual annuities. *American Economic Review* 89: 1299–1318.

Musgrave, R. A. 1959. *The Theory of Public Finance.* New York: McGraw Hill.

National Association of Insurance Commissioners (NAIC). 2008. 2006 Profitability Report. NAIC Store: Statistical Reports. http://www.naic.org/store_pub_statistical.htm#profitability (accessed December 9, 2008).

2006. A Shopper's Guide to Cancer Insurance. http://oci.wi.gov/pub_list/pi-001.htm (accessed July 10, 2010).

National Highway Traffic Safety Administration (NHTSA). 2007. *Traffic Safety Facts 2007.* Washington, DC: National Center for Statistics and Analysis, U.S. Department of Transportation. http://www-nrd.nhtsa.dot.gov/Pubs/811002.PDF (accessed November 5, 2010).

Office of Fair Trading (OFT). 2002. Extended warranties on domestic electrical goods: A report on an OFT investigation. http://www.oft.gov.uk/shared_oft/reports/consumer_protection/oft387.pdf (accessed November 18, 2010).

Palm, R. 1995. *Earthquake Insurance: A Longitudinal Study of California Homeowners.* Boulder: Westview Press.

Pauly, M. V. 1968. The economics of moral hazard: Comment. *American Economic Review* 58: 531–7.

1970. *Medical Care at Public Expense.* New York: Praeger.

1990. The rational nonpurchase of long-term care insurance. *Journal of Political Economy* 98: 153–68.

2010. *Health Reform without Side Effects: Making Markets Work for Individual Health Insurance.* Stanford: Hoover Institution Press.

Pauly, M. V., and F. Blavin. 2008. Moral hazard in insurance, value based cost sharing, and the benefits of blissful ignorance. *Journal of Health Economics* 27: 1407–17.

Pauly, M. V., and B. Herring. 2006. Incentive-compatible guaranteed renewable health insurance premiums. *Journal of Health Economics* 25: 395–417.

2007. Risk pooling and regulation: Policy and reality in today's individual health insurance market. *Health Affairs* 26: 770–9.

Pauly, M. V., B. Herring, and D. Song. 2006. Information technology and consumer search for health insurance. *International Journal of the Economics of Business* 13: 45–63.

Pauly, M. V., A. L. Hillman, M. S. Kim, and D. R. Brown. 2002. Competitive behavior in the HMO marketplace. *Health Affairs* 21: 194–202.

Pauly, M. V., H. Kunreuther, and R. Hirth. 1994. Guaranteed renewability in health insurance. *Journal of Risk and Uncertainty* 10: 143–56.

Pauly, M. V., and R. Lieberthal. 2008. How risky is individual health insurance? *Health Affairs* 27: w242–w249 (Web exclusive, May 6, 2008). http://content. healthaffairs.org/cgi/reprint/27/3/w242.

Pauly, M.V., K. Menzel, H. Kunreuther, and R. Hirth. 2011. Guaranteed Renewability Uniquely Prevents Adverse Selection. *Journal of Risk and Uncertainty* 43(2): 127–39.

Pauly, M. V., and L. M. Nichols. 2002. The nongroup health insurance market: Short on facts, long on opinions and policy disputes. *Health Affairs* 21: w325–w344. Web exclusive, October 23, 2002. http://content.healthaffairs.org/cgi/reprint/ hlthaff.w2.325v1.

Pear, R. 2010. Health executive defends premiums. *New York Times*. February 24.

Piao, X., and H. Kunreuther. 2006. *Object-oriented affect in warranty decisions*. Manuscript. New York, NY: Columbia University.

Poterba, J., S. Venti, and D. Wise. 2011. The draw down of personal retirement assets, January. NBER Working Paper No. 16675. Cambridge, MA: National Bureau of Economic Research.

Rabin, M., and R. Thaler 2001. Anomalies: Risk aversion. *Journal of Economic Perspectives* 15: 219–32.

Retzloff, C. D. 2005a. *Trends in Life Insurance Ownership among U.S. Households*. Windsor, CT: LIMRA International.

2005b. *Trends in Life Insurance Ownership among U.S. Individuals*. Windsor, CT: LIMRA International.

Roth, Jr., R. J. 1998. Earthquake insurance protection in California. In *Paying the Price: The Status and Role of Insurance against Natural Disasters in the United States*. Eds. H. Kunreuther and R. J. Roth, Sr. Washington, DC: The Joseph Henry Press, 67–96.

Rothschild, M., and J. Stiglitz. 1976. Equilibrium in competitive insurance markets: An essay on the economics of imperfect information. *Quarterly Journal of Economics* 90: 629–49.

Rottenstreich, Y., and C. K. Hsee. 2001. Money, kisses, and electric shocks: On the affective psychology of risk. *Psychological Science* 12: 185–90.

Samuelson, P. 1964. Principles of efficiency: Discussion. *American Economic Review, Papers and Proceedings* 54: 93–6.

Samuelson, W., and R. Zeckhauser. 1988. Status quo bias in decision making. *Journal of Risk and Uncertainty* 1: 7–59.

Sandroni, A., and F. Squintani. 2007. Overconfidence, insurance, and paternalism. *American Economic Review* 97: 1994–2004.

Schade, C., H. Kunreuther, and P. Koellinger. 2011. Protecting against low probability disasters: The role of worry. *Journal of Behavioral Decision Making*. Article first published online: September 26, 2011. DOI: 10.1002/bdm.754 (accessed October 28, 2011).

Schaus, S. 2005. Annuities make a comeback. *Journal of Pension Benefits: Issues in Administration* 12: 34–8.

Schulze, R. and T. Post 2010. Individual annuity demand under aggregate mortality risk. *Journal of Risk and Insurance* 77(2): 423–49.

Shafir, E., I. Simonson, and A. Tversky. 1993. Reason-based choice. *Cognition* 49: 11–36.

Shapira, Z., and I. Venezia. 2008. On the preference for full-coverage policies: Why do people buy too much insurance? *Journal of Economic Psychology*, 29(5): 747–61.

Shiller, R. J. 2003. *The New Financial Order: Risk in the 21st Century*. Princeton: Princeton University Press.

Silverman, R. E. 2005. Getting paid for getting sick: As health costs rise, insurers market policies that make payments for specific illnesses. *Wall Street Journal*. July 14.

Singletary, M. 2003. Renters insurance worth the cost: The color of money. *Renter's Insurance: Business*, September 21, 2003. http://www.cvoeo.org/downloads/housing/renters-insurance.pdf (accessed October 28, 2010).

Slovic, P. 1995. The construction of preference. *American Psychologist* 50: 364–71.

Slovic, P., B. Fischhoff, and S. Lichtenstein. 1978. Accident probabilities and seat belt usage: A psychological perspective. *Accident Analysis and Prevention* 10: 281–5.

Slovic, P., J. Monahan, and D. G. MacGregor. 2000. Violence risk assessment and risk communication: The effects of using actual cases, providing instruction, and employing probability versus frequency formats. *Law and Human Behavior* 24: 271–96.

Smetters, K. 2004. Insuring against terrorism. *Brookings-Wharton Papers on Financial Services: 2004*. Ed. R. Herring and R. E. Litan. Washington, DC: Brookings Institution Press, 139–87.

Smith, A. 1759/1966. *Theory of Moral Sentiments*. Repr., New York: Augustus M. Kelley

Social Security Administration. 2009. Social security basic facts. Social Security Online: Press Office Fact Sheet. http://www.ssa.gov/pressoffice/basicfact.htm (accessed October 28, 2010).

Sonnenberg, A., and F. Delco. 2002. Cost effectiveness of a single colonoscopy in screening for colorectal cancer. *Annals of Internal Medicine* 162: 163–8.

Spindler, M. 2011. Asymmetric information in insurance markets: Does this really exist? *Geneva Association Insurance Economics* no.64, July 2011.

Starmer, C. 2000. Developments in non-expected utility theory: The hunt for a descriptive theory of choice under risk. *Journal of Economic Literature* 38: 332–82 (also cited in Chapter 3).

Steele, J. 2003. No coverage is a risky policy. *Chicago Tribune* (online), December 2, 2003. http://articles.chicagotribune.com/2003-12-02/business/0312020113_1_renter-s-insurance-insurance-information-institute-insurance-industry (accessed November 5, 2010).

Stone, J. 1973. A theory of capacity and the insurance of catastrophic risks: Part I and Part II. *Journal of Risk and Insurance* 40: 231–43 (Part I); 339–55 (Part II).

Sulzberger, A. G. 2011. They dropped their flood insurance, then the "mouse" roared. *New York Times.* June 24. http://www.nytimes.com/2011/06/24/us/24flood. html?_r=1&ref=agsulzberger (accessed October 13, 2011).

Sun, L. H. 2010. Report: Millions in area at risk of being denied insurance. *The Washington Post* (online), May 13, 2010. http://www.washingtonpost.com/ wp-dyn/content/article/2010/05/12/AR2010051202047.html (accessed October 27, 2010).

Sunstein, C. R. 2003. Terrorism and probability neglect. *Journal of Risk and Uncertainty* 26: 121–36.

Sydnor, J. 2010. (Over)insuring modest risks. *American Economic Journal: Applied Economics* 2: 177–99.

Taleb, N. 2007. *The Black Swan: The Impact of the Highly Improbable.* New York, NY: Random House.

Thaler, R. 1985. Mental accounting and consumer choice. *Marketing Science* 4: 199–214.

Thaler, R., and C. R. Sunstein. 2008. *Nudge: Improving Decisions about Health, Wealth and Happiness.* New Haven, CT: Yale University Press.

Tobias, A. P. 1982. *The Invisible Bankers: Everything the Insurance Industry Never Wanted You to Know.* New York: Simon & Schuster.

Tobin, R. J., and C. Calfee. 2005. *The National Flood Insurance Program's Mandatory Purchase Requirement: Policies, Processes, and Stakeholders.* Washington, DC: American Institutes for Research.

Travel Insurance Center. 2010. FlightGuard AD&D overview. http://www. travelinsurancecenter.com/eng/information/cm_home.cfm?line=tguard_fac (accessed July 10, 2010).

Truffer, C. J., S. Keehan, S. Smith, J. Cylus, A. Sisko, J. A. Poisal, J. Lizonitz, and M. K. Clemens. 2010. Health spending projections through 2019: The recession's impact continues. *Health Affairs* 29: 522–9.

Tversky, A., and D. Kahneman. 1991. Loss aversion in riskless choice: A reference-dependent model. *Quarterly Journal of Economics* 106: 1039–61.

Tversky, A., S. Sattath, and P. Slovic. 1988. Contingent weighting in judgment and choice. *Psychological Review* 95: 371–84.

Tversky, A., P. Slovic, and D. Kahneman. 1990. The causes of preference reversal. *American Economic Review* 80: 204–17.

U. S. Census Bureau. 2004. Current Housing Reports, Series H150/03. *American Housing Survey for the United States: 2003.* Washington, DC: U.S. Government Printing Office.

———. 2008. Current Housing Reports, Series H150/07. *American Housing Survey for the United States: 2007.* Washington, DC: U.S. Government Printing Office.

———. 2010. Statistical Abstract: the National Data Book. http://www.census.gov/ compendia/statab/ (accessed June 25, 2010).

U.S. Department of Labor. Bureau of Labor Statistics. Consumer Expenditure Survey, 2004: Interview Survey and Detailed Expenditure Files.

U.S. Government Accountability Office (GAO). 2002. *Flood Insurance: Extent of Noncompliance with Purchase Requirements is Unknown.* Washington, DC: GAO-02-396.

2008. *Flood Insurance: FEMA's Rate-Setting Process Warrants Attention.* Washington, DC: GAO-09-12.

Viscusi, W. K., W. A. Magat, and J. Huber. 1987. An investigation of the rationality of consumer valuations of multiple health risks. *Rand Journal of Economics* 18: 465-79.

Volpp, K., L. K. John, A. Troxel, L. Norton, J. Fassbender, and G. Loewenstein. 2008. Financial incentive based approaches for weight loss: A randomized trial. *Journal of the American Medical Association* 300: 2631-7.

Wakker, P., R. Thaler, and A. Tversky. 1997. Probabilistic insurance. *Journal of Risk and Uncertainty* 15: 7-28.

Weinstein, N., K. Kolb, and B. Goldstein. 1996. Using time intervals between expected events to communicate risk magnitudes. *Risk Analysis* 16: 305-8.

Wharton Risk Management and Decision Processes Center (2005), *TRIA and Beyond: Terrorism Risk Financing in the U.S.* Philadelphia: Wharton School, University of Pennsylvania.

Winter, R. A. 1994. The dynamics of competitive insurance markets. *Journal of Financial Intermediation* 3: 379-415.

Wu, G., and R. Gonzalez. 1996. Curvature of the probability weighting function. *Management Science* 42: 1676-90.

Yaari, M. E. 1965. Uncertain lifetime, life insurance, and the theory of the consumer. *Review of Economic Studies* 32: 137-50.

Yegian, J., D. Pockell, M. Smith, and E. Murray. 2000. The nonpoor uninsured in California, 1988. *Health Affairs* 19: 171-7.

Zeckhauser, R. 1970. Medical insurance: A case study of the tradeoff between risk spreading and appropriate incentives. *Journal of Economic Theory* 2: 10-26.

Author Index

Subject Index

A. M. Best rating agency, 62, 157–9
accidental death insurance policies, 125–6
accurate information, public provision of
  consumer behavior and, 204–5
  demand-side anomalies strategies using,
    209–10
  policy evaluation using, 192–3
actuarially fair premiums, 30–1
  adverse selection, 76–8
  benchmark model of supply and, 20–7
  multiyear flood insurance, 239–40
  mutual insurance, 90–1
  rental car insurance purchases and, 127–8
  search costs and, 70–1
  term-life insurance modeling, 62–4
  warranties, 130–2
actuaries
  ambiguity aversion, 153–4
  earthquake insurance and, 173
  insurance supply models, 284n5
  reinsurance and, 177
  terrorism risk assessment, 38
  wind damage risk assessment, 150–1
adaptive measures, 110, 236, 242
administrative costs
  annuity anomalies and, 138–40
  imperfect information about risk and,
    74–5
  optimal deductibles and, 30–1
  overpriced insurance and, 177–80
adverse selection
  annuity anomalies and, 138–40
  asymmetric information and, 75–8, 92–3
  crowding-out effects and, 200–1
  imperfect information and, 146–9, 159–61

mandated coverage as solution to, 218–19
  "non-essential," 79
  real-world complications and, 78–80
affordability
  of health insurance, 263–5
  overpurchasing of insurance and, 36
  public policy framework for, 272
Affordable Care Act, 189
Aflac insurance company 128–30
aggregate premiums, mutual insurance,
  90–1
"all perils" coverage, 71
  bundling of low-probability events,
    demand-side anomalies management
    using, 213
  insurance ratings and, 158
  renters' insurance, 57–61
  search costs and interest in, 70–1
  terrorism insurance, 12–13, 17
Allstate insurance, 169
Alternative risk transfer instruments, 279–80
ambiguity aversion
  insurance decision-making and, 9–10
  insurer pricing and coverage decisions
    and, 152–4, 159–61
  insurers, 149–52
  probability of adverse events and,
    205, 221
  securitization of insurance risk and, 175–7
  terrorism insurance supply anomalies and,
    162–5
American Community Survey data, 116–18
American Council of Life Insurers, 62
American General Life Insurance
  Company, 62